THE OPEN UNIVERSITY
A Second Level Course

The changing experience of women

Unit 5
Reading women writing

Prepared for the Course Team by
Richard Allen

The Open University Press

U221 Course Team

Richard Allen
Francis Aprahamian (*Editor*)
Madeleine Arnot
Else Bartels
Veronica Beechey
Sylvia Bentley
Frances Berrigan (*BBC*)
Lynda Birke
Maria Burke
Ruth Carter
Barbara Crowther
Judy Ekins
Susan Himmelweit
Barbara Hodgson
Gill Kirkup
Diana Leonard
Vic Lockwood (*BBC*)
Judy Lown
Joan Mason
Perry Morley (*Editor*)
Rosemary O'Day
Fran Page (*Designer*)
Michael Philps (*BBC*)
Stella Pilsworth
Ann Pointon (*BBC*)
Sonja Ruehl
Mary Anne Speakman
Elizabeth Whitelegg

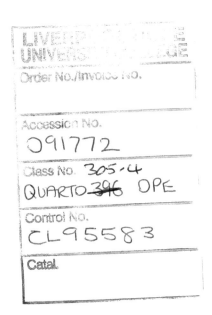

Consultants

Lesley Doyal (*Polytechnic of North London*)
Mary Ann Elston (*N.E. London Polytechnic*)
Catherine Hall (*Essex University*)
Jalna Hanmer (*Bradford University*)
Janice Winship

The Open University Press
Walton Hall, Milton Keynes
MK7 6AA

First published 1983

Designed by the Graphic Design Group of the Open University.

Typeset and printed in Great Britain by Archway Press Ltd., Poole, Dorset BH15 2AF.

ISBN 0 335 10300 6

This text forms part of an Open University course. The complete list of Units in the course appears at the end of this text.

For general availability of supporting material referred to in this text, please write to Open University Educational Enterprises Limited, 12 Cofferidge Close, Stony Stratford, Milton Keynes, MK11 1BY, Great Britain.

Further information on Open University courses may be obtained from the Admissions Office, The Open University, P.O. Box 48, Walton Hall, Milton Keynes, MK7 6AB.

1.1

Contents

Acknowledgements

This Unit would not have been possible without the stimulation and example of the many women feminist literary critics. I owe a particular debt to the works of Ellen Moers, and Sandra Gilbert and Susan Gubar cited in the Unit. In preparing the Unit I have also received very helpful comments from Cora Kaplan of the University of Sussex and other members of the Course Team.

Grateful acknowledgement is also made to the following sources for material used in this Unit:

Text

'Papa Loves Baby', 'Not Waving But Drowning', 'Lightly Bound', 'The Fool' and 'She Said ...' from Stevie Smith (1978) *Selected Poems*, ed. James MacGibbon, Penguin. Reprinted by permission of James MacGibbon, Executor of Stevie Smith's Estate; 'Tampax' and 'Frustration' from Francis Landsman (1979) *Hard Feelings*, ed. Alison Fell, The Women's Press; 'The Farmer's Bride' and 'The Quiet House' from Charlotte Mew (1953) *Collected Poems*, Duckworth; 'On Writing *Benefits*' from Zoë Fairbairns (1981) in *No Turning Back*, ed. Feminist Anthology Collective, The Women's Press.

Illustrations

pp. 11 and 12 from, Opie, I and Opie, P. (1974)*The Classic Fairy Tales*, Oxford University Press, illustrations supplied by Robert Harding Associates; *p. 16* from Charlotte Mew (1953) *Collected Poems*, Duckworth; *pp. 41 and 43* Courtesy of Colorado Historical Society.

Introduction and Study Guide

This Unit is about women's writing, about reading, and about literature. It is based on a number of texts which are set reading and, in particular, it introduces Agnes Smedley's novel *Daughter of Earth*. Feminist criticism is central to the Unit because most of the new work on the topics we discuss has been done by feminist critics. But the Unit is not a survey of feminist criticism. The contents of the three main Parts of the Unit are briefly described below.

Part A   Women, literature and writing

Sections 2 to 9 raise general issues about women's writing and about literature, and introduce you to the kind of attentive and aware reading that is crucial to your work throughout the Unit. We explore the argument that individual readers can find and develop meanings in what they read, and consider whether this is a purely individual, subjective, or aesthetic process, as well as whether the fact that the writer or reader is a woman (or a man) is important. You will have a chance to consider the ideas you encounter in the context of a fairy story *Snow White,* a poem by Stevie Smith 'Papa Love Baby', and a short story by Doris Lessing 'A Woman on a Roof'. I suggest that, if you find the more abstract expression of the ideas in Sections 2 to 5 difficult, you should press on to reading the texts in Sections 6 to 9. You will find an Exercise after Section 9, designed to consolidate your work in this Part of the Unit. You might like to return to Sections 2 to 5 before or after attempting that Exercise, depending on your own assessment of your progress.

Part B   Women writers and feminist critics

Sections 10 to 14 consider what being a writer has meant for particular women in the last 150 years. Section 11 is about Charlotte Brontë and particularly about her novel *Jane Eyre,* arguably the most influential piece of women's imaginative writing ever published. Section 12 is about Mrs Humphry Ward, now scarcely known, but in her day an extremely prominent person and a highly successful novelist. Section 13 discusses Charlotte Mew, a woman poet whose work is again little known now. You should notice similarities in the accounts of these women writers. To each writing was a trade, a way of earning money, and a way of breaking out from the confining world of the home and the family. But you should also notice the different experiences and aims of each writer. Finally, in Section 14, we look briefly at a contemporary feminist writer Zoë Fairbairns, and in particular at her account of the writing of her novel, *Benefits.*

Part C   *Daughter of Earth*

The final Sections of the Unit are an introduction to an American novel, Agnes Smedley's *Daughter of Earth.* It was written in 1927 but remained unpublished in Britain until 1974; it is now established as a feminist classic. Your work here is text based, and depends on further use of the skills of attentive reading introduced in Part A. I explore certain early sections of the novel in detail but leave the reading of the book as a whole for you to develop your own conclusions and emphases.

You will probably find that Parts A and C will take you longer than Part B. It is easy to spend a considerable amount of time on a quite short extract from a text. You might then like to divide up your time on the Unit as follows:

Part A	Women, literature and writing	40 per cent
Part B	Women writers and feminist critics	20 per cent
Part C	*Daughter of Earth*	40 per cent

At various points in the Unit, I ask you to read all or part of a text before continuing. Often I ask you to make notes on what you read; often my own discussion of the passage follows. To be fair to the text, the Unit and yourself you *must* read what I ask you to read *when* I ask you to read it. If you do not, my discussion will almost certainly remove the suspense from the texts and spoil your enjoyment of them. If you have not experienced the texts for yourself you will have no basis on which to engage with my discussions.

If you have time, you will almost certainly find it advantageous to read quickly at least to the end of Part 6 of *Daughter of Earth* before beginning Part C. It is not essential that you do this, however, and you should take care to allow enough time to work through the Unit.

PART A Women, literature and writing

2 Women and writing

'Writing' refers to an activity; when we learn to write, we learn how to make marks on some sort of surface, which form letters and words. We do this in such a way that others can recognize our marks, which can communicate meaning. Writing is inextricably linked to language. Learning to write is not a characteristic feature of all societies. In British society in the Middle Ages, being able to write was an uncommon skill, associated with a particular social status. In certain parts of the world today sophisticated societies exist where writing is not known, and only an oral culture exists. If no one writes in a society, then the statement 'she cannot write' is more or less meaningless. But, in the sort of society common in Europe and North America today, to say 'she cannot write' indicates that the person referred to is handicapped within society and has limited social power or freedom. Being able to write in a culture where most business and most legal transactions involve being able to write means that one can enter into social activity. The ability to use written language fluently and in certain particular ways may be part of belonging to a particular class or occupational group. An ability to write in a style based, for example, on a knowledge of Latin and Greek has been for some time in Britain a mark of the male upper class and the higher echelons of the Civil Service. The ability to write in the language of computer systems indicates now membership of a different kind of managerial group. The list of different groups of people, each with its own internal shared common language, could be prolonged and could range from advertising copywriters to radical sociologists, and from space engineers to cookery writers.

Creative writing forms one of those groups, although one would be hard pressed to define a single unified style by which the group could be recognized. Many of these writing groups would claim that their writing was not simply for their own group but for the good of society as a whole. Even then, however, the particular language internal to that group distinguishes members of the group from the rest of society. Sometimes writing may be a means of communication only for people within the group and exclude others from membership of a charmed circle. A doctor's prescription acts as a confidential communication with a pharmacist, and excludes anyone else (including the patient who is to take the medicine). The language of a legal contract may often be meaningful only to the lawyer who writes or reads it and not to the layperson for whom it is drawn up. This kind of distinct and distinguishing language does not just occur in occupational groups. Language and writing are common within individual social classes and the language of one distinguishes it from another. Literature and the kind of writing we shall read in this Unit are activities associated with the aristocracy, the middle class and the bourgeoisie much more than with working-class life.

Much attention has been given to the question of whether men and women form distinct groups with distinguishing languages in speech or in writing. The investigation has taken a number of forms. Recently, for example, feminist linguists have explored the detail of everyday speech patterns and have tried to place those patterns in a broader context of social relations. Feminist critics have asked whether there are specifically female kinds of imagery in women's writing, stemming perhaps from a specifically female imagination. In all these investigations, differences have been found between men and women. But such investigations — like those of physical differences discussed by Else Bartels' article in the Reader – do not yield simple results. In speech, for example, women may be found to be more polite and less assertive than men, but the nature of the differences may be also heavily influenced by social class. In writing too, social class may seem at least as important a determining factor as sex or gender.

In simple terms, most research suggests that more writing by men is published and circulated than writing by women; if one narrows the investigation to writing that is described as literary or literature the same remains true. But as far as literary writing is concerned, more writing by women of the middle classes is published than writing by men from a working-class background.

3 Women and literature

The second term I want to introduce here — literature — is based on the results of language and writing. But the term has shifted its meaning over the last 300 years. Some hint of the older meaning survives in the associated word 'literate'. 'Literate' still means being generally competent at writing and reading and may be applied to almost any subject. We may still speak of the literature on a particular topic, or ask for literature describing a particular product but, in most usages, literature has come to indicate a distinct kind of writing with a particular significance in society. 'She is literate' indicates that a person is a fluent reader and writer. 'She is a creative writer' indicates that a person writes from her own thoughts and imagination; the results may be poetry or advertising, etc. 'She writes literature', on the other hand, seems an odd formulation, the more recognizable phrase is 'she reads literature'. Our unease about the first formulation is because literature depends upon more than an individual act of writing. It requires an act of what is generally called criticism. Among other things this serves to place the writing on some kind of scale of values and declares it worth reading.

Criticism is a complex process and may depend simultaneously on a number of different scales of value. It may depend on aesthetic criteria — and here academic work may claim the lead in directing judgement — or it may depend on social and moral criteria — and here book buyers and readers, and newspaper and magazine writers may lead. Criticism is also a continuing process and works are often revalued, not only because of changes in fashion but also because of changes in social conditions and ideas. In a totalitarian state, the dominant forms of criticism may classify as literature only material that serves the state and echoes its own propaganda. In a state that values the pursuit of wealth and material advancement, the dominant criticism may applaud a grand and flamboyant literature reflecting its own values (the equivalent of the Albert Memorial in London, for example). But, in such a society, criticism may also give value to a literature that condemns materialistic values as philistine (the poetry of Tennyson for example). In any society, in universities and 'literary' circles the emphasis may be on some technical skill of the writer or on the ability to meet certain ideal standards based on 'classical' practice.

In most societies, then, loosely formed ranges of works exist, called literary canons. A canon is a loose list of works that comply with a particular standard of value. More than one canon may exist in a society but one will usually be dominant. Canons and the standards that govern them are the subject of debate, and arguments often range over which works and which standards are best.

If language and writing can be seen as embodying differences in society, so too can the literary canon. Arguments about women in society produce arguments about literary standards and the literary canon. Feminist criticism is centrally concerned with questioning the place of women's writing in the existing system of values on which the canon rests and the canon itself, in the same way as feminists question the situation of women in society generally*.

In 1971 Tillie Olsen gave a seminal lecture entitled 'One out of Twelve: Women who are Writers in our Century'. She spoke of the way women's horizons had

---

* Another word often associated with the literary canon is tradition. A writer will be said to work within a particular tradition if his or her work appears to adhere to certain standards. A critic may argue that certain standards have existed over a long period of time and have particular importance; F. R. Leavis called his book on the novel *The Great Tradition*. In it he argued that certain writers — George Eliot, Henry James, D. H. Lawrence, etc. — were the most important novelists writing in English. Their work exemplified standards by which all other novels were to be judged.

broadened in the nineteenth and twentieth centuries through education, and of how many women had begun to write. Men's work still dominated, but women were responsible for approximately 20 per cent of all books published. She contrasted this with women's recognized achievement. Her published notes on the lecture read:

> Achievement: as gauged by what supposedly designates it: appearance in twentieth-century literature courses, required reading lists, textbooks, quality anthologies, the year's best, the decade's best, the fifty years' best, consideration by critics or in current reviews — *one woman for every twelve men* (8 per cent women, 92 per cent men).   (Olsen, 1980, p.24)

In her notes, Olsen quotes Elaine Showalter, one of the most influential feminist critics of the novel, writing on the same topic:

> . . . eclipsing, devaluation, are the result of critical judgements, a predominantly male domain. The most damaging, and still prevalent, critical attitude remains 'that women's experience, and literature written by women are, by definition, minor.' Indeed for a sizable percentage of male writers, critics, academics, writer-women are eliminated from consideration, conciousness, altogether.   (ibid. p.232)

The feminist critic's task involves looking with a new eye at individual works, bringing women writers out of silence and reassessing the principles on which choices are made. This work has been particularly striking in relation to poetry, where men have continued to dominate the canon even while women have taken a higher place in the novel. In her anthology, *The World Split Open: Four Centuries of Women Poets in England and America, 1552–1950,* Louise Bernikow states her aim as follows:

> My desire is to bring out into the open many poets now lost to our eyes, and also to bring [into the open] some specific kinds of content, things that have been said and experiences that have been shaped into various poetic forms now lost to our ears. I do not think the loss has been an accident, but rather a result of the patriarchal structure of literary life and work in both countries . . . this collection has been made by an ardent lover of poetry who, because she is also a feminist, has made choices that are political . . .   (Bernikow, 1979, p.xxi)

As this extract suggests, feminist work often involves more than simply looking again at key figures and famous works, or the addition of new names to the literary canon. It also involves research into women's culture, often seen as a specific subculture existing within male-dominated society. Showalter uses the title *A Literature of Their Own* for her study of *British Women Novelists from Brontë to Lessing.* The emphasis is less here on establishing women within a dominant canon and more on exploring links between women writers; in her opening chapter she discusses these links and the women's subculture of which women's writing is part as follows:

> For women in England, the female subculture came first through a shared and increasingly secretive and ritualised physical experience. Puberty, menstruation, sexual initiation, pregnancy, childbirth, and menopause — the entire female sexual life cycle — constituted a habit of living that had to be concealed . . . Women writers were united by their roles as daughters, wives, and mothers; by the internalised doctrines of evangelicalism, with its suspicions of the imagination and its emphasis on duty; and by legal and economic constraints on their mobility. Sometimes they were united in a more immediate way, around a political cause.   (Showalter, 1978, p.15)

When some critics discuss writing, reading and criticism, they may link the three terms together and refer to 'literary production', implying that writers are producers and readers consumers in a system analogous to other forms of manufacturing production. They may also call the process 'literary practice', emphasizing the exchange of meanings and the establishing of cultural conventions within society. You will learn more about these kinds of ways of looking at writing in the next Unit. Here I want only to stress that many factors are involved in the process of writing, literature and reading. Education, both for the writer and the reader, plays a crucial part. So too does technology; the cheap circulation of books, which we now take for granted, depends on large printing presses and mass production, usually controlled by a few large companies. But basic technology now allows small groups of people to produce small quantities of books and pamphlets at a reasonable cost. The marketing strategies of publishers can also be crucial to the availability of writing; books are aimed at particular markets, and production style varies accordingly; paperback publication invariably increases circulation.

Public policy is also important; libraries are substantial buyers of books and also often the only source of people's reading. Public subsidy often determines whether a writer can write at all. Finally, critics in universities, colleges and schools, as well as reviewers in newpapers and magazines, can crucially affect whether writings will be available. At all points in this process, differences based on sex are significant: men can control the process at most points and discrimination against women can and does occur.

 ## 4 Women and the literary process

Yet — for all the possibilities of discrimination — reading, writing and literature have been of paramount importance among the arts for women for the last 200 years or so. More than any other medium the literary process has allowed women space to create their own meanings and communications among themselves, forming their own tradition, *and* has been an esteemed form within a male-dominated society. Women writers have been able to gain public success and recognition through their own work.

Reading novels became, from the late eighteenth century on, an increasingly popular way of filling time for middle-class women, whose lives were more and more confined to the home or to idle society life. In her novel *Northanger Abbey*, Jane Austen describes and satirizes the effect of novels, especially on young women. Catherine Moreland, the heroine of the novel, finds the imaginative world of Ann Radcliffe's novel *The Mysteries of Udolpho* preferable to the idle world of Bath. In an early chapter she exclaims to her friend:

> I am got to the black veil . . . I know it must be a skeleton . . . I am delighted with the book! I should like to spend my whole life in reading it. I assure you, if it had not been to meet you, I would not have come away from it for all the world . . . (Chapter 6)

Jane Austen makes her less agreeable male characters in the novel view this female enthusiasm and the novels themselves with disdain. But the future of novels is more accurately foreshadowed by the opinions of Henry Tilney who remarks: 'the person, be it gentlemen or lady who has not pleasure in a good novel, must be intolerably stupid' (Chapter 14).

Increasingly through the nineteenth century, writing became an accepted profession for women and their success was great enough for male critics to speak of the world being swamped by a tide of female novels. The truth was that the numbers of titles by women never exceeded those by men, but that certain individual women (the Brontës, Mary Ann Evans*, Elizabeth Gaskell, etc.) did dominate the literary scene at various times. Books written specifically for children were also produced for the first time in large numbers in the mid-nineteenth century. This kind of morally pure work was felt to be highly suitable work for women. Although moral standards have changed, women still dominate this genre. In the nineteenth century, women were also encouraged not to write until after they were married and had had children, lest their vital force be dissipated or they be corrupted. Again, ideas have changed, but many women critics have pointed out how many women writers either have not married, or have not had children. Tillie Olsen speaks eloquently of her own situation in *Silences;*

> In the twenty years I bore and reared my children, usually had to work on a paid job as well, the simplest circumstances for creation did not exist. Nevertheless writing, the hope of it, was 'the air I breathed, so long as I shall breathe at all.' In that hope, there was conscious storing, snatched reading, beginnings of writing, and always 'the secret rootlets of reconaissance'. (Olsen, 1980, p.19)

The rise of the novel in the eighteenth and nineteenth centuries — with its predominantly female readership and with a large number of women writers — was inextricably involved with the development of the publishing industry. That development would not have been possible without technological advances in the nineteenth century that improved the speed and increased the scale of printing and book making. Yet none of these advances would have occurred without readers able to buy the books.

*The real name of the novelist George Eliot.

Later, the industry was further stimulated by the development of the private, and then the public libraries. The private libraries in particular depended on woman subscribers from the bourgeoisie and lent out only the sort of respectable material they thought those subscribers should read. Some of the great publishing houses that catered for these new markets exist no longer. But others survive, and those that have disappeared have been absorbed into other names so that it is still true to conclude that without women readers and writers the publishing industry as we know it would not exist. More recently Virago, The Women's Press, and other smaller feminist publishing houses such as Onlywomen and Sheba Publications have begun to explore a distinctively feminist market. Here, too, literature and fiction have been important: new novelists such as Michèle Roberts and Zoë Fairbairns have been published, and the work of existing writers given a new lease of life. Virago in particular has developed a list that combines modern work with a substantial list of Virago Modern Classics. In numerical terms, women also more or less dominate employment in publishing houses, book selling, and libraries, although few attain to positions of real power and, in publishing for example, the work of female editors remains under the ultimate control of male financial and managerial staff. The actual printing of books is also largely a male province; the printing trades have for the last 150 years consistently operated rigidly discriminatory practices against women in printing companies of any size.

Finally, education offers evidence for the view that in some way literature is important for women. In 1978 in England and Wales more than twice as many women passed A-level English Literature as men (31 646 women as compared to 14 471 men); by contrast women passing A-level Physics were outnumbered four to one by men. In polytechnics and universities more than twice as many women undergraduates study literature as men, and only at postgraduate level is the situation reversed.

◧ Reading a text

Reading involves three essential elements: first and most obviously, the reader; second, what is read, which I call here the text; and, third, the producer of that text, that is, the writer. The writer creates the words on the page and gives them meaning but, particularly as time passes, readers may find alternative meanings in those words. The broad meaning of the text may remain unchanged but the variety of emphases possible are immense.

The meanings that readers and writers choose to emphasize depend upon factors such as education, social class and gender. Literary forms too are not neutral: a topic that can be conveyed by the novel cannot be easily embodied in a poem and vice versa. But the idea of what is appropriate for certain forms changes over time. The most important point to note is that this view of reading emphasizes that writer, reader and text are all part of a social process, and if criticism aims to elucidate the meaning of a 'text', it must aim to elucidate the whole of this process since all parts contribute to meaning. Such a view avoids the idea that either the writer, the reader or the critic can claim the authority to give a correct view of the text based either on subjective or objective truth, or that any text has one meaning. It emphasizes that the history and the present of the writer, the reader and the literary form are all important. Subjective assertion ('I think this means . . . ') and objective counter-assertion ('words used in this order always mean ...') are not opposed; rather, both are part of the process of reading. The reader has the freedom to define specific meanings in reading the text. But with this freedom goes the responsibility to allow the words of the text and the writer their own identity. Sex differences are again significant at all points in this process. Whether the writer is a woman or a man affects their experience of the world; whether a literary form can be, or has been, used by women is equally important; and finally whether the reader is a man or woman affects their perception of the text. Whether a woman writer or reader is a feminist may, at times, seem to affect the process even more.

I hope that these issues expressed in the abstract here will be clarified in the next Section. I hope too that looking back to this Section from the details of the next will also be helpful.

6 Snow White

The story of Snow White* had existed for many years and in many countries before becoming part of written culture. An image of the essence of the story may still be passed on by word of mouth — not least because of the Walt Disney film produced in 1937 — but the details of the story depend on the numerous printed versions, all based on the original version written down by the Grimm Brothers in 1811. The first English translation of their work followed in 1823, and this version is still in print. The version of the story we know from the Grimms features seven dwarfs and the step-mother's use of a lace, a comb, and an apple, and of disguise in her attempts to kill Snow White. This version has driven out the alternative — and perhaps native English or Irish — version, which involves three robbers instead of the dwarfs, and different temptations.

Rescue. An illustration from *Snow White.*

Snow White is an interesting text with which to begin, partly because of its extra-ordinarily wide circulation. It is particularly interesting for us here too because of the context in which it is usually read or told. A child will first hear the story at a young and impressionable age, when his or her identity as male or female is being formed. The child will normally hear the story from an acknowledged figure of authority — most often a parent and perhaps most often a woman. The situation is very much a learning situation. *Snow White* has some strong lessons to teach — particularly to girls, but to boys as well.

The story appears simple and innocent, but its fantasy and its happy ending gloss over blunt lessons for women. In the world of the fairy tale, Snow White grows up to be a passive pure, dutiful wife. The only alternative seems to be becoming an evil, cruel witch, who aims to destroy the pure young woman. The pure woman can only survive with the help of men. Marriage, to a prince, is the only really safe place, and the only place where she can have enough power to strike back at the witch. The story suggests too that a girl must leave home, since there she can only be a rival to her mother. If she does take this step, running first through the dark wood of the unknown, she will learn that being a wife and housekeeper is not a terrible experience. Snow White must serve the dwarfs, but these men are harmless. Snow White's experience of men here is of innocence and benevolence. At the end of the story, marriage is described as rescue by the prince from a glass coffin of deathly purity.

* You will find the text in the *Supplementary Book (SB)* for this Unit.

Men are rescuers not oppressors. *Snow White* — like *Sleeping Beauty, Cinderella, King Grizzlebeard, The Frog Prince* and other classic fairy stories — takes as a central, but perhaps less than obvious, theme the entry of a woman into society. In all cases, the society is dominated by men, families and fathers. The stories praise domestic virtues and marriage, suggest that men are shining princes underneath, and condemn those women who do not conform. These stern truths are concealed beneath a bewitching sugar coating of fantasy and timelessness.

Sleeping Beauty about to be disturbed by the Prince.

6.2 The writers

The work of Jacob and Wilhelm Grimm was intended, like that of most collections of folk tales, to preserve something that might otherwise be lost. Their delight in the stories and the desire to give pleasure to their readers also shines through the collection. But nationalism and moral teaching were also strong motives. In the introduction to the first edition they wrote:

> . . . these tales deserve better attention than they have received so far, not only because of their poetry which is of a particular charm, and bestows on those who have heard the tales in childhood a *precious lesson* and a happy memory *throughout life*, but also because they belong to the national literature.   (Quoted by Michaelis-Jena, 1970, p.51; my italics)

But the final responsibility for the story does not rest with the Grimm brothers. Their folk tales were not drawn from ancient manuscripts but taken from the dictation of people for whom the stories were very much alive; almost all of these people were women and in general they were nannies or servants. *Snow White* was told to the Grimms, together with *Sleeping Beauty* and *Little Red Riding Hood,* by a nanny in the family of friends. Women were generally responsible for passing on these stories from generation to generation by word of mouth but, when they were written down, they became the property of men. Almost all the great collectors of fairy tales in European culture were men — Jacob and Wilhelm Grimm, Charles Perrault, Hans Christian Andersen, Joseph Jacobs, Andrew Lang — and it is by their names that the stories are known.

6.3 The reader

What kind of meaning can women and children find in *Snow White?* Are readers constrained by the stern meanings I have described above, and by the patriarchal attitudes of the Grimms? Does the enchantment of the story allow enough space for women to neutralize the fierce moral message? And are different meanings available for girls and women and boys and men?

One of the few critics who have looked seriously at fairy tales is Bruno Bettelheim. In his book *The Uses of Enchantment* published in 1976 he sees fairy tales as very much part of the development of a child's perception of the world and as designed to build up the child's capacity to deal confidently with strangeness. For him, the meaning and importance of *Snow White* for a child is as follows:

> Like *Snow White*, each child in his development must repeat the history of man, real or imagined. We are all expelled eventually from the original paradise of infancy, where all our wishes seem to be fulfilled without any effort on our part . . .
> But before the 'happy life' can begin, the evil and destructive aspects of our personality must be brought under our control . . . Symbolically the story tells that uncontrolled passion must be restrained or it will become one's undoing. Only the death of the jealous Queen (the elimination of all outer and inner turbulence) can make for a happy world . . .
> The stories also convince the hearer that he need not be afraid of relinquishing his childish position of depending on others, since after the dangerous hardships of the transitional period, he will emerge on a higher and better plane, to enter upon a richer and happier existence . . . (Bettelheim, 1976, pp.214–15)

Did you notice that Bettelheim refers throughout to the child as male? The possibility that a girl/woman might read the story in a different way from a boy/man is not considered. The detail of the story is ignored. Bettelheim explicitly locates his account of fairy tales within a sophisticated psychoanalytical framework but fails to respond to the way the story is about the different destinies men and women are likely to experience★.

He also fails to note how details of the story, which appear on the surface to be merely part of its fantasy world, are particularly relevant to women's lives and experiences.

1   The looking glass, which drives the Queen on, and the lace and comb, with which she tempts Snow White, all play a part in the rituals of making-up, which implicitly turn women into objects for men to view.

2   Is it not significant then that it is the good dwarfs — benevolent men — who free Snow White from the power of these magic spells? Women at both points seem merely the objects of the process.

3   In contrast the dwarfs are powerless against the bewitched apple, created by a kind of black-magic parody of cookery. Magic associated with women's arts is ultimately the most evil. Snow White is rescued from this last spell almost entirely by accident, when the men carrying the glass coffin stumble over a root.

4   The last spell involving the apple may be a little ambiguous; it appears to kill Snow White, which can hardly be good. But it merely puts her to sleep and saves her from

---

★ Bettelheim reads *Cinderella* in a similarly sex-blind way, 'the child' he writes 'learns from *Cinderella* that to gain his kingdom he must be ready to undergo a Cinderella experience for a time' *(op.cit,* p.276). He ignores the fact that Cinderella is a woman and that his account of the story does not apply to its heroine. He shows a less sure grasp of the way fairy stories can reflect the everyday world than Charles Perrault, who attached the following moral to his original version of the story in 1697:

> . . . it is certainly a great advantage to be intelligent, brave, well-born, sensible and have other similar talents given only by Heaven. But however great may be your God-given store, they will never help you to get on in the world unless you have either a godfather or a godmother to put them to work for you . . . (Perrault, 1977, p.96; translation by Angela Carter)

the endless chores of cleaning, cooking, making beds, sewing, washing and knitting. Does becoming a frozen object of male veneration have some advantage?

But once opened up in this way, other possibilities may appear for the reader. Glass, in the form of the mirror, is the means whereby the step-mother's pride is made visible and is thus implicated in her evil acts. The voice the step-mother hears, on the other hand, may be thought to be *more* involved in the evil, and this surely is the voice of the absent king and father. It is his taunting rather than her reflection which drives her on. The coffin in which 'dead' Snow White is put is also glass; the dwarfs use glass because they cannot bear to be parted from Snow White. Because the coffin is glass, the prince can see her, fall in love, and rescue her. But the act cannot avoid the sense that the dwarfs wish to dote on their possession still, or the suggestion that the coffin is a glass case in which Snow White is set out for exhibition or for sale.

This kind of detail may perhaps implicitly allow women readers to emphasize that the story is about men's oppression as well as about women's evil and purity. It is presumably open to women also to emphasize the sheer strength of the step-mother figure who broods over the whole story. Evidently, however, it is harder for women to find good and active images of themselves in the story than for men to bask in the triple images of themselves as rescuers (as huntsman, dwarfs and prince).

It is also open to women to emphasize the cruelty in the story, particularly if all the details of the ending of the story are preserved in the translation. The final image crystallizes the implicit misogynism of the story. As the prince stands sheltering his innocent and compliant bride, the step-mother receives a final savage retribution; now that Snow White is established in her perfection, the old Queen must die: 'Just then a pair of red-hot iron shoes were brought in with a pair of tongs and set before her, and these she was forced to put on and dance in them till she fell down dead' (Grimm, 1896, p.169).

Perhaps this ferocity and the anti-woman nature of the story make it impossible for the story ever to be comfortable for women. The Merseyside Women's Literature Collective have accordingly rewritten the story, changing the actions but basically retaining the characters. Snow White is a more powerful and active character, who joins with the dwarfs in a kind of women's rebellion against the jewel-encrusted, exploitative Queen. This version is reprinted in the *Spare Rib* anthology, *Hard Feelings*. You might look at that version, and consider it as a fairy story, comparing the messages it has for girls and for boys with those of the dominant version. Angela Carter has 'rewritten' the story in a more enigmatic form as 'The Snow Child' in a collection of similar stories called *The Bloody Chamber*. There the emphasis is on sexuality and the male violence latent in the story.

 ## 'Papa Love Baby'

As a second and very different example of reading and of the literary process, let us now look at a poem by Stevie Smith.

● Read the poem now, which is on p.15.

I hope you enjoyed the poem. You will probably need to read it a couple of times to make sense of it, and you may find it helpful to read — or even mutter — it aloud. Poetry often makes more sense that way. If the poem does not interest you and seems boring, or trivial and not funny, then there is a problem. In technical terms, the literary process involving writer, text and reader has been cut short. If you were reading for your own pleasure, you would turn to another poem or simply put the book down. If you were with a friend who was keen on the poem, you might go along with their interest. If the poem occurred in a class, you might also feel the need to pursue it though you might think your response would be of a particular, perhaps limited or academic, kind. Obviously, the search for meaning will be affected too.

Thinking about how or why a text does not interest you can be part of the act of criticism. It may be that the writer had deliberately flouted or set out to redevelop ideas

Papa Love Baby

My mother was a romantic girl
So she had to marry a man with his hair in curl
Who subsequently became my unrespected papa,
But that was a long time ago now.

What folly it is that daughters are always supposed to be
In love with papa. It wasn't the case with me
I couldn't take to him at all
But he took to me
What a sad fate to befall
A child of three.

I sat upright in my baby carriage
And wished mama hadn't made such a foolish marriage.
I tried to hide it, but it showed in my eyes unfortunately
And a fortnight later papa ran away to sea.

He used to come home on leave
It was always the same
I could not grieve
But I think I was somewhat to blame.

(Smith, 1978, p.22)

of what you recognize as a poem. It may be, on the other hand, that the writer has chosen to adopt a particularly arcane or academic style which you do not like or find unfamiliar. It may be too that the writer sets out to express in a dominating way a meaning that you find unacceptable. In choosing the material for this Unit, I have tried to select texts that will create enthusiasm and pleasure in students rather than resistance, but the fact that I am a man and that I have worked for most of my academic life in literature is not irrelevant. I hope you will be interested enough to pursue the readings and the criticism, and compare my choices of meanings and relevant facts with your own ideas.

'Papa Love Baby' seems to me a successful and funny poem. The humour begins with the odd title. As we go on to read the poem we realize that there is a gap between the clumsy baby talk of the title of the poem and the sophistication of the poetry. The title then signals the gap between the incident described in the poem and the actual telling: the baby has grown older and the experience 'was a long time ago'. The narrator first sets down a direct memory of the incident — the words 'Papa Love Baby' — and then matches that by describing and analysing her feelings. The tone of the poem then remains comic until the last verse, when it suddenly becomes serious and poignant. The language becomes plainer, but the lack of punctuation in the last verse makes it also appear a little inarticulate.

In a literary reading of the poem, one might notice the way that the strong rhythms and rhymes contribute to the comedy. Easy rhyming in a poem helps to move the language and sense forward, and may unobtrusively emphasize links between words, themes, and feelings. Exaggerated and uneven rhyme calls attention to itself, and to the verse as an artificial language. In 'Papa Love Baby' Stevie Smith creates the sense of a speaker who is, first, unused to poetry and, second, a little embarrassed by the feelings she is expressing. The third and fourth lines of the third verse, for example, would read quite well enough without the word 'unfortunately' although the rhyme would not be strictly correct. Adding the word completes the rhyme with 'away to sea' but creates quite a different impression for the reader. The second verse begins with two lines which, as set out on the page, rhyme and even turn into comic doggerel: 'Al-ways-sup-posed-to-be' can be read with exactly the same di-dum-di-dum rhythm as 'was-n't-the-case-with-me'. But, written as prose, the lines have a much plainer and straightforward feeling: 'What folly it is that daughters are supposed to be in love with Papa. It wasn't the case with me'.

The second verse continues with four lines (rhyming: all/befall, me/ three) that, to me, have the feel of a nonsense poem or a limerick. The final verse restores a serious tone, but even here the use of the word 'somewhat' in the last line gives again a shifting feel to the verse, which we can now see catches exactly the ambiguous feelings of the woman. Is she rather amused by the whole thing, throwing away the final blame by including 'somewhat', or is this a plain statement of regret which the joking assuages? It is easier, for me, to allow the two meanings to lie, and to

15

leave the poem open, than to resolve the ambiguity. In her novel, *Novel on Yellow Paper**, Stevie Smith wrote 'the thoughts come and go and sometimes they do not quite come and I do not pursue them to embarrass them with formality — to pursue them into a harsh capacity' pp.25-26). The remark might mean that as a poet she recognises that poetry can have a certain formality which imprisons the life it describes and that she is trying to preserve the contradictions of experience. But the remark might also mean that she aims to keep a measure of distance from what she describes, not pursuing the subject matter to the ultimate, and leaving the reader not with a statement, however complex, but a puzzle.

A Doré illustration of Little Red Riding Hood.

Poetry is then an area where a certain irresponsibility rules. One of her best poems, 'Not waving but drowning', shows this well. The poem describes someone getting into difficulties in the sea. In the first verse we hear the dying man's words and the voice of someone describing the scene:

Nobody heard him, the dead man,
But still he lay moaning:
I was much further out than you thought
And not waving but drowning.

In the second verse the voice describing the scene speaks of the dead man in conventional tones: 'Poor chap, he always loved larking . . . It must have been too cold for him his heart gave way, They said'. But in the last verse the voice of the dead man breaks in, echoing but redefining the first stanza:

Oh, no no no, it was too cold always
(Still the dead one lay moaning)
I was much too far out all my life
And not waving but drowning.

As with 'Papa Love Baby' the verse seems to achieve a final twist as the dead man confesses to have been 'too far out all my life'. Reading the poem we grasp at this final perception but almost as soon as we have caught it, the poem ends with the reiterated line 'not waving but drowning', apparently cutting off further thought on the matter.

This quality in the verse was also part of Stevie Smith's life, 'the poetry wasn't so much a projection of her personality as an integral part of it. It was her voice itself', as one of her friends said. The film *Stevie* reflects quite accurately what must have been a conscious love of paradox. While writing her poems she worked as a secretary in a publishing firm that produced mainly popular material, but since she came from a relatively exclusive girls' school — the North London Collegiate — it is not surprising that for most of her working life she was secretary to Sir Neville Pearson and Sir Frank Newnes. They did not allow her work to interfere too much with her poetry; *Novel on*

* The novel's subtitle is, 'Make of it what you will'.

16

Yellow Paper takes its title from the office paper on which it was written in office hours, and it is said that they engaged typists to do her work so as not to disturb her poetry. She lived all her life from the age of three in the same house in the archetypal suburb — Palmers Green — at a time when suburban life was synonymous with an absence of culture. During that time the house remained exactly as it has been when she was a child. The hero of her life was an aunt who lived with her in the house after her parents' death — 'the Lion' Stevie called her. But most of her friends were women who were firmly part of artistic society in London. Kay Dick, one of these friends, wrote that she had 'an immense capacity for non-sexual love' and 'a sadness that human beings, in spite of reason, were all too prone to savage one another' (Smith, 1972, p.168). Janet Watts writes that Stevie Smith 'was tigerishly proud of the powerful feelings behind her spinsterish exterior'.

Her poems about women often show the same love of paradox. Here are three short examples:

Lightly Bound

You beastly child, I wish you had miscarried,
You beastly husband, I wish I had never married.
You hear the north wind riding fast past the window? He calls me.
Do you suppose I shall stay when I can go so easily?

The Fool

A couple of women is one too many,
Oh, how I wish I could do without any!

She Said . . .

She said as she tumbled the baby in:
There, little baby, go sink or swim,
I brought you into the world, what more shall I do?
Do you expect me always to be responsible for you?

(Smith, 1978, pp.148, 115, 101)

The meaning of each is plain and requires no lengthy explication, but it is worth remarking that both 'Lightly Bound' and 'She Said' end on a question to the reader. The reading of the poems is not complete until the reader has answered.

'Papa Love Baby' is also about women's experience; a 'romantic girl', it says, will inevitably make 'a foolish marriage' to a man 'with his hair in curl'. The poem offers one explicit reason why Papa should leave home — his daughter does not return his love — but implicitly also suggests that Papa no longer feels he has a place in the household now that it contains a mother and a daughter. Jealousy lurks beneath the surface. The poem also relates to Freud's ideas about the way girls grow up to a sense of a female sexual identity; technically, some would say, the girl is failing to complete the Oedipal process. But Stevie Smith suggests that this is not something that can be seen only in personal psychoanalytical terms. Sitting 'upright in my baby carriage', sharply assessing mama and papa, shows the strong will of the child. But, in a sense, the adult middle-class women is also always upright in the carriage, holding queenly court over all around, but is also an object incapable of independent movement and dependent on the will of others. The lines 'I could not grieve/But I think I was somewhat to blame' catch the feelings of a woman in the family. It may be in her interests for it to go wrong — the breaking up may liberate her — but her responsibility is to hold it together. It will be her fault if it fails. The poem suggests that romantic feelings carry women into marriage where they stay; a man's romantic feelings are likely to carry him away to sea and freedom.

Reading and rereading the poem opens out these kinds of meanings in the inter-action between writer, text and reader. Interpretations that appear to depend on textual detail flow into issues about the family and sexuality, and interpretations that begin with the reader's response or the writer's life flow into the text itself. The apparently private act of reading *Snow White* seems on reflection to develop a clear relation to the process of socialization as experienced by girls and boys. 'Papa Love Baby' sets out, in a rather mischievous way, a perspective on growing up and relationships within a family. The particular, private event which the poet imagines takes on a new and more public life on the printed page. Reading the poem allows women briefly to take that experience as a possibility in their own lives.

The third piece in this Part of the Unit is Doris Lessing's short story 'A Woman on a Roof'.

● Please read the story, which you will find in the Supplementary Book, now.

Try to make some notes as you read or when you have finished the story. Ask yourself, for example, what you think the story is about, and as we did in the preceding Sections, ask yourself what the details of the story convey. Then compare your notes with my reading. In my account you will find I have worked through the story character by character, but you may decide that method does not fit your reading best. It is important that you develop your own reading of the story rather than simply being a passive observer of mine.

When you have read the story and made your notes, pause a moment and try to recollect how you read the story. Try not to spend more than 30 minutes on reading the story and on the exercise as a whole.

Do not read further until you have read the story.

It is interesting to reflect on how you read because this can have an effect on the emphasis you find in the story. Did you read the story quickly, wanting to know what happened? Or did you read slowly, questioning each detail as you went? Most people's reading falls somewhere between these two extremes. Most literature students, I suspect, read a text quickly to get some overall sense of the whole, and then go back over the text more slowly questioning detail. On the other hand, it may be that you read the story quickly and it triggered intense feelings. The story could then project your thoughts out into the world beyond its specific environment into your own personal world. A number of literary critics would say that such a move was undesireable, and that reading should inspire you to return to the details of the story and examine each in turn. Their aim would be to set down the craft of the storyteller. Another response to the story might be to consider the attitudes expressed there in relation to Lessing's other work and what we know of her life.

In all of these approaches, as I have said already, we must try to respect the text and the writer's own identity, and not to turn the text into something it is not. Having said that, I would emphasize again that no single reading should be taken to exclude the others, but that all exist as possibilities within the reading of the text.

When I read the story for the first time, I wanted to know what happened. Violence against women is sufficiently common, the woman harassed by three men is in a vulnerable position, and it is perfectly feasible that the story will end in physical assault. I was worried that the situation depicted could easily be exploited for some pornographic and violent fantasy, although my knowledge of Lessing's work, the context in which I found the story, and some of the details in the first paragraph reassured me that the story would not develop in that way. But the possibility of physical and mental violence remains until the last page and gives a real tension to the story.

When I read the story again, more slowly and less nervously because I know the woman escapes unharmed, the plot still seemed to offer scope for further investigation but I also found myself beginning to think more in terms of the motives and acts of the individual characters, and in the end I wrote my notes in this way. I found too that, although it was my concern for the woman which propelled my reading forward, my notes were more about the three men. The story seemed to tell me much more about them and to open out from there easily to general points about society. Talking to other members of the Course Team about the story led me to wonder if this emphasis sprang from the story, or from the fact that I am a man, interested in images of masculinity.

Woman on a Roof

9.1 Tom, Stanley, and Harry

Stanley, mentioned first in the story, is obviously the villain of the piece. His feelings are from the first the most violent. Like some member of the Social Purity League, he is annoyed that the woman is stark naked. Lessing stresses that this anger builds to a climax through the story: on p.250 (*SB*, p.6)* he calls the women 'Bitch', on p.251 he is furious 'his . . . face . . . screwed into rage as he whistled again and again . . .' On the same page his 'face was hard, really angry'. His rage is then reduced a little, on p.252 (*SB*, p.7) he is 'bitter', on p.253 only sullen. But this is the calm before the storm of his final explosion of anger:

> Stanley whistled again. Then he began stamping with his feet, and whistled and yelled and screamed at the woman, his face getting scarlet. He seemed quite mad, as he stamped and whistled, while the woman did not move, she did not move a muscle. (p.255)(*SB*, p.7)

> On the pavement Stanley said: 'I'm going home.' He looked white now, so perhaps he really did have sunstroke. (p.256)(*SB*, p.8)

Like the others, he is annoyed by the woman's failure to respond to their whistles, but they are 'uneasy' (p.251) about his anger, feeling that the rage is disproportionate. Both Harry and Tom too feel somehow that the woman needs to be protected from Stanley. But Stanley is not a simple misogynist or a psychopath, since he talks easily to Mrs Pritchett when she gives them tea.

The link Lessing wants to make is between the anger and Stanley's own situation as a newly married man. 'What about your missus?' Harry says at the beginning as Stanley whistles when the woman first appears. Stanley ignores the possibility that his behaviour may have a double standard: 'Christ,' said Stanley virtuously, 'if my wife lay about like that, for everyone to see, I'd soon stop her.' (p.250); and again: 'I tell you if she was my wife!' (p.251) . . . 'I bet her old man has put his foot down,' said Stanley, and Harry and Tom caught each other's eyes and smiled behind the young married man's back (p.252).

The possibility that a woman can behave in this free way makes Stanley jealous and suspicious that his own wife may do the same. By the familiar double standard, his own freedom to pursue another woman is perfectly acceptable to him.

Lessing also wants to show the woman on the roof as challenging his own sense of superiority. If she does not respond to Stanley's male sexual cries, his wolf whistles, his own power is challenged. The challenge affects him particularly as a newly married man — the newly established patriarch in his own family and among the other men. In his final breakdown, his rage at the woman slides beyond the sexual challenge into a rage against those who are his real superiors and at the world in general. The rage, and his need to reassert his power, expresses itself in personal sexual terms as he threatens the woman.

> They had to wrench another length of guttering that ran beside the parapet out of its bed . . . Stanley took it in his two hands, tugged, swore, stood up. 'Fuck it,' he said, and sat down under the chimney. He lit a cigarette. 'Fuck them,' he said. 'What do they think we are, lizards? I've got blisters all over my hands.' Then he jumped up and climbed over the roofs and stood with his back to them. He put his fingers either side of his mouth and let out a shrill whistle . . . Then he began stamping with his feet, and whistled and yelled and screamed at the woman, his face getting scarlet. (p.255)(*SB*, p.7)

His rage disguises a fear of impotence — also embodied in the final suggestion that he might have sunstroke — as a worker, and more challengingly, as a husband.

Harry, as an older man, has achieved the status of patriarch; he has 'grown-up children' and Tom 'trusted and looked up to him . . .' (p.252). In the story he is a moderating influence, trying to restrain Stanley's temper, to remind him that he is a married man and not a free-running wolf. In the end it is he whom Lessing has break up the situation and assert his authority — 'to save some sort of scandal or real trouble over the woman' (p.255). But his concern can only be provoked by the visible and obvious violence of Stanley; Tom continues to pursue his inward fantasies untouched even after the men have stopped work.

*Reference to the page in the *Supplementary Book (SB)*.

Harry does not respond to the woman with the same threat of violence as Stanley, but Stanley's behaviour seems wrong to Harry only when it becomes extreme:

'She's on her back,' Stanley said, adding a jest which made Tom snicker, and the old man smiled tolerantly. (p.249)*SB*, p.6)

[Mrs Pritchett] . . . had an eye for the handsome sharp-faced Stanley; and the two teased each other while Harry sat in a corner, watching, indulgent, though his expression reminded Stanley that he was married. (pp.254) (*SB*, p.7)

When Stanley almost makes the woman fall (p.252), Harry does not speak with concern but 'facetiously'. Harry's place in his family is long established, one speculates, as is his place in the work crew. His power is consolidated by moral authority — the right to mediate and make overall judgements. He is angry with the woman for being undressed. He also mocks the men for being too involved. 'What's eating you? What harm's she doing?' he says to Stanley. But Stanley's final outburst, and the threat of 'real trouble' does knock Harry off balance. Here he has no simple moral to make and no facetious response. The way Lessing describes his final departure — 'He fitted himself into the open square in the roof, and went down, watching his feet on the ladder' (p.255) — speaks of his uncertainty and a sense of personal crisis; he is shocked by Stanley's behaviour but the shock is doubly unsettling because it emphasizes that he has earlier tolerated behaviour that was different only in degree. His own self-confidence in his virtue is under attack.

Tom adds another dimension to the images of men in the story by showing the apparently glamourous fantasy world created by men around women. The three ages of man, according to Lessing in the story, seem to be first the fantasist, second the sexual tyrant, and third the moral judge; woman plays audience, servant and then the guilty party. Tom's fantasies insidiously involve an apparently innocent pleasure, tenderness and strength.

. . . she looked like a poster, or a magazine cover . . . Tom imagined himself at work on the crane, adjusting the arm to swing over and pick her up and swing her back across the sky to drop her near him . . . Last night he had thought of the unknown woman before he slept, and she had been tender with him. (pp.250–1)(*SB*, p.6)

. . . he knew from his nightly dreams of her that she was kind and friendly . . . Last night she had asked him into her flat; it was big and had fitted white carpets and bed with a padded white leather head top. She wore a black filmy negligé and her kindness to Tom thickened his throat as he remembered it. (pp.252–3)(*SB*, p.7)

. . . thinking of how she had held him in her arms, stroked his hair, brought him where he sat, lordly, in her bed, a glass of some exhilarating liquor he had never tasted in life. (p.256) (*SB*, p.8)

He felt as if he had protected her from Stanley, and that she must be grateful to him. He could feel the bond between the woman and himself. (p.254)(*SB*, p.7)

The dreams are so pleasant to Tom that when the woman doesn't respond to being thus incorporated into his dream world he is resentful and feels the victim:

She hadn't understood him. He felt her unfairness pale him . . . She lay there. He stood there. She said nothing. She had simply shut him out. (pp.256–7)(*SB*, p.8)

Tom's feelings are warmer and less violent than those of Stanley, but his aim is still power and exclusive possession of the woman as a willing servant to his needs. Tom feels in himself 'the devout conviction that he was there to protect the woman from Stanley . . .' but earlier we have read of his own desire to take her with his crane, like some kind of mechanical King Kong seizing Fay Wray.

9.2 The woman

The behaviour and motives of the men and the way in which they may be typical of society in general can be read off from the story in a more or less straightforward and unambiguous way. The same is true of Mrs Pritchett. But the woman of the title is much more of a puzzle, which readers must negotiate in the text, choosing their own emphasis for particular readings.

Early descriptions of the woman are limited to descriptions of the extent of her sunburn. Anger is almost the only positive emotion allowed her in the story too; the fierce response to Tom echoes her 'straight . . . angry' look when Stanley almost makes her fall. But what is principally reiterated after the second day of the events of the story is her indifference:

> The woman stayed on her blanket, turning herself over and over. She ignored them, no matter what they did . . . They whistled. She looked up at them, cool and remote, and went on reading. [Tom] . . . watched the indifferent, healthy brown woman a few feet off . . . (pp.250–1)(*SB*, p.6)

The men's fantasies and anxieties depend upon women to bring them into expression, but they exist independently of the individual woman; her personality is hardly necessary. At the end she outfaces and dismisses Tom; there is no physical resistance.

> 'Listen,' . . . 'If you get a kick out of seeing women in bikinis, why don't you take a sixpenny bus ride to the Lido? You'd see dozens of them, without all this mountaineering.' (p.256) (*SB*, p.8)

Lessing obviously wants us to feel an increasing self-confidence in the woman. And the danger she faces from the men is physical and the confidence she gains is depicted in terms of her body. She gains poise and power as she tans.

> She had turned brown in the night. Yesterday she was a scarlet and white woman, today she was a brown woman. Stanley let out a whistle. She lifted her head, startled, as if she'd been asleep, and looked straight over at them. The sun was in her eyes, she blinked and stared, then she dropped her head again. (p.249)(*SB*, p.6)

Her ability to stand the heat — 'she must have the hide of a rhino' Stanley exclaims — contrasts with the pink and sweating men. But the strength she gains from the suntan, ironically, seems to make her more of a sex object. By ignoring the fact of the men's desire, she becomes the thing they most desire. At the end of the story, her curt dismissal of Tom — 'why don't you take a sixpenny bus ride to the Lido' — expresses a contempt for his action in daring to pursue *her,* not the distaste for his actions you might expect; Lessing, that is, chooses not to have her say 'You men are all the same'.

The alternatives for the woman — of withdrawing from the man's world or of involvement in it in some assertive way — enable the story to be read as embodying the situation of a woman in male culture. The language and structure of such culture depends on the assumption that man is powerful and that his view of the world is somehow the normal one. Women, in response to this kind of culture, must either speak man's language and find themselves continually defined as second, or remain silent, or form a subculture of their own with its own language. In 'A Woman on a Roof', Lessing seems not interested in this last possibility — the woman on the roof has no communication with Mrs Pritchett — and concentrates on the first two. Mrs Pritchett engages easily with the banter of the men as she serves them tea and protects them from the heat. The woman on the roof, on the other hand, is first silent and indifferent, withdrawing from the exchanges, which assert the men's dominance. As the story and her suntan develop, she engages with an assertive way of behaviour which is conventionally male. The price of maintaining her self and her integrity would seem to be a kind of isolation.

The system of roofs is a further source of accumulated but unresolved meanings in the story. By the structure, the woman is placed on one high point and the men on another; the gap between the roofs is made directly impassable by the drop to the street and it preserves the woman from any physical contact and harassment for much of the story. The location allows the story to express Stanley's violence and the woman's indifference. It can also have other significances: the gap embodies the gap between men and women in society, the woman may be put in a high place open to view as a sex-object, but the danger of the ladders to the roof may signify the exposed position of the woman. The gap between the roofs and the drop to the street suggests the power of conventions in society that check the violence implicit in men's attitudes to women.

The fact that the woman prefers to sunbathe on the roof rather than in the park also speaks a desire to be alone. That she can visibly spend her time at home not engaged in household work angers the men who must work. Stanley's feelings are personal and relate to his own marriage, but there is a clear possibilty of an element of class hostility too. Even then, it is unclear whether the woman *is* idle and middle-class, living in a flat in an area lived in by an airline pilot, which provokes the men who must work in the heat, or whether the working men are hostile to her because she is indifferent to them and thus *identify* her with the idle rich. The story leaves all this open; there is no direct evidence about whether the woman works, whether these few days on the roof are her hard-earned holiday, whether she is unemployed, just as there is no direct evidence that she is married, single or childless.

9.3 Writer, reader, text

One way of reading these unresolved aspects of the text would be to say that there is a single complex meaning that must be pursued. Such a reading would aim to exhaust the meaning of details in the story. Another might be to say that the parts of the story dealing with the woman express a view that a woman's position is fragmentary and shifting and of no account by the side of the dominant place of men in male culture. A third way might be to rephrase both of these views and say that the story contains a reservoir of meanings and that particular ones spring to life within the context of a particular reading. In this case, whether the reader is a man or woman may have a crucial effect on the reading. The perceptions I bring to my reading, for example, are those of a man; whatever this may imply, it certainly means that my reading is that of a non-woman. I registered my initial concern for the woman but passed from that to points about male culture and to the view that a hostile culture prevents the woman from speech. Both men and women experience sexual harassment and can respond to the fear of the woman, but men and women experience harassment in different ways and different responses are possible. It is easier, for example, for a homosexual man to slip into silence and to hide the differences that provoke hostility behind a conventional male image. For women sexual harassment is directly and indirectly part of everyday experience. A woman reader then may well feel the wordless depiction of harassment in the story in a quite different way from a man reader; for her the silence may exist in words, but the situation speaks loudly and clearly. These 'male' and 'female' readings are, of course, not automatic or biologically determined by the reader's sex; it is possible no doubt for both men and women readers to feel that the woman on the roof is willingly or foolishly indulging or encouraging the men.

The writer's role in creating the various possibilities of meaning in the text is obviously important. In my reading of the text the portrayal of the men is clear and explicit, whereas that of the woman is unresolved and inexplicit. There is obviously no single way that one can say authoritatively that Doris Lessing's view of men and women is one thing or another, or that such a single view is automatically translated into the text. Writers, as much as anyone else, have minds and ideas that develop and change over time. The short story is also a form that writers have used for experiment; testing themselves to see if they can project themselves into a particular situation or idea without the worry of having to sustain the notion for a whole novel. But there is evidence to suggest that the ambiguity of the story does express Lessing's own ambiguity about women and feminism.

In the few comments she has made about her own life, Lessing is clear about the relative position of men and women and how this affects their minds as well as their bodies. In her own family she says:

> It was my mother who suffered. After a period of neurotic illness which was a protest against her situation, she became brave and resourceful. But she never saw that her husband was not living in a real world, that he had made a captive of her commonsense . . . (Lessing, 1975, p.91)

Throughout her early work she is concerned with the power structures which exist in individual relationships and in groups. Her novels have also centred on women. The story of Martha Quest in the earlier volumes of the *Children of Violence* series and *The Golden Notebook* have particularly explored women's lives. But throughout runs an uneasy turning away from feminism or any idea that there may be specifically feminine perspectives on women's situation. This stance affects her style too. In her introduction to a collection of her *African Stories*, Lessing referred to two of her early stories 'The Trinket Box' and 'The Pig':

I see [these stories] as two forks of a road. The second — intense careful, self-conscious, mannered — could have led to a style of writing usually described as 'feminine'. The style of 'The Pig' is straight, broad, direct, is much less beguiling, but is the highway to the kind of writing that has the freedom to develop as it likes.   (Lessing, 1964.)

I shall return in my discussion of Charlotte Brontë and Agnes Smedley to the issues involved in the choice of styles. Here it is sufficient to note that Lessing's early work in the first Martha Quest novels follows the 'straight, broad, direct' road; in that style an escape from a sense that a woman's life and her personality are fragmented seems possible through an involvement in politics. However, as Lessing's work proceeds, there is a turning away from politics. The style of her writing shifts too. From *The Four-Gated City* onwards, Lessing seeks to present her women characters as achieving wholeness at an individual or a personal level, but that wholeness is very much a spiritual or a mystic wholeness. Increasingly Lessing's heroines hear voices and find peace in some kind of transcendental unity that transcends history, class and politics.

This account of Lessing's work is extremely skeletal and compressed; if you have read any of her novels, you will no doubt be able to supplement it, or disagree with my point of view. I should want to argue, however, that this view of politics and of personal life is relevant to and expands one's ideas of the way the woman hardly speaks in 'Woman on a Roof' and to the fact that her character is left empty of detail.

Revision Exercise

The following Exercise is designed to consolidate your work on the previous Sections. You should complete it before going on to Section 10. When you have completed the Exercise, check your notes against the answers at the end of the Unit. Answer each of the following questions.

1   What has to happen before writing can become literary? (If you are in doubt look back at Section 2.)

2   What is meant by a literary canon? What is added to that meaning if one speaks of it as 'dominant'? (If you are in doubt look back at Section 3.)

3   What attitudes might a feminist critic have towards the literary canon? (If you are in doubt look back at Section 3.)

4   How has literature been important for women since 1800? (If you are in doubt look back at Section 4.)

5   In the view of this Unit, what are the three elements in the literary process? (If you are in doubt look back at Section 5.)

6   How might *Snow White* have a different meaning for a girl than for a boy? (If you are in doubt look back at Section 6.)

7   What is your reaction to the poem 'She Said' quoted on p.17? (If you are in doubt look back at Section 7.)

8   How did *you* read 'Woman on a Roof' when you read it for the *first* time? Look back on your notes or try to remember what seemed the most striking thing. Do you think your choice was because of something in you or in the text, or both, or even in the writer? (Look back to Section 8 for guidance.)

My discussions of *Snow White,* 'Papa Love Baby', and 'Woman on a Roof' aim first to demonstrate and then to get you to practise something of the way one may self-consciously unravel a particular text. A second or even a third reading may well be necessary before one can be aware of the choices that lie behind particular readings. I use the word 'choice' here advisedly. Much of what I have suggested about the literary process may seem to you over deterministic, or over-elaborate. It may seem that I am saying that if a writer is a woman that *must* be the most important consideration in what she writes, or again that being a woman dictates how one reads and what *will* be of great importance. Using the word 'choices' counters that by emphasizing that in reading and writing — however social factors, or the fact of gender, or education, etc. may tend to reduce or to weight the options available — being a writer in our culture means choosing a particular form to express *your* particular point of view, and being a reader means being able to choose to emphasize particular meanings that are important to *you.* One may also read with pleasure a text that implicitly embodies a point of view you do not share, or refuse to value a text that is aesthetically judged to be good because you find its points of view unacceptable.

PART B Women writers and feminist critics

10 Introduction

Part A has concentrated on reading specific texts; in general we have worked out from the texts to other considerations about literary form or the writer, etc. In Part B I want to reverse this perspective. We shall still be looking at some texts but in a context of writing as a trade for women, and of what 'being a writer' means for a woman. I want to explore some simple connections one may perceive between these kinds of issues and the texts themselves.

My choice of writers is designed to highlight different meanings and situations rather than to assemble some kind of composite or essential 'woman writer'. No such being exists, not least because, as we understand it in our society, being a writer of imaginative literature means being creative, which in turn means being an individual taking an individual perspective. However, I think you will see that certain reference points do emerge — particularly in relation to earning money, being a wife or a daughter, or being recognized as a writer.

I shall consider the work of four women writers: Charlotte Brontë, Mrs Humphry Ward, Charlotte Mew, and Zoë Fairbairns.

In terms of women's writing, Charlotte Brontë is the most important of the women we shall consider. Her novels, and in particular *Jane Eyre,* may be said to have inspired innumerable women writers and readers. A whole tradition of novels — such as Daphne du Maurier's *Rebecca* and Jane Rhys's *The Wide Sargasso Sea* — make direct reference to *Jane Eyre* and see it as quintessentially a woman's novel.

Mrs Humphry Ward is now a much less known figure but, in her time, her own public reputation and that of her novels were immense. Her novels were published too at a time when the sales of novels by women were at their highest — sales of novels by Mrs Ward, by Marie Corelli and Mrs Henry Wood were regularly numbered in hundreds of thousands of copies.

The market for poetry was generally much smaller, and Charlotte Mew's work achieved only a tiny sale. But she is an important and interesting figure, not least because she played a part in the renaissance of poetic writing in England after 1900. Furthermore, it is interesting to consider her work because poetry, much more than the novel, is seen by publishers and the majority of male critics as an area where women have a lesser place.

Women's writing has played a key part in the revival of feminism since 1970. The novelist's capacity to explore the situation of the individual woman and to link those personal feelings with wider social meanings have matched the women's movement's emphasis on the personal and the political. Poetry has also been a way whereby women can express and celebrate their own feelings. The heightened language can convey the full emotional weight of feeling of a situation. But more often it is the energy, intellect and wit that is most striking. Poetry allows mischief, as we have seen in Stevie Smith. Two poems that stick in my mind from many are 'Tampax' and 'Frustration'. Both are by Frances Landsman and appeared in *Spare Rib* in 1976* and both, as you may guess, deal with menstruation.

Tampax

you can swim in tampax
you can ride
and sail
and more,
even if you couldn't do
any of these things before

Frustration

do you struate?
a little girl
asked my youngest son
no, he said
it doesn't sound like fun
it's not she said
it's not at all
it hurts like hell below
s'pose that's why only men struate, he said
with a proud brave manly glow

---

*Both are reprinted in the Spare Rib Anthology, *Hard Feelings* (1979).

The new women's publishing houses have made possible the publication of a good deal of poetry in small pamphlets and in anthologies like *The World Split Open* and *One Foot on the Mountain*. They have also published a number of new novels. One of the most successful of these is *Benefits* by Zoë Fairbairns. The writing of this last novel is the subject of Section 14. To single out one writer in this way is undoubtedly unfair to the many other skilful and successful feminist women writers. My choice is prompted in part by the fact that after finishing her novel Zoë Fairbairns wrote an article, 'On Writing Benefits', describing her own thoughts and feelings on some of the issues you will come across in relation to the other women writers we discuss.

But what originally prompted my four choices was not literary or social representativeness but the fact that I have found all these writers and their work fascinating. They have all given me pleasure. Ellen Moers conveys what I feel, and expresses the point better than I can in *Literary Women*:

> First I thought that not all, that far from all women writers would require or benefit by a critical approach through the fact of their sex; to my surprise, many more than I expected came to life for me as women writers as they had not done before. Mrs Gaskell and Anne Brontë had once bored me; Emily Dickinson was an irritating puzzle, as much as a genius; I could barely read Mary Shelley and Mrs Browning. Reading them anew as women writers taught me how to get excited about these five, and others as well.
>   In fact, the greatest surprise has been richness of this approach to literature in general, and to much besides literature. Every subject I have had to consider — Romanticism, opera, pronouns, landscape, work, childhood, mysticism, the Gothic, courtship, metaphor, travel, literacy, revolution, monsters, education — has broadened and changed in the light of some knowledge of the women's issues and the women's traditions that have been shaping forces in all modern literature. (Moers, 1978, pp.x–xi)

11 Jane Eyre

The essential features of the lives of the Brontë sisters — Charlotte, Emily and Ann — are probably the best known of all English novelists. Haworth Parsonage, where they were born and lived most of their lives, has become a tourist centre and a place of pilgrimage in a way no other British writer's birthplace has. The lives of the sisters have run together in many accounts with details from the novels to create a kind of super-novel peopled by characters from the books, the three sisters, their wastrel brother Branwell and their ruggedly-individual Irish father, the Reverend Patrick Brontë. The super-novel is inspired by a wild untutored female imagination that speaks with the voice of wind from the Yorkshire Moors. The lives and the novels become legends to be savoured from the comfort of our armchairs.

Charlotte Brontë

The mythologizing is not a recent event. It began with the first publication of *Jane Eyre* together with novels by Emily and Ann in 1847. The sisters concealed their identity with the pseudonyms, Currer, Ellis, and Acton Bell. The mysterious authors of *Jane Eyre* and *Wuthering Heights* were seen as some kind of wild voice from beyond society; the publication of *Jane Eyre* was 'the most alarming revolution of modern times'*. When rumours that *Jane Eyre* had been written by a woman became current, informed opinion, such as that of the *Quarterly Review*, said that if this was true the author was a woman who had 'long forfeited the society of her own sex' (Moers, 1978, p.146). When the truth was revealed, Charlotte's demure presence contradicted the rumours for those who met her.

After Charlotte's death the wild character of her novels was attributed first to 'her residence in a foreign school, her observation of foreign manners, and her analysis of the thoughts of foreigners' *(Saturday Review,* quoted by Showalter, 1977, p.93). Mrs Gaskell's *Life of Charlotte Brontë* appeared two years after Charlotte's death. For all its detailed accuracy, it cannot be said to be free from a tendency to shade in the descriptions of the Brontë family with colours drawn from Lucy Snowe in Charlotte's *Villette*, from Cathy and Heathcliff in Emily's *Wuthering Heights*, or from Jane Eyre and Rochester in *Jane Eyre*.

*The comment is that of the novelist Mrs Oliphant writing eight years after the first publication of *Jane Eyre*.

The reality of Charlotte's life was far from the supranatural world. Her own view of creativity may well have coincided in part with elements of the myth — there is evidence that much of her writing was done in some kind of trance — but the writing was also done for a very definite financial end. The details of Charlotte's life are easily accessible in the introductions to the Penguin or the World's Classics editions of *Jane Eyre*, as well as in longer biographies which you will find in most libraries. That by Winifred Gérin is the most substantial. Charlotte's plight was that of many middle-class women of her time. Men had considerable freedom to determine their own lives, to marry or stay single, and to earn their own living. Women, on the other hand, were confined by the inevitability of marriage and financial dependency upon a husband. Inherited wealth could help preserve their independence but the only respectable work open to them was to become a governess or a teacher in a school. Domestic service, which was the most common employment for women at the time, or factory work, meant an almost unthinkable and desperate break with class and family identity. Writing for the expanding publishing market, for all its low rewards, was an attractive way out of the trap. The Brontë sisters tried desperately to earn their livings as governesses and teachers before considering writing for publication. They even started their own school but with little success. After a difficult start, the sisters' novels did bring them more rewards but, considering the time it took to write a novel, Charlotte's income when she was a quite famous novelist moving in London society was not remarkably more than her brother Branwell's had been as a chief clerk in a small railway station in the North.

A fragment of Emily Brontë's diary showing Emily and her sister Anne writing at the kitchen table.

The first inspiration for the sisters' writing came from within their family. Their father was a cultured and well read man, who encouraged his children in a similar passion for literature and for the intense and romantic art in vogue in the 1820s. But there were six children in the family and no money to pay for the girls to go to school. They did briefly attend a charity school at Cowan Bridge. There the bright imaginings of Howarth met a darker world. The school was a grim place, where education went hand in hand with suffering. The children's imagination was fed by fierce morals and even fiercer reality — when one of their fellow pupils died in pain from an inflammation of the bowels, the headmaster gave the other children a grim warning:

> I bless God that he has taken from us the child of whose salvation we have the best hope and may her death be the means of rousing many of her schoolfellows to seek the Lord while he may be found . . . (Quoted by Gérin, 1976, p.13)

Two of the Brontë daughters died within eighteen months of starting at the school from infections contracted there. Charlotte, Emily and Ann were then kept at home, to educate themselves with whatever time and help their father could spare.

In the family — inspired by each other and by what they read and saw — the children's imaginations blossomed; writing and painting became the means not only of expressing their imaginings but of expressing their sense of belonging in the tight family web. Charlotte's first work, illustrated by herself, was a story she wrote for her sister Ann at the age of 8. It was tiny, measuring 2½ inches by 2½ inches, perhaps because paper was precious or because they themselves were small; but the paper had a proper sewn binding and was fully bound with brown paper. The stories and paintings of the three sisters and their brother Branwell depicted larger than life heroes, heroines and villains, living in a number of imaginary countries, the most important of which was called Angria. In the case of the girls, all this was done at the same time as they ran their father's house. There was always a paid servant to do the heaviest work but most of the cooking, sewing and careful housekeeping depended on the three sisters. Her upbringing and the childhood dreams of Angria filled Charlotte with high standards and clear ideas about personal relationships. In explaining her feelings and after rejecting an offer of marriage from a friend's brother, she wrote that she did not feel 'that intense attachment which would make me willing to die for him; and, if ever I marry, it must be in that light of adoration that I will regard my husband . . . ' (letter, 12 March 1839, quoted by Gérin, p.126). Submission to the highest love was something of a problem too. This letter implies what Angrian romances spell out: that to a considerable extent love meant for Charlotte a mutual passion based on the 'possessive and tyrannical' nature of man's love and the 'disinterestedness and adoration of a woman's love' (Gérin, p.132).

The stress and frustrations which Charlotte Brontë felt are plainly embedded in *Jane Eyre*. The novel speaks eloquently of the horrors of Lowood school, of the plight of the governess, and of the dangers and attractions of relationships with men. For some women the descriptions of Jane's childhood seemed totally true, but for others the book was too disturbing. Harriet Martineau, a social reformer not given to wild rages or irrationality, still remembered that when reading *Jane Eyre* she had been 'convinced that it was by some friend of my own, who had portions of my childish experience in his or her mind' (quoted by Moers, 1978, p.65). But the majority of women reviewers were hostile. Lady Eastlake (writing as Elizabeth Rigby) in *The Quarterly Review* fiercely denounced the character of Jane: 'she has inherited in fullest measure the worst sin of our fallen nature — the sin of pride . . . Jane Eyre is proud, and therefore she is ungrateful . . . ' (quoted by Gilbert and Gubar, 1979, p.338).

Lady Eastlake's opinion was obviously inspired by a dislike of the antireligious tone of the book, but Sandra Gilbert and Susan Gubar in *The Madwoman in the Attic: The Woman Writer and the Nineteenth-Century Literary Imagination* argue that:

> . . . what horrified the Victorians was Jane's anger. And perhaps they, rather than more recent critics, were correct in their response to the book. For while the mythologizing of repressed rage may parallel the mythologizing of repressed sexuality [seen by modern critics] it is far more dangerous to the order of society. The occasional woman who has a weakness for black-browed Byronic heroes can be accommodated in novels and even in some drawing rooms; the woman who yearns to escape entirely from drawing rooms and patriarchal mansions obviously cannot. And Jane Eyre, as Matthew Arnold, Miss Rigby, Mrs Mozley, and Mrs Oliphant suspected, was such a woman.
>
> Her story, providing a pattern for countless others, is . . . a story of enclosure and escape . . . in which the problems encountered by the protagonist as she struggles from the imprisonment of her childhood towards an almost unthinkable goal of mature freedom are symptomatic of difficulties Every-woman in a patriarchal society must meet and overcome; oppression (at Gateshead), starvation (at Lowood), madness (at Thornfield), and coldness (at Marsh End). Most important, her confrontation, not with Rochester but with Rochester's mad wife Bertha, is the book's central confrontation, an encounter . . . not with her own sexuality but with her own imprisoned 'hunger, rebellion, and rage'. (ibid. pp.338—9)

The central confrontation to which the authors refer comes after Jane has agreed to marry Rochester. The arrival of a mysterious acquaintance of Rochester prevents the wedding. Rochester is compelled to reveal to Jane that his first wife is still alive but hopelessly mad:

> He lifted the hanging from the wall, uncovering the second door . . . In a room without a window there burnt a fire . . . and a lamp suspended from the ceiling by a chain. Grace Poole bent over the fire, apparently cooking something in a saucepan. In the deep shade at the far end of the room, a figure ran backwards and forwards. What it was, whether beast or human being , one could not, at first sight tell: it grovelled seemingly, on all fours; it snatched and growled like some strange wild animal; but it was covered with clothing, and a quantity of dark, grizzled hair, wild as a mane, hid its head and face . . . (Chapter 26)

This 'beast or human being' is Bertha Rochester, 'the madwoman in the attic'. The images here and elsewhere of Bertha are so striking that they take on a life of their own, defying simple explanation. But one can suggest that before her marriage they simultaneously confront Jane — whose whole being is devoted to a rebellion against society — with the twin damnations that face her in her society and in her time. On the one hand is a warning image of what the surrender to masculine sexuality in marriage could mean in the future, on the other is a black vision of how rebellion can mean violence and a different kind of confinement.

At this point I can only sketch in some of these possibilities which account for the absolutely central role that *Jane Eyre* has played in women's writing and reading. If you want to follow this discussion further, I suggest you first of all read the novel, if you have not already done so, and then read the discussion of the novel in Chapter 10 of *The Madwoman in the Attic*. What I hope to hint at here — after emphasizing through the discussion of Charlotte Brontë's life how important it is to approach the book through 'the ground of her sex' — is the force and resonance of the images Charlotte Brontë creates in Jane Eyre's mind and experience. These jolt the reader, and particularly the woman reader, from any chance of a passive reading, or one that ignores the fact that this is a woman writing, into an intense involvement with the story and woman's issues and experience.

Virginia Woolf describes her reading of *Jane Eyre* in her pioneering essay of feminist criticism *A Room of One's Own* (1928). She too seizes on the stress in the book and the tension between writer, book and reader. She quotes a passage from Chapter 12 of the novel, which describes how Jane would go up to the roof of Rochester's house and gaze at the surrounding countryside. It seems to Woolf that in the novel we hear the voice of Charlotte Brontë not that of one of the characters; Jane Eyre says:

> 'I longed for a power of vision which might overpass that limit; which might reach the busy world, towns, regions full of life I had heard of but never seen: that then I desired more of practical experience than I possessed; more of intercourse with my kind, of acquaintance with variety of character than was here within my reach. I valued what was good in Mrs. Fairfax, and what was good in Adèle; but I believed in the existence of other and more vivid kinds of goodness, and what I believed in I wished to behold.
>
> 'Who blames me? Many, no doubt, and I shall be called discontented. I could not help it: the restlessness was in my nature; it agitated me to pain sometimes . . .
>
> 'It is in vain to say human beings ought to be satisfied with tranquility: they must have action; and they will make it if they cannot find it. Millions are condemned to a stiller doom than mine, and millions are in silent revolt against their lot. Nobody knows how many rebellions ferment in the masses of life which people earth. Women are supposed to be very calm generally: but women feel just as men feel: they need exercise for their faculties and a field for their efforts as much as their brothers do; they suffer from too rigid a restraint, too absolute a stagnation, precisely as men would suffer; and it is narrow-minded in their more privileged fellow-creatures to say that they ought to confine themselves to making puddings and knitting stockings, to playing on the piano and embroidering bags. It is thoughtless to condemn them, or laugh at them, if they seek to do more or learn more than custom has pronounced necessary for their sex.
>
> 'When thus alone I not unfrequently heard Grace Poole's laugh . . . '

And Woolf comments:

> That is an awkward break, I thought. It is upsetting to come upon Grace Poole all of a sudden. The continuity is disturbed. One might say, I continued, laying the book down beside *Pride and Prejudice,* that the woman who wrote those pages had more genius in her than Jane Austen; but if one reads them over and marks that jerk in them, that indignation, one sees that she will never get her genius expressed whole and entire. Her books will be deformed and twisted. She will write in a rage where she should write calmly. She will write foolishly where she should write wisely. She will write of herself where she should write of her characters. She is at war with her lot. How could she help but die young, cramped and thwarted? . . . [In the passage above Charlotte Brontë] puts her finger exactly not only upon her own defects as a novelist but upon those of her sex at that time. She knew, no one better, how enormously her genius would have profited if it had not spent itself in solitary visions over distant fields; if experience and intercourse and travel had been granted her. But they were not granted; they were withheld; and we must accept the fact that all [the Brontë] . . . novels . . . were written by women without more experience of life than could enter the house of a respectable clergyman; written too in the common sitting-room of that respectable house and by women so poor that they could not afford to buy more than a few quires of paper at a time upon which to write *Wuthering Heights* or *Jane Eyre.* (Woolf, 1967, pp.69–71, quoting *Jane Eyre.* Chapter 12)

12 Mrs Humphry Ward

Mrs Humphry Ward, or to give her more of her own name, Mary Augusta Ward, is today almost unknown and unread as a writer, though the political activities of her later life maintain some place for her in women's history. She was born Mary Augusta Arnold in 1851. Her background was quite different from that of Charlotte Brontë. Money was still a strong motive for writing, but she was a member of the Arnold family and part of a great Victorian intellectual oligarchy. Even as a woman she would hardly have felt the same threat of poverty as the Brontës. Education was regarded with almost supreme veneration in her family. Her father was a school inspector and an educationalist, her grandfather was the great boys' school reformer Thomas Arnold of Rugby. Her uncle was Matthew Arnold, whose moral and cultural pronouncements on Culture and Anarchy and on Literature echoed across the Victorian decades. Yet her own formal education was minimal and, as a young woman, attendance at a university as student or teacher — which was the main fulcrum of her male relative's lives — was almost unthinkable. As a girl, her experience of such a world had to be at second-hand. But to be a woman, even in the light of her own later, rather conservative, ideas, did not mean that she, or other women in her family, felt incapable of the same reforming zeal and energy as men. By listening to, and talking with, the men of her own family and their friends in Oxford, she educated herself in academic subjects and political thought.

In 1872 she married Humphry Ward, then a Fellow of Brasenose College in Oxford. She had three children, born in 1874, 1876 and 1879. Her first published story — moral and religious in tone — appeared in the *Churchman's Magazine* in 1870. She continued to write while her children were very young. After the birth of her third child she became one of the first women students to enroll at Oxford University and studied for two years at Somerville College. She gained a 'woman's first'; by then she was also fluent in French, Spanish, German and Latin. Her intellectual stature was testified by requests to review books from the eminent and serious *Saturday Review*. Despite not having an official degree, she was from 1882 to 1888 examiner for the Taylorian Scholarship in Spanish at Oxford.

Meanwhile Humphry Ward had decided to leave Oxford and accept the post of Art Critic for *The Times* — a post he held for 25 years. Both Humphry and Mary were inspired by Matthew Arnold's doctrine that education must be part of Life. Culture was essential to a healthy society, and the role of writer or critic had a special social responsibility. Although they pursued this public goal, moral duty demanded that Mrs Humphry Ward still be Mother in the Ward family, with responsibility for the spiritual integrity of the home and her children. Fortunately, servants took most of the burden of physical work. After she finished her studies Mrs Humphry Ward began to work, energetically and full-time, writing both fictional and intellectual works. Her first novel, *Miss Bretherton,* appeared in 1883. In 1885 her translation of the French writer Amiel's influential work about morality and philosophy, *Journal Intime,* brought her further notice. Real success, however, came in 1888 with the publication of her second novel, *Robert Elsmere.* The novel dealt with topics of social concern and religious doubt — themes which crystallized the growing crisis of confidence among Victorian intellectuals as 'progress' and 'good', which had been watchwords, became more obviously at variance with social economic reality. Mr Gladstone, one of the leading guides of opinion of the day, read and admired the book *and* publicly said so. The novel became a bestseller in Britain and North America. By 1891 British sales totalled 70 500; the American edition sold 500 000 within a year. Such was its success and fame that, in America, it is reported, a 'condensed' version of the novel was given away as a sales gimmick with soap.

Although a great many of the American editions were pirated, and brought no royalties, writing made Mrs Humphry Ward a wealthy and prestigious woman, and gave her entry into society in her own right. She pursued her writing and became prominent in public work. Her next novel *David Grieve,* published in 1892, was almost as great a success as *Robert Elsmere.* In 1890 she began a long and prominent involvement in settlement work; Toynbee Hall in the East End of London was the original settlement, which set the pattern whereby young men of privilege who also

Mrs Humphry Ward.

had a social conscience went from Oxford and Cambridge to live in what they saw as a community among the poor. There they studied in a kind of secular monastery, working to improve the material and moral state of the poor. The settlements were born from genuine humanitarianism — many felt that in 'progressive' industrial society the lot of the working class was little better than that of savages — and from fear that a revolutionary pressure was building up among these 'savages' which would destroy civilized society. Many of those working in the settlements sought to reawaken what they saw as a mediaeval spirit of community to combat alienation and materialism. Mrs Humphry Ward helped found settlements for men, but she was particularly interested in women and children. She was instrumental in the Play Centres for London movement begun in 1897, and later in the Women's Settlement of 1915 and the Infant Welfare Centre. She is commemorated in the Mary Ward Centre in London.

None of the settlements were wholly successful or enduring, not least because the organizers' idea of what the working class ought to enjoy was not the same as those of the workers themselves. They were also far from self-supporting, and subscriptions from the rich were always needed. Mrs Humphry Ward's books allowed her to be generous, although this generosity also required her to be industrious. Her output continued with *Marcella* in 1894 and *Sir George Tressady* in 1896. Her labour was rewarded by a status and an income which far exceeded that of her husband. She financed the purchase of a large house in Sussex with the proceeds of *Robert Elsmere*, but sold it soon afterwards to move to Stock's House in the Hertfordshire village of Aldbury. This she had completely rebuilt in 1908 on the best modern principles*.

Her last novel appeared in 1908, but her style and techniques as a writer were by now rather old fashioned. Times had changed. Her readers could not find new meanings or identify with her heroes and heroines as they could with *Jane Eyre*. In 1917, in the rather guarded memoirs of a famous person, she wrote that her interests were 'contemporary literature, religious development, and social experiment'. However, in acknowledging her writing and settlement work, she had rather passed over another aspect of her public life that had been of vital importance to her from 1899 to 1914. For although she — a woman — was the major financial supporter of her family, a major public figure and a worker for women, she was also an active opponent of women's campaign for the vote. In 1899 she joined other wives of the famous in an 'Appeal against Female Suffrage'. In the years that followed she was principal speaker on many anti-suffrage platforms. She urged instead that women should influence society as wives and mothers. Inspired perhaps by current ideas of mediaevalism and 'community', and a desire to see the Victorian bourgeois family unit take on the strength and permanence of mediaeval social organization, she preached that women had their own separate spheres, functions and skills. Women should not join in the rat race, which Victorian free enterprise decreed for men. Such ideas could, of course, have different consequences. In social terms, working-class women could be encouraged to attend classes in home economics and hygiene so as to improve family life and support the wage earner better. Separate, improving gatherings for women could be organized, where the demon drink — and probably also, therefore, men — were not permitted. Women should do good works rather than claim the right to vote. If women wished to play a part in government, it should be in local government, where social and welfare work were the main topics, not in national government, where foreign policy and finance should remain men's work. In their separate sphere women could form strong bonds with other women; one might be more heartbroken at the death of one's closest woman friend than at the death of male members of one's own family.

In the end, Mrs Humphry Ward took a lesser part in the Anti-Suffrage League, largely because she felt it had been taken over by men with only negative ideas. She continued to work for women, helping found a Joint Advisory Council of MPs and Social Workers to scrutinize legislation affecting women and children.

A quotation from *Robert Elsmere* might, finally, exemplify how the role of wife and homemaker — which Virginia Woolf was to see as a bar to any kind of independence and creativity, and to name 'the Angel in the House' — was to Mrs Humphry Ward a

*After her death, the rebuilt house eventually became a girls school, before being bought by the Playboy organization in the 1960s. It must surely count as a twist of fate that bunny girls should be trained in the chapel Mrs Humphry Ward had had built near the house.

strength to women. The central event of the novel is Ellesmere's realization that, although he is a priest, he no longer has any faith. His wife, who retains her belief, is at first aghast. But after a brief alienation they are reconciled, although the move comes entirely from her:

> 'I will not preach to you [she says to Robert] — I will not persecute you — I will only live beside you — in your heart — and love you always. Oh, how could I — how could I have such thoughts [of separating from you] . . . '
>
> 'Robert' she said presently, urged on by the sacred yearning to heal, to atone, 'I will not complain — I will not ask you to wait. I take your word for it that it is best not, that it would do no good. The only hope is in time — and prayer. I must suffer, dear I must be weak sometimes; but oh, I am sorry for you! Kiss me, forgive me, Robert; I will be your faithful wife unto our lives' end'.
>
> He kissed her, and in that kiss, so sad, so pitiful, so clinging, their new life was born . . .
> (Chapter 29)

13 Charlotte Mew, 'said to be a writer'

Charlotte Mew was born in 1869. Her first published works were stories which appeared in a number of popular magazines such as *Temple Bar*, *The Egoist*, *The English Woman*. She also wrote poems for the same magazines, which were published in 1916 in book form with the title *The Farmer's Bride*. Eventually she gave up prose to concentrate on poetry, and the stories were not reprinted until 1981. A second edition of *The Farmer's Bride*, which included additional poems, appeared in 1921 but no further volume appeared until after her death, when the poems written after 1921 were published as *The Rambling Sailor*. In 1923 — on the recommendation of John Masefield, Walter de la Mare and Thomas Hardy — she was awarded a small civil list pension (then almost the only form of direct state subsidy for writers) of £75 a year. She committed suicide in 1928. Unlike Charlotte Brontë and Mrs Humphry Ward, she did not achieve fame or wealth by her writings. Only 500 copies of *The Farmer's Bride* were published for sale at one shilling each, and these took some time to sell. When her local paper recorded her death, it wrote of 'Charlotte New (sic), said to be a writer'. To some extent the lack of fame was dictated by her decision to concentrate on poetry. In the 1920s some poets did still achieve high sales, but novels and stories were a much safer risk. The Poetry Bookshop, which published *The Farmer's Bride*, normally printed only 250 copies of their books of poetry.

Charlotte Mew.

After her death her work received little attention until the publication of her *Collected Poems* in 1953. In 1981 Virago published her *Collected Poems and Prose*. In her lifetime she did not reach that level of fame which would have led others to write about her; very little is known about her. Such information as is available is summarized in the Introduction to the Virago collection by Val Warner. We often depend heavily upon the recollections of her friend Alida Monro which preface the 1953 *Collected Poems*. Yet there is no doubt that individually and collectively her poems are as compelling as many from her time that have achieved a much wider circulation.

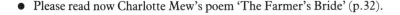

● Please read now Charlotte Mew's poem 'The Farmer's Bride' (p.32).

This was the first poem by Charlotte Mew read by her publishers, and it provided the title for the first published volume of her verse. The voice that speaks in the poem is that of the farmer; his bride does not speak. But in contrast to 'A Woman on a Roof', we feel her silent terror at her plight and her fear of sexuality. You might have noticed in reading the poem the consistent way in which Charlotte Mew describes the bride in terms of an animal or in association with animals: 'sheep . . . hare . . . mouse . . . birds . . . and rabbits . . . beasts in stall . . . leveret . . . magpie'. All identify the bride with nature, whereas the farmer is identified with society and culture. All too are animals that man keeps for his own gain and purpose or hunts. This idea is carried on for me in 'her wide brown stare . . . ', 'a shiver and a scare', and 'The soft young down on her', as well as in the more open 'We chased her . . . We caught her . . . And turned the key upon her, fast'. To me, the key represents part of an arch of sexual and procreation images which frame the poem, beginning with the last line of the first verse and ending in the open longing of the last verse. In the first verse, the word 'Fall' may mean autumn (although this is not its usual meaning in England), but the word is used among farmers to mean the birth of the new lambs or other farm animals. Finally it may well also carry a reference to the Biblical Fall into knowledge of sexuality. The 'some other' in the last line of the penultimate verse may well refer to the man's longing for a child.

The Farmer's Bride

THREE Summers since I chose a maid,
  Too young maybe—but more's to do
At harvest-time than bide and woo.
    When us was wed she turned afraid
Of love and me and all things human;
Like the shut of a winter's day
Her smile went out, and 'twadn't a woman—
    More like a little frightened fay.
        One night, in the Fall, she runned away.

"Out 'mong the sheep, her be," they said,
'Should properly have been abed;
But sure enough she wadn't there
Lying awake with her wide brown stare.
So over seven-acre field and up-along across the down
  We chased her, flying like a hare
Before our lanterns. To Church-Town
    All in a shiver and a scare
We caught her, fetched her home at last
And turned the key upon her, fast.

She does the work about the house
As well as most, but like a mouse:
    Happy enough to chat and play
    With birds and rabbits and such as they,
    So long as men-folk keep away.

"Not near, not near!" her eyes beseech
When one of us comes within reach.
    The women say that beasts in stall
    Look round like children at her call.
    I've hardly heard her speak at all.

Shy as a leveret, swift as he,
Straigh. and slight as a young larch tree,
Sweet as the first wild violets, she,
To her wild self. But what to me?

The short days shorten and the oaks are brown,
    The blue smoke rises to the low grey sky,
One leaf in the still air falls slowly down,
    A magpie's spotted feathers lie
On the black earth spread white with rime,
The berries redden up to Christmas-time.
    What's Christmas-time without there be
    Some other in the house than we!

    She sleeps up in the attic there
      Alone, poor maid: 'Tis but a stair
    Betwixt us. Oh! my God! the down,
    The soft young down of her, the brown,
The brown of her—her eyes, her hair, her hair!

When I reread the poem, I feel the situation of the woman with increased force and pity, even though it is so indirectly expressed. On the other hand, in the farmer himself, I find, particularly in the first three lines, arrogance rather than the naïveté I found on the first reading. This arrogance continues in the third verse: 'She does the work about the house/as well as most'. The man's own feelings are most directly expressed in the fourth and last verse. These are short with a simple pattern of rhyme and rhythm that is quite different from the other narrative verses*. The last verse expresses the man's longing for the woman: ''Tis but a stair/Betwixt us. Oh! my God!' The fourth verse seems to show more appreciation for her beauty. After the evocation of man as hunter and intruder in the first-line reference to the shy leveret (and the odd use of 'he'), the woman is compared less possessively and less intimidatingly to a larch tree and to wild violets. The last broken line perhaps expresses the man's loneliness and also his frustration that she is 'wild' and unapproachable.

The poem reflects the admiration Mew felt for Thomas Hardy. His poems often show a similar intricate rhyming pattern with marked changes from verse to verse, and are often dramatic in the sense that, like 'The Farmer's Bride', they are written as if someone is speaking. These dramatic poems contain a narrative that often extends and develops the meaning of what the characters say. But, more importantly, they convey the emotion the speakers feel. Mew's admiration of Hardy may also be detected in the way the plight of the bride in 'The Farmer's Bride' echoes indirectly the situation of Sue Bridehead in Hardy's novel *Jude the Obscure*. Hardy and Mew both question the prevailing assumption that marriage, sexuality, and procreation are for

*A short but revealing exercise might be to go through the other verses and mark the rhymes. In the long verses, Mew creates a remarkably fluid and interesting pattern that is unrepetitive but binds the verses together.

women part of a naturally blessed state; for the woman in the poem, the rather unromantic marriage means only restriction, and the possibility of defilement. If you know Hardy's novel, you might notice a particular parallel between the last stanza of the poem and Sue Bridehead's fear of a sexual relationship with Mr Phillotson.

Mew seems to have shared Hardy's attitude to the relative value of poetry and prose. One wrote prose as trade to earn money; poetry was an altogether higher and more serious art, of interest to a more select and sensitive audience. Mew's poems might have appeared in the same magazines as her stories, but their real audience was the small group of people who gathered at the Poetry Bookshop.

Charlotte Mew lived almost all her life with her family in London. Her closest friend was her younger sister, Anne, whose death in 1927 precipitated the depression which led to Charlotte's suicide. Alida Monro described Charlotte as having:

> . . . inherited from her mother a view of life that was very prevalent during the last century, namely that appearances must be kept up at all cost. When I first knew Charlotte, the top half of their house was let to some people, but it was a long time before this was disclosed to me in confidence, as it was felt that such a circumstance was a matter of which to be deeply ashamed . . .
>
> Charlotte would always say, when speaking of her mother, that family ties meant everything to her; but it is probable that she adored the idea of a mother rather than the woman herself, for there was little in common between them. 'Ma' was a tiny woman, scarcely more than four feet, very shrivelled and with tiny claw-like hands. There was a portrait of her painted in oils hanging on the wall, which showed that in her youth she had been pretty and bright, like a little bird.   (Mew, 1953, p.ix)

Until 1890 the family had generally risen socially. Charlotte's paternal grandfather was a yeoman farmer whose son became a successful architect; her maternal grandfather was a successful surveyor in London. But her own father squandered his inheritance and all his capital. When he died in 1898 he left his family penniless. Charlotte's mother had never worked for money, and the family depended upon the money which Charlotte earned by writing and the pittance Anne earned renovating and handpainting antique English furniture. Poverty caused the family to turn in on itself. Charlotte's mother, and to a lesser extent Charlotte herself and Anne, clung desperately to the respectability of their class — almost perhaps as a way of preserving their identities. They zealously guarded a family secret more threatening to their sense of respectability than the presence of lodgers. There were two other children in the family: a son older than Charlotte and a younger daughter. But both suffered mental illness throughout their lives and were looked after in asylums. At that time, views of mental health and insanity would have stigmatized the two absent children as a stain on the character and integrity of the whole family. Within this closed world, writing offered Charlotte Mew, as it had Charlotte Brontë, financial and imaginative escape and freedom.

The relationship between this family and class background, and the desire to write cannot, one feels, have been easy. Alida Monro writes of a fiercely moral puritanism in Charlotte, which could lead her to cut any of her friends to whom a whiff of scandal became attached. She tells of a 'very complete friendship' between Charlotte Mew and the writer May Sinclair, which Charlotte then broke off because of something she heard about Miss Sinclair (ibid. p.xv). Other writers since then have speculated about whether Charlotte had lesbian relationships. Her work was very much influenced by French poets, whose work was far from respectable. Her poems speak openly of sexuality, prostitution and death, etc. — all taboo subjects. Something of the tension may also be seen in the strongly religious, but rather romantic, spirit that can be found in some of her poems. Finally, and perhaps most strikingly, the intense reticence of her own private life contrasts with the existence of a number of poems in which a particular private and personal moment in a woman's life is transformed into the public life of a poem. One example of this is a poem called 'The Quiet House'. Here personal and deeply private feelings about loss and unhappiness are cast into a dramatic situation in a poem that almost wilfully calls attention to the technical skill of its author.

● Please read 'The Quiet House' now.

WHEN we were children old Nurse used to say,
 The house was like an auction or a fair
Until the lot of us were safe in bed.
It has been quiet as the country-side
Since Ted and Janey and then Mother died
And Tom crossed Father and was sent away.
After the lawsuit he could not hold up his head,
 Poor Father, and he does not care
 For people here, or to go anywhere.

To get away to Aunt's for that week-end
 Was hard enough; (since then, a year ago,
 He scarcely lets me slip out of his sight—)
At first I did not like my cousin's friend,
 I did not think I should remember him:
 His voice has gone, his face is growing dim
And if I like him now I do not know.
 He frightened me before he smiled—
 He did not ask me if he might—
 He said that he would come one Sunday night,
 He spoke to me as if I were a child.

No year has been like this that has just gone by;
 It may be that what Father says is true,
If things are so it does not matter why:
 But everything has burned, and not quite through.
 The colours of the world have turned
 To flame, the blue, the gold has burned
In what used to be such a leaden sky.
When you are burned quite through you die.

 Red is the strangest pain to bear;
In Spring the leaves on the budding trees;
In Summer the roses are worse than these,
 More terrible than they are sweet:
 A rose can stab you across the street
  Deeper than any knife:
 And the crimson haunts you everywhere—
Thin shafts of sunlight, like the ghosts of reddened swords have struck our stair
As if, coming down, you had spilt your life.

I think that my soul is red
Like the soul of a sword or a scarlet flower:
 But when these are dead
 They have had their hour.

I shall have had mine, too,
 For from head to feet
I am burned and stabbed half through,
 And the pain is deadly sweet.

The things that kill us seem
 Blind to the death they give:
It is only in our dream
 The things that kill us live.

The room is shut where Mother died,
 The other rooms are as they were,
The world goes on the same outside,
 The sparrows fly across the Square,
 The children play as we four did there,
 The trees grow green and brown and bare,
The sun shines on the dead Church spire,
 And nothing lives here but the fire.
While Father watches from his chair
  Day follows day
The same, or now and then a different grey,
  Till, like his hair,
Which Mother said was wavy once and bright,
  They will all turn white.

 To-night I heard a bell again—
Outside it was the same mist of fine rain,
The lamps just lighted down the long, dim street,
  No one for me—
 I think it is myself I go to meet:
I do not care; some day I *shall* not think; I shall not *be*

 Feminist writing: Zoë Fairbairns

Soon after her novel *Benefits* was published, Zoë Fairbairns wrote an article, 'On Writing Benefits', in the *Women and Writing Newsletter*. The article which has since been reprinted in the Feminist Anthology Collective's *No Turning Back* (1981), is reproduced on p.35. I hope that it will recall to you certain topics that have figured in my discussion of Charlotte Brontë, Mrs Humphry Ward and Charlotte Mew. You may well feel that in this case some of the issues are more important than others.

● Read it now and try to make some notes that relate this extract to what you have read in previous Sections. You may find the following questions useful in prompting your notes — although the list is by no means inclusive and some questions overlap. You may have other ideas of your own that you want to add:

1 Does Zoë Fairbairns suggest that writing is somehow special for a woman?

2 What might stimulate a woman to write? Might it be money? Or the particular subject matter? (cont. on p.36)

ZOË FAIRBAIRNS

On Writing *Benefits*

First published in *Women and Writing Newsletter*, 1980

In the summer of 1976 I was working at the Women's Research and Resources Centre, collecting feminist literature for a library. I read newsletters and pamphlets from all over the WLM; and the argument about wages for housework made my head spin.

'Pay housewives and free them from dependence on their men,' said one group, 'It's a good idea.'

'Yes,' I thought, 'it is.'

'Don't pay housewives, it'll only institutionalise their position in the home,' said another group, 'it's a bad idea.'

'Yes,' I thought, 'it is.'

It's not very comfortable holding opinions that are mutually contradictory, but that is the sort of niggling mental discomfort that gives birth to novels. The best stories are those that ask a question (what will happen to her? will they fall in love and live happily ever after? whodunnit?), and the question that I wrote *Benefits* to examine (though perhaps not answer) was this: what would actually happen, to you, me and the woman next door, if a British government introduced a wage for mothers? Inevitably, because I did not want to avoid the challenge of asking how such a thing might come to be, in what circumstances might a British government do it?

I started writing *Benefits* early in 1977. I lived on savings and income from part-time jobs at first, then I got a fellowship from the Greater London Arts Association. I enrolled in an evening class in Social Policy & Administration to understand the history and mechanisms of the welfare state and to get a feel for its jargon; and was supported by the interest and enthusiasm of my women writers' group (the group that wrote *Tales I Tell My Mother*, Journeyman Press, 1978) and the man I live with. I finished it in mid-1978, then finished it again in early 1979; Virago promised to publish it in January 1980 but in fact brought it out three months early, which must be some kind of record.

The book has been widely reviewed. The straight press response has ranged all the way from *The Birmingham Post*: 'Zoe Fairbairns is not really interested in the insights afforded by the novel. She is first and foremost a champion of Women's Lib, and her need to present the case...takes priority over any need to explore and question her views' and *The Sunday Telegraph*: 'She writes vividly and wittily when she forgets her overall political scenario' (i.e. and not at other times), to the *Observer* which thought the book 'intelligent and energetic' the TLS: 'ambitious but not pretentious' and the *Sunday Times*: 'successful and upsetting'. The main concern of straight press reviewers (and I agree it is important) has been the extent to which I have, or have not, presented characters who are real, saying and doing real things, rather than just mouthpieces for 'my views.'

Six feminist journals (that I know of) have reviewed the book. (I also got a footnote in *Ms*!) *Women's Voice* didn't like the absence of humour, nor the 'dangerous assumption that we are involved in a gender struggle and not a class struggle'. The *Women, Literature and Criticism Newsletter* and the *Rev/Rad Newsletter* gave extensive space to long, thoughtful, balanced reviews which cannot be classified as 'pro' or 'anti' because they did not set out to give or withold a seal of approval, rather to discuss the ideas, and the ways of their presentation. This kind of review is rewarding too when it gives me insights into my own work that I was not specifically conscious of, e.g. 'Neither Marsha nor Lynn is by herself more important than the political group she's connected to.' Of course this is true, but I don't remember actually deciding to express it.

I received many letters too: from friends, long-lost friends and strangers, men and women. One of my favourite comments was scribbled on the bottom of a christmas card from a woman relative whom I rarely see and hardly know: 'I enjoyed your book uncomfortably'.

The response that most depressed me was neither favourable nor unfavourable. It came from a woman I met at a party; she said, 'I was so glad to know from your book that you'd left the Wages for Housework campaign.' Putting aside the facts that (a) it soon emerged that she had not actually read the book and (b) that I have never been in the WfH campaign, even though I have agreed with many of the things they said, what depressed me was her assumption that I had written *Benefits* in order to 'prove' that the WfH demand is 'wrong'. (I would have felt the same if she had thought it proved them 'right'.) If I thought I had found an answer to the dilemma outlined at the start of this article, I would not have expressed it in a novel, I would have written a manifesto. A novel that set out to 'prove' the rightness or wrongness of a general principle would be pretty boring, even though it can successfully show that principle working in practice for the individuals with whom it is concerned. For instance (as a woman pointed out at a meeting I went to, yet another instance of feminist critics seeing things in the book that I had not deliberately intended but immediately saw were right) Lynn's relationship with Marsha shows that even a happy marriage to a supportive man was not enough for her; she could love a woman too. It does not make a general statement about 'why' married women 'in general' might become lesbians. When writing fiction I think it's important to avoid thinking in terms of people 'in general' and concentrate on *this particular individual*. Reconciling this artistic imperative with my equally strongly held belief that people and relationships are shaped by the balance of sexual, economic and political power in their lives, was one of the most difficult technical problems of writing *Benefits*.

I started with a time and place – London 1976. I set my characters down there and examined the forces at work that seemed chiefly relevant to my theme – a collapsing welfare state, economic decline, a fascistic/sentimental concern with 'familial values' and – I believe we have to face this – a feminist movement that has very little to say to the woman who actually *wants* to have children and look after them as the major commitment of her life. We all know such women exist and I think it is simply not good enough to say that they suffer from conditioning and if they don't want to go out to work they damn well should. As long as feminists treat them as if they (a) are fools or (b) don't exist, they will inevitably join the factual equivalents of the Family Movement. Having set up this background I tried to give the narrative its head and see where it ended up.

For me a certain inevitability attaches to where it does end up, not least because I didn't plan it, it just went that way. But if I look at it now, as a completed work, and ask (trying to forget I wrote it – which isn't always as difficult as it sounds) what it means – which is very different from having started with a 'meaning' and tried to move everything in that direction – I come to this conclusion. It is not the payment of 'Benefit' as such that oppresses the women. On the contrary: it makes life easier for the wife of the working-class man, the wife of the middle-class man, the single mother and the feminists in the tower. But of course it is not given for that purpose. A divided and inadequate feminist response to the plight of the dependent mother allows a cost-cutting government to believe that instead of paying for work done, it has bought shares in the women's wombs. At no point do feminists stand together and say: mothers work as hard and as vitally as anybody else, and deserve their own money *for that reason*. There's a suggestion at the end of the book that they might come together and do that, and more, now that the horrific implications of patriarchy's treatment of motherhood as an optional extra activity on the sidelines of real life becomes clear. But I'm not optimistic. The novel ends with the moon in the sky at the same time as the sun; but they are both 'racing with the clouds'.

This seems to be where I came in. Writing the book has cleared my head a little but I'm still believing contradictory things and still depressed by them. Yes, I still think mothers should be paid for their work and freed from having to choose between degrading dependence or a compulsory second job. Yes, I also think such a payment could be used against women in horrific ways. What's missing is a feminist response to motherhood and family life that is just enough and realistic enough to acknowledge that some women might actually want to live that way.

I'd like to conclude by saying that all responses to the book have been welcome, moving and supportive, and that includes the adversely critical ones. Writing is a solitary business; I have the 'room of my own' (though not, unfortunately, the private income) that Virginia Woolf prescribed for women writers, and will defend it against all comers, but it's good and important to be part of something wider.

3 Does Zoë Fairbairns consider that her novel deals with subject matter that relates specifically to women? (If there is such a thing.)

4 Can one draw any conclusions from the way *Benefits* was published? (Think especially about in what form and by whom it was published.)

5 Does Zoë Fairbairns suggest there was any tension between her own individual creative writing and the political demands of the Women's Liberation Movement?

6 Are the views that — (a) a novel tells a story; and (b) characters in novels should be free and not simply embodying a particular message – relevant here?

7 According to its author, is *Benefits* a novel with a thesis?

8 What does Zoë Fairbairns tell us about the reactions of readers and reviewers to the novel?

9 Did she as a writer assume a certain kind of reader?

PART C Daughter of Earth

The last part of this unit is an introduction to Agnes Smedley's novel *Daughter of Earth*. You may have followed the suggestion in the *Undergraduate Courses* entry and have read the novel through already. My discussion is based on particular parts of the book, and you will need to have read those parts in order to understand it*. If you are just starting the book, I hope that my discussions will not remove the suspense from the story as a whole and will encourage you to read on. I remember that when I first read *Daughter of Earth* I found it hard to put down — I hope you will have a similar reaction.

15 A distant voice or a classic of all time?

Why should we read a novel which was first published in the United States in 1928, but which remained unpublished in Britain until 1977, and which deals almost entirely with American life. And why choose it for this Open University Course? The answer to both these questions might be simply that it is a literary masterpiece that has lain undiscovered, at least in Britain. I hope your reading of the novel convinces you that this is the case. It may be also that the rediscovery of the novel is an important part of a rediscovery or redefinition of a literary canon of women's writing — the kind of process discussed in Section 1. But probably more important than either of these facts for most readers is the power that the subject matter of *Daughter of Earth* has as an account of a woman's experience and of her struggle to survive.

The story tells of a woman struggling for freedom in a family she both loves and hates, pursuing an education and work because they offer freedom, and becoming involved in political struggles from the same desire for freedom for the individual, regardless of her or his sex, class or race. It appeals particularly to women but also to men, despite the fact that the circumstances of Marie Rogers' life may well be very different from those of most readers of the novel in Britain today. Her contradictory feelings about men and about her own sexuality, and men's responses to her as a woman also still provoke a response of recognition from readers. Again though Phoenix, Colorado, and New York may well be strange to readers, we can still respond directly to the inspiration that Smedley has Marie derive from nature and to her longing for travel.

*As I wrote in Section 1, you will almost certainly find it advantageous to read quickly at least to the end of Part 6 of *Daughter of Earth* now.

We can also respond to the novel with pleasure because it is different from much of what we read in British (and European) novels. There is considerable truth in the generalization that these novels are essentially, particularly as far as women characters are concerned, about achieving a successful marriage. *Jane Eyre* traces the growth in mind and moral spirit of its heroine, but that growth, paralleled by a similar growth in her man, Rochester, prepares them for marriage. George Eliot's great novel *Middlemarch*, like Tolstoy's *Anna Karenina* and *War and Peace*, charts the failure of a bad marriage. But that failure is part of a process of education whereby characters may make a true and proper marriage at the end of the novel. In fiction, as in life, the number of failed marriages may rise, but so too does the rate of remarriage. The theme is related to another whereby the novel charts the education of a hero and heroine to take his or her place in the life of their own society. Both themes continue in popularity to the present day. In European novels, a rejection of society and family with a move to a completely new place — such as we find in *Daughter of Earth* — are not appropriate social responses. Characters who opt for such a course often decline into madness, suicide, or unthinking religion.

16 The pioneer tradition in American writing

Typically, the European novels that chart the growth of the hero or heroine to marriage and their entry into a more or less preexisting society have what one might call a socially settled and realistic mode. In them we are concerned with individual moral choices set against a more or less fixed social world. *Jane Eyre*, again, provides an example. Jane does move from place to place but the growth in her character is signalled by her ability to *return* with a new self-confidence to places from which she has fled, such as Gateshead and Thornhill. Her marriage to Rochester also follows a long, settled period at Thornhill. Aimless wandering signals only failure. Novels of this kind exist in American writing, for example in the work of Hawthorne, Henry James and Edith Wharton. *In The Scarlet Letter, The Golden Bowl* and *The House of Mirth,* the society of the place has a vital role to play in the heroine's decisions and ideas. Social life and the family are somehow basic to such novels (and this marks them as a middle-class cultural form); one cannot escape their influence even by travel. The rules of New York or Boston society extend equally to the lives of the characters, whether they are in Rhode Island, London or Italy. But such writing belongs more typically to the more settled, urban and Europeanized, Eastern United States. Even in that culture, novels that break out of these social forms are not untypical. Melville's *Moby Dick* and *Typée,* and Fenimore Cooper's *Leather Stocking Tales* are examples of a very different, and American, novel of the individual. They draw not upon settled community life but upon the New England experience of whaling and sailing and the history of the early settlers' struggles with the native Indians, and on a strongly religious and transcendental spirit. This spirit continues, particularly in the 'Western' genre, to the present. The North European culture of the Eastern United States spread South and West, where it met the African and Mediterranean culture already established in the Southern and Western States. All this helped to create new forms and styles that have now taken their place in Western culture generally.

In the vastness of North America, the restless individual is not doomed to tragedy, crushed by the slow progress of change, but may strike out into what, ignoring the Indian tribes, was a New Territory and new possibility. American culture is not wholly utopian about these adventures; pioneers died in the parching desert, or found only the Purgatory River, but there was always a chance of finding a dream — Canaan (in Connecticut), Phoenix (in Arizona), or Big Timber in the Country of Sweet Grass in Montana. The quests for a new land may also be — as in modern examples of the Western like *Bonnie and Clyde* or *Hud* — far from virtuous, but the possibilities of a new life are there. In Twain's famous novel, Huckleberry Finn travels to freedom down the Mississippi to Cairo and beyond, only to discover that where he ends up is not so different from where he started from; yet he can still turn to a new wilderness in search of meaning and fulfilment.

More often than not, this cultural tradition is male — women are identified with confinement and settlement rather than exploration. Huckleberry Finn aims to keep himself well clear of Miss Watson, school and regular washing. The male pioneer prefers the solitary life in close communion with nature, keeping far from the world of towns, houses, schools, children and women. For the gold-rush pioneers, women represented a restriction on freedom or a chance of wild pleasure in the saloons. For women the choice lay between being revered and avoided by men — perhaps as the pure schoolmistress, renouncing their womanhood and working 'like a man' — or the life of the saloon and gambling hall. All these strands can be seen in *Daughter of Earth*.

Marie Rogers's growing up forms the structure of *Daughter of Earth*, but that frame is filled with restless travelling, as first her father and then she herself search for a new life. In setting Marie in the centre of the story, Agnes Smedley claims for a woman a place conventionally occupied by a man.

The reader joins in the experiences of the young Marie Rogers in her quest. We also share the perspective of the older Marie looking back on a life which seems now a 'grey and colourless' sea with no sun, and now a 'crazy quilt' jumping with colour which holds her attention for hours. We are fully committed to an individual point of view, and remain so even though that individual point of view may on occasion be closely involved in political and public events. In the book, the mine disaster at Primero stands hard up against, and is swamped by, Marie's rush to her mother's bedside. The reader thus joins in Smedley's attempt in writing out her own life through Marie Rogers to give her own life that 'sense of coherence and continuity' which Rosalind Delmar, in the Afterword (p.271), sees as a powerful motivation for the writing of the novel. Through our reading and imagining we gain, not just insight — on how a woman may adjust to a position in a society dominated by marriage, the family and patriarchal order — but pleasure at an individual woman's overcoming of suffering, her creation of her own identity, and understanding of herself.

12 An autobiography in fiction — can it be true?

The life of Agnes Smedley is set out in the clipped tones of *Who Was Who in American History* as follows:

> SMEDLEY, AGNES, author, born Northern Missouri, 1894; daughter of Charles H and Sarah (Ralls) Smedley; student summer school University of California 1915, New York University night school, University of Berlin 1927-28; divorced. Has spent 23 years in foreign countries, of these 12 years in China; in War Zones of China with regular and guerilla armies, and Chinese civilian organizations engaged in war work, 1937-40; special correspondent in Far East for the *Frankfurter Zeitung* of Germany until Hitler's rise to power; special war-time correspondent for *Manchester Guardian* of England, 1938-41. Has been foreign correspondent, field worker for Chinese Red Cross Medical Corp, lecturer in Chinese Armies. Interpreter of China to Western world and vice versa. Active participant in China's war for liberation. On death list of Japanese Secret Service during World War II. Member Progressive Citizens of America, American Veterans Commission, East and West Association; P.E.N; Author Daughter of Earth, 1929; Chinese Destinies, 1933; China's Red Army Marches, 1935; China Fights Back, 1939; Battle Hymn of China, 1943; The Great Road, The Life and Times of Chu Teh (1956); Chapter XI of China, the United Nations Series . . . Contributor to Asia, New Republic, nation, Vogue, etc. Lecturer, Address Palisades, New York. Died May 6 1950; buried Peking China.

It is a life to impress anyone; the tumultuous events of *Daughter of Earth* pass in the gaps between the first two semicolons.

In her book *Battle Hymn of China*, first published in 1943, Agnes Smedley describes some of her later experiences in China. She prefaces that account with a narrative of her early life. The account is much more compressed than in the novel and the style is here appropriate for an enthusiastic but factual account of her work in China. Perhaps the novel has influenced the later account, but I think 'Glimpses of the Past' may still be taken as a broadly reliable 'factual' account.

Comparison of the accounts is illuminating; I have picked out three points to illustrate how they differ and how they coincide:

1 *The description of Marie's mother's death.* Compare the following paragraph with *Daughter of Earth*, pp.86–9:

When I was sixteen, my mother lay down and died from hard labour, under-nourishment, and a disease which she had no money to cure. My father fell on his knees and wept dramatically, then rifled her old tin trunk. With the forty-five dollars he found hidden between the quilt patches he went to the saloon and got drunk with the boys. My elder sister had just died in childbed, leaving a baby boy, and I was thus the eldest child, with responsibility for this baby, as well as for my younger sister and two brothers.

As well as the inevitably more dramatic tone of the novel, you will notice differences of detail which indicate a difference of emphasis, and a desire to stress a different pattern in the novel. The father taking money from his dead wife is not to be found in the novel — perhaps because the kind of poverty stressed there makes it inconceivable that Marie's mother would have forty-five dollars — whereas all the details of Marie's feelings and the subsequent funeral scene are not to be found in 'Glimpses of the Past'. Marie is not the detached narrator of the later account, and her father is not a robber of the dead but a hypocrite who responds to the minister's vicious words:

My father arose and went up to the preacher and knelt down, the imprint of a bottle in his hip pocket showing through his coat as he bent. The preacher reached down and laid his hand piously on his head — one soul saved! . . . with a gasp of disgust and anger, Helen arose and walked out of the room . . . I followed her . . .   (p.89)

2 *Learning to be a stenographer.*   Now compare the following paragraphs with the account on pp.93–4 of the novel:

At the beginning of the second stage the primary need was, as always, to earn a living. An aunt helped me learn stenography, but I could seldom hold a job for more than a few days or a week. I might have learned to spell and punctuate correctly had I not seen girls about me who did it very well. Uncomplainingly they spent their lives taking down the thoughts of bosses, then turning away to type them out.

This resentment prevented me from becoming a good stenographer, and for years I wandered from one job to another — stenographer, waitress, tobacco stripper, book agent, or just plain starveling. My mother's voice urging me to "go on an' git an edjicashun" sent me libraries, but I did not know what to read. Now and then I found a school where I could work as a waitress and attend lectures, and one year I managed to spend as a special student in the Normal School at Tempe, Arizona.

The main difference here is that the aunt plays a prominent and important role in the novel, and is a fully developed personality in her own right. The rather ambiguous resentment against bosses and successful stenographers that Smedley describes in 'Glimpses of the Past' is also replaced by a more focused hatred of the sexual favours demanded from the stenographers:

. . . he was a nice old man and so educated. Still everything became mixed up when he put his arm around me — it crept around like a snake — the pictures, the arm, the typewriting all became confused.   (p.94)

3 *Aunt Mary.*   Finally compare the following paragraph with pp.8–10 of the novel:

If Aunt Mary had lived in an earlier period, her abilities might have caused her to be burned as a witch. Instead, she was well over ninety before she laid down her corncob pipe for the last time. People said she sped around the country in a Ford until her dying day, her white hair flying, her pipe in her mouth. She was so tall that when she died a special coffin had to be built for her. I have not yet heard just how many men were needed to carry the coffin, but by the time I get around to investigating the story, I'm sure the number will be fabulous. I've heard it said by the gentle branch of our family that Mary is most certainly not taking any back seat in the Hereafter.

A great deal of detail is given in the novel which will not fit into compressed 'factual' account but, in other respects, the tone is remarkably similar. This may be because Aunt Mary has a comparatively slight role in the novel, or it may be that she fits easily into the scheme of things that mattered. Or is it perhaps because, even in life, Aunt Mary's life has acquired something of the quality of a novel?

It is not possible to show that in any single way Smedley transforms her own life into Marie Rogers. The process of writing the novel is rather one in which particular memories are organized into a narrative that has fictional and symbolic unity, as well as the unity that follows from the fact that the events and feelings are all of those of one woman. Searching out quite what the sources of the 'organization' are is a hopeless and, in the end, rather sterile task. Yet one might speculate that it was fuelled by, for example, an immense amount of reading; a direct experience of, and joy in, nature; a passionate desire to set down the horrors and oppressions inflicted not just by the police and secret service but within 'ordinary' families intent on the honourable aim of making good. The structure is also influenced, no doubt, by Smedley's later attempts to resolve the internal conflicts which the book charts. Rosalind Delmar writes that after leaving America in 1919 and after some years of intense suffering, 'she was introduced to a German woman associate of Freud's and began psychoanalysis' (pp.274–5). Becoming a 'fictional character' in the process of writing the novel meant that Smedley consciously works through her experiences but also absorbs them into a broad web of cultural symbols that help to give them a wider meaning. In writing the novel, Smedley claims both truth for her narrative and success for herself. The novel asserts that her American youth is past, and as far away as America is from Denmark. But whether the power of the novel testifies to this, or the ability of events still to disturb her imagination, remains an open question. Writing and publishing the novel also has clear class implications, and again Smedley claims success. Becoming a writer establishes a final social as well as artistic distance between her present self and her former life.

18 'The Kingdom of the Women' (*Daughter of Earth,* Part 1*)

Part 1 of *Daughter of Earth* covers the first nine years of Marie Rogers's life in a series of 'crazy quilt' patches — the image occurs on p.2 of the novel. The following two Sections of the Unit depend upon a reading of that part of the novel and, if you have not yet begun reading the novel, you must now read Part 1 to make sense of my discussion. As you read, note the sections — or patches — of the narrative indicated by gaps in the text, then check your list against the list below. There is no secret motive behind asking you to do this, other than perhaps to get you to see for yourself how economical Smedley's 'patch' method is, and how much she manages to convey in each section. Making notes in this way will also help you to remember the novel, and in the end to see something of its overall shape.

- Please do not proceed further until you have read Part 1.

The sections of the narrative as I noted them are,

pp.1–2   Introduction to writer, looking back from Denmark
pp.2–3   First memories; secret flowers and the harsh land
pp.3–7   Marie's mother; the escape from the cyclone
pp.7–8   Brother George; first furtive knowledge of sex
pp.8–11   Grandmother, Aunt Mary, Cousin Helen
pp.11–16   Harvest supper
pp.16–21   Molasses pulling; family leaving farm and returning for winter
pp.21–22   First school
pp.22–26   Father's return and departure; town life, urban grind begins

At the end of the first section, Marie speaks of herself as part of the class of people who are 'of the earth' and whose 'struggle is the struggle of earth' (p.2). Much of the first half of the novel is a struggle played out against a harsh scenery that echoes the harsh life of the miners and sharecroppers who scratch a living under and from the earth; work invariably involves tilling the earth, mining the earth or even, in Marie's father's case, simply moving it from one place to another. But the beauty of the wild country is also seldom forgotten; at the beginning, this beauty — as fleeting in a whole year but as powerful as the 'flowers so fat and velvety that a ray of sunshine withered

*The quotations in the titles of this and the following Sections are all taken from the parts of the novel discussed in the Sections.

them' (p.2) — is concentrated into the description of the harvest supper and the molasses pulling. The colour and the light of both events is also matched by a sense of some kind of social meaning:

> Everyone seemed to hover close to some tantalizing, communal racial memory. Then work began again and continued, sometimes one day, sometimes two, sometimes three. It was a time filled with happy, cheerful, although hard labour. (p.14)

The event are shown to have a particular significance for women at the harvest time:

> Alone before their husbands, these women were complaining, obedient and dull, and the men spoke little; when they did speak it was to assert the age-long rights and privileges of their sex. But here in a crowd! My, how the women ordered the men folks about! And how the men stepped around, calling upon everybody to witness their martyrdom! (p.13)

At the molasses pulling a temporary and romantic equality is symbolized in the way:

> . . . men and women alike put on big long aprons and with screams of laughter at the transformation, buttoned each other up the back. They chose partners . . . Facing each other they pulled the soft candy . . . They pulled and laughed and gossiped and flirted. (p.18)

Mine buildings in Colorado around 1900.

By using the images of the 'two soft mounds, as gentle as the breasts of a woman', which store the apples and potatoes, Agnes Smedley implies that this bright, sweet and fruitful life is successful for the women. But to me, the image strains between an image of fruitfulness and an image of the exploitation that women suffer on the farm, and threatens briefly the general picture. The harvest supper can have a different meaning for Marie's father, and this contrasting male meaning is conveyed for me particularly in the scene of the dance. For her father it is an opportunity to hold 'his position as leader' and to dare 'what no one else dared' (p.15). He becomes 'the living, articulate expression of their desires' (ibid.), extending the meaning of the supper beyond its function as a festival of thanksgiving into a colourful dream of 'rhythmical abandon' far from the reality of the hard field work.

The pull of these desires eventually begins the break-up of the Rogers family when the father begins to insist that they leave the farm:

> Our life there had indeed been poor, but as I see it now, it had been healthy and securely rooted in the soil. My mother was satisfied to work ceaselessly and to save a few pennies a year, but for my father such an existence was death, and he had stood it as long as he could. (p.19)

In these descriptions Smedley seems to want to extend the title of the story to imply some sort of dual structure in which the woman, Marie's mother, is somehow linked to the earth, whereas the man is a wanderer. But Smedley is also careful in the opening section to balance the image of the earthbound woman against the earlier image of Marie's grandmother:

> She was a woman with the body and mind of a man. Once married she assumed control of her new husband and all that he possessed. When her word failed with her own or his children, she used her hand. It was a big hand. She milked the cows each morning and night with the sweeping strength and movements of a man . . . when she kneaded bread for baking, it whistled and snapped under[her] hands, and her arms worked like steam pistons. She awoke the men at dawn and she told them to go upstairs to bed at night . . . In the autumn she directed the slaughtering of beef and pork, and then smoked the meat in the smokehouse (p.9)

The woman here is not just the housekeeper but the homemaker, for Smedley stresses her 'managing ability', building the character to the final climatic sentence: 'She was like an invading army in a foreign country'. Note too that Marie's cousin Helen is introduced in this same patch of the crazy quilt. She has a comparable strength, walking 'immune through her stepmother's wrath'. The 'mean, spoilt' Mildred also figures here for the first time. These two women, with Marie, carry the torch of women's strength of will and independence through the later part of the novel.

19. 'The shining railway tracks'

On first reading, the 'adventure' of the variety and pace of the crazy quilt carries most readers I suspect relentlessly forward. But, in the first section, Smedley carefully builds and elaborates a symbolic structure as part of a picture of a society where, although characteristics may not be tidily divided, the sexes have separate and unequal destinies. Farming and nature images are generally associated with Marie's mother.

● What images does Smedley use in this part to convey the position of men in this world?

You might pick on the power of the black stallion brought to the farm, or the 'big sweeping hat' that her father wears. You might also note the story of Marie's great-aunt, particularly the lover named Wolf or the great-uncle who kills him, and perhaps too how Marie's father claims to have killed a man to justify abandoning his family. But the images that stick most in my mind are those which refer to him actually travelling:

> One evening at sunset as I stood watching the hard, white, dusty lane, a carriage turned the curve. It was drawn by two snow-white horses travelling with sweeping ease and swiftness. In the carriage sat two dark figures. They came soundlessly as a dream comes, the horses tossing their heads against the painted sky. The click of hooves grew clearer, then the carriage rolled in at our gate and my father leaped over the wheel . . . My father's broad brimmed soft hat was pulled down over his left eye and he wore a black tie that flew in the wind. As he turned I saw the shining buckle of his many-coloured belt. (p.22)

The same atmosphere pervades the end of the chapter:

> . . . The next day my father left us again. He went away on a railroad hand-car. A number of men sat around the edge . . . We watched until he was a black speck in the distance. Even then we strained our eyes to catch a last glimpse of him . . . then he was gone. The shining railway tracks stretched to the horizon, melted together, and plunged over the edge of the world . . . and over there my father had gone . . . into the distance where happiness was. (p.26)

Smedley also establishes the division between men and women, and husband and wife, in similarly graphic images, as when Marie's father returns with his present of black silk, trying now to buy back his wife's approval:

> 'Ain't you even got a kind word?' he continued bitterly, when she made no answer.
> 'It's awful purty', she answered, and her tears began to fall on the gleaming silk. (p.23)

Marie's own realization of this ultimately fiercely patriarchal society is caught first in her perceptions of the stallion and then of the different value her brother's birth has on the family:

> Strange men from beyond the hills came to our farm and brought a huge black stallion. The women could not follow the men to the field where our horses ran loose, and we children were told to play behind the house . . . My father came to my mother, took money and went back to the field again. Then the men took the stallion away. Mystery hung over everything; and a secrecy of which no one spoke . . .

> Slowly I was learning of the shame and secrecy of sex. With it I was learning other things — that male animals cost more than female animals and seemed more valuable . . .

> The next day my father brought a box of cigars from the town and distributed them among the men who drove up to congratulate him . . . A *son* had been born! I felt neglected . . . my father . . . shook me off . . . There seemed to be something wrong with me . . . (pp.6 and 7)

The father shows a dominance that is linked to the power to dream out the unconscious desire of escaping society, travelling from the farm, and being a success. Marie's mother lives the kind of pioneer life where individuals, escaping from a life of powerlessness, create a new world for themselves on their own land with their own hands; it is not the trekking but the settling that matters. Her father is a different kind of pioneer, driven forward to the horizon by romantic dreams which can ultimately only survive in solitude. The patch of the quilt which describes the cyclone deftly catches the different worlds. The mother is intent on keeping the essentials of her home, her material and ideological self, and her family in the safety of the cave — a place of safety made by themselves under the house; survival and preservation of meaningful society by one's own efforts is how one might describe it. The father is much more the gallant hero, filling others with some of his bravery:

> 'I'll cut us out, I'm tellin' you. There aint no need losin' your head until somethin' happens'. I listened to his voice and knew that I could put him up against any cyclone that existed. (p.6)

In his own imagination he dares not the real wind that blows that day but the legendary cyclone that:

> . . . cut right across the country fer sixty miles an' they tried to dynamite it to break it up. You could see it comin' fer miles, a long black funnel . . . it sucked up a smokehouse in one place an' left the house, ten feet away, standin' as clean as a whistle! (p.6)

Trinidad, Colorado, at the turn of the century.

Immediately after this, the older Marie, looking back, tells how she, the child who likes to play with fire, echoed her father's imaginings, 'For I was my father's daughter!' The episode brings to my mind the storm which sweeps up Dorothy from Kansas in Frank Baum's *The Wizard of Oz*, first published in 1900. The land of Oz, where desire is released, is the same magic world for which Marie's father longs — over the rainbow, beyond the horizon, and reached by the erect spiral of the twister. He dreams of a land not on the wrong side of the tracks, which is where they end up, but at the end of the railroad's magic ribbon of steel. Marie's mother joins with him in the dream, as she rides with him on 'the two snow-white horses . . . ' (p.5) and whirls with him in the dance; but, in the end, the cash rewards associated with jobbing work are seen to be reserved for men rather than women*. On the farm, where work is shared, women can find rewards, but taken from there to the town their dreams are confined by circumstances to more limited and enclosed worlds. Marie tells how:

> I dreamed dreams: my mother was away and she returned to find I had plastered the two rooms with lovely plaster! She stood in the centre of the front room with its single window in the corner, and exclaimed: 'Well, I *do declare!* Who plastered the house?' Then I would look at her slender figure and beautiful eyes and proudly reply: 'I did!' (p.24)

> . . . My attention was riveted on the packet of coloured cards [showing religious scenes] which the woman held . . . in my imagination I saw our house papered with them — long rows of gorgeous red pictures. (p.25)

 ## 'On the road' (*Daughter of Earth,* Parts 5 and 6)

In the previous two Sections we have discovered the beginnings of a system of values and symbols based on the structure of the family and nature. Smedley uses this throughout the book as one way of creating the 'unity in diversity' of the novel. We shall now move on in the story and look at Part 5 and the first part of Part 6.

● Please read from p.91 to p.149 before going further.

At the beginning of Part 5 Marie has survived the agony of the deaths of her mother and sister, and the hellish life of the mining camps. Her demand for independence has sought out and found wanting the only avenue that seems open — to be a low-grade teacher. She has fled from her father's brutality to Helen, her older cousin, in Denver. Remember that in Part 1 it was foreshadowed that Helen and Marie would not accept the settled life of women; the lives they live are more related to those lived by men. Helen, as a wage-earner, was able to claim equal rights in the Rogers's household with Marie's father. 'I pay for my room and board here!' is her proud boast, rather than the begging and wheedling words of Gladys, the sick young wife, 'Damn it, kid, you know I love you!' (p.45). In Part 5, Helen has become a prostitute, earning money from the sexual services men want from women. She shares with Marie's father a desire for freedom and success, and in money she has been more successful than he. Her desire and her sharp-sighted view of the world cheats the men who want to dominate her . . . 'if any man struck her, she could call the police — no wife could do that. She was pledged to obey no man.' (p.92). But success here destroys Helen's own best chance of happiness when she refuses to marry Sam and be a mother to his child. Sam.

> . . . had failed to induce her to . . . marry him because — as she said — when a woman marries a man and can no longer make her own living, he begins reminding her of her past. (p.91)

> . . . her arms were empty since he had taken the child and gone and sometimes she walked the floor and cried. Her voice was dull when she said she could not see how she was going to stand the loneliness. (p.93)

Smedley thus makes Helen dramatically show some of the hazards of women's search for freedom. Marie's quest for freedom follows a different path. Helen helps her decide to become a stenographer. But Smedley holds the two options together by making Helen's money pay for Marie's training and by using the phrase 'to learn my profession' (p.93), which describes Marie's work as a stenographer, and also refers to Helen's trade as a prostitute.

---

*Marie's mother tries to join her daughter in her dream of being educated (p.82) but her efforts here too are doomed to tragic failure.

But, at the same time as Helen and Marie claim the rights of women, Marie shows herself to be her father's daughter. Like him, freedom seems to need to involve travelling, adventures and social success. So, having been a stenographer, she gives up that steady work and goes 'on the road', working at the more hazardous, but potentially more lucrative, work of selling magazine subscriptions. The shining white horses which spirit her father away and bring him back to amaze those left on the farm are replaced by the more prosaic but equally powerful: 'free pass on all the trains in the state. The pass was not only for going, but for returning . . . ' (p.98). The rejection of the desire to return is the most hard fought battle Marie faces in the book. Dealing in a man's world, and competing with other men, gives her 'a confidence and mastery such as I had never felt before . . .' (p.98). The pioneer, wanderlust spirit is much in evidence as Marie goes from town to town with gun and dagger, far from the office world of the stenographer. The freedom, however, has a limit; the free pass expires, just as her father's white horse had once to be sold.

In Part 6 Marie becomes a stenographer again: now not in the city office but in the Southern Californian desert. Sexual relations with men again seem as much part of Marie's 'profession' as they were of Helen's. One man demands 'What's yer price? . . . 'but you need'nt pitch it too high just because you've got the monopoly. I never pay more'n five dollars a night.' (p.133). But the pioneer town allows Marie more freedom to insist, without violence, that the transaction be strictly cash:

> Another land speculator, connected to a Los Angeles newspaper, adopted the attitude of a philanthropist. He was willing to make me the correspondent for his newspaper — for a consideration . . . It was an opportunity for making money and it appealed to my ambition . . . 'No "consideration," ' I said, 'but you can take a percentage of what I earn . . .' (p.133)

Overlapping with this are Marie's first opportunities for real study. Access to it initially seems like a dream, travelling to the school in the suitably significantly named town of Phoenix, she sees the town springing 'out of the desert like a mirage . . . ' (p.115). Confidence and mastery are again the rewards as 'ideas and thoughts take form in my mind . . . ' (p.117) but:

> I began to see that a girl could be beautiful, or she could command respect by intellectual ability, a show of power, a victory. But intellectual ability, a show of power, and victory, are dry, tasteless things. It was a tragic lesson to learn. I yearned for beauty, grace and love. (p.117)

Escape and success again carry within themselves the seeds of doubt and despair; Marie is as much the fierce, unhappy and unwomanly girl from 'beyond the tracks' as at her first school. The music and light of the dance at Phoenix echoes the party when she found her proudly bought three bananas placed amongst 'presents of books, silver pieces, handkerchiefs and lovely things such as I had never seen in my life' (p.32). Then, as now, it is 'my desire to know everything in the world even if it hurt' (p.33) that holds her in the school.

 ## Strangled emotions: Love between men and women

The bond to her family holds Marie back more than any outward sign of poverty or lack of social graces, The figures that reach from the past to pull her down are described particularly on pp.98–101 and pp.125–6. First she meets her father in the street, then George's letter again punctures her present life. What do you make of these scenes? Why do you think Smedley places them here? And what do they convey?

- Look again at those pages before reading further.

In my reading, on both occasions, the past and the family place burdens on Marie specifically because she is a woman. When Marie's father goes away, the family he leaves behind is forgotten. They are supported by Marie's grandfather. His return home always comes as a surprise (e.g. pp.25 and 83). By contrast, first Helen and then

Marie give the money they earn to Marie's mother. And when Marie goes away after her mother's death, her savings — designed to fulfill her own ambitions — are repeatedly depleted by the insistent demands of her father and brothers. She takes her mother's place in the family and feels her obligations, even though these are entirely one way and no reciprocal feelings to be found. On p.101 the images testify violently to the crisis she feels. Her own ambitions drag her on to the train 'as a chain would drag a dog', while she feels herself committing the greatest betrayal of all :

> It was early dawn and I know that somewhere a cock was crowing . . . once . . . twice . . . thrice.
> But a black curtain descended softly and erased from my memory the faces of those I loved. So deeply did I love them that I even forgot them . . . except for the dreams that awoke me at night and sent me further and further away, where I did not know . . . Where I often did not care. (p.101)

The violent immediacy returns when she receives George's letter: 'my heart sank within me and the veil of forgetfulness that I had so carefully constructed fell apart' (p.125). In her consciousness we see Marie's sense of obligation construct the letter as an indictment against herself. The imagery again takes its tone from Marie's vision of herself as Peter betraying the tortured and whipped Christ — 'always before me in the desert walked my wounded brother . . . ' (p.125). Smedley controls both these images, allowing them to spring from Marie's mind but emphasizing that they are not merely sick and frustrated imaginings. She emphasizes too that, when Marie meets the brothers in the attic room, they have become strangers. Those whom she loved now identify with their father rather than their sister, colluding in casting over Marie a cloak of dependent obligation.

In commenting on the two passages, I also want to refer to the way Marie's father's pursuit of his dream has degenerated into the search for his next drink. The aesthetically fine figure of the early chapters has become the stooped-shouldered grotesque — the town drunk mumbling to himself. Marie can no longer see herself, I think we understand, as her father's daughter. Apart from a brief sardonic mention on p.235, these are the last mentions of him.

Between the two scenes are four others which again reveal the careful construction of the book:

1 pp.101–109   On the road Carlsbad; in the hotel where a woman is raped
2 pp.109–115   Big Buck, Arizona; meeting the Mormon, etc.
3 pp.115–118   Phoenix and school
4 pp.118–122   Karin Larsen, Knut Larsen introduced; a different world?

The first two scenes look back, whereas the second two look forward. They echo the pivotal choice which faces Marie: which road should I follow — 'to the East or the West?' (p.125). Her eventual journey to the East and her political life are still only foreshadowed by the school in Phoenix and by her first meeting with the Larsens — they are further developed in the rest of the part of Part 6. The possibility of a life in the West other than one of sexual service, or in 'that gaunt house on the plains, accepting food from a father I hated' (p.125) is shown in the scenes describing Marie's time in Carlsbad, her return to Big Buck and her life in Arizona. The men involved here do not show the brutality towards Marie which she so often meets, but in all cases it is her and her ambition that are to be sacrificed. With Big Buck, the best of all the men, Smedley even implies that Marie's own ambition — rather than some aspect of the man — renders the marriage impossible. However good and kind, Buck is just 'too big and too dignified' (p.112) to share in the excitement and pursuit of desire which drives Marie onward.

 'the broken fragments . . . '

There is another — and perhaps finally more damaging — way in which the shadow of Marie's family falls across her life, which you might have noticed in the second of the two passages you have been looking at. In the agony of her choice Marie asserts:

> Love and tenderness meant only pain and suffering and defeat. I would not let it ruin me as it had ruined others! I would speak only with money, hard money . . .

I threw up fortifications to protect myself from the love and tenderness that menaced the freedom of women; I did not know then that one builds fortifications only where there is weakness (pp.100 and 101)

But love and tenderness do break through the barrier almost immediately when she meets the Larsens. And perhaps because she is so determined to control them, she shows herself easily swayed:

I stood at the back and watched them take notes and talk of those things to which I was a stranger. The love, the comradeship and understanding between them was very deep and very beautiful . . .

Could love really be beautiful and free, I wondered . . . Could human beings be tender and not be weak? Could there be love free from danger and subjection for a woman?

. . . I returned to the school to stare steadily at that hemmed-in road of my life. I would break all obstacles . . . work, money, study! (p.120)

The dream offered by Knut is remarkably seductive:

He was whispering as if the lonely desert might hear him . . . elemental things, ecstatic things. A great peace swept through my body and mind in the all-embracing gentleness of his touch . . . and his lips were caressingly tender as the moonlight falling on a quiet sheet of water. (p.122)

Smedley abruptly shatters the dream with the beginning of Part 6: 'Sex had no place in love. Sex meant violence, marriage or prostitution and marriage meant children . . . ' (p.123). And so when Marie becomes pregnant while married to Knut all her terrors return:

'Yer goin' to have a baby!'
   I turned and left the room when she said that. Fear, bitterness, hatred, gone from me for weeks, swept through me again like a hurricane. Everything that was hopeful vanished — I saw myself plunged back into the hell from which I was struggling — the hell of nagging, weeping women . . . I looked upon my baby with concentrated hatred. (p.134)

Nevertheless, the dream of a relationship with a man based on 'romantic friendship' (p.126) persists no matter how strong a poison her upbringing has implanted. We see Marie searching for it again in her relations with Ranjit Singh and Anand Manvekar later in the book. On this topic Smedley seems to speak directly through her created character, for the words and sentiments are closely echoed by her own words in 'Glimpses of the Past' written fifteen or so years later than *Daughter of Earth*:

I have always detested the belief that sex is the chief bond between man and woman. Friendship is far more human. I personally have never been able to reconcile myself to the sex relationship, for it seemed to me only a trap which limited women in every way. (p.12)

Writing later Smedley also remembers a dream which recurred during a period of psychoanalysis she underwent in Berlin. She dreamt she held a perfect Chinese vase 'and contemplated its beauty'. Suddenly a crack appears in the perfection and the vase is shattered. The dream, here ascribed to the period of writing *Daughter of Earth* (i.e. 1927), is in the novel transposed earlier and becomes part of the fictional character. It is now placed around 1918–19 before Smedley/Marie left New York:

I stood comtemplating a bowl in my outstretched hand . . . a beautifully shaped flower bowl, curved gently, broad and low, and about it was painted a wreath of flowers as delicate as all the art of ancient China. So beautiful and delicate it was that I held it far from me to see it shimmer as a ray of sunlight fell upon it. As I stood wondering at its beauty, a crack crawled down the side . . . I had not broken the bowl . . . nobody has broken it . . . but it was broken irrevocably broken by something I knew not what. (pp.259–60)

To me this image cuts across the whole of the book, providing the 'unity in diversity' in the portrayal of Marie which Smedley hopes for in the first paragraphs and which testifies to her own understanding of the fictional character that is herself. If you have time, continue your reading of the book if you have not finished it already. When you have finished, turn to Appendix 1, where you will find notes on the image I have just quoted. As you read my interpretation, ask yourself if it tallies with yours. Try to identify any differences, or any ways in which you think my argument might be expanded.

23 Conclusion and Study Objectives

This Unit cannot have a conclusion in that it is not designed to introduce you to a single argument about women's writing. Hopefully, indeed, it will be open ended, in that your reading of *Daughter of Earth* will not stop at the end of Part 6 but will continue to the end of the book. In my discussion of *Daughter of Earth,* and also in the earlier Parts of the Unit, I have aimed to introduce some of the questions raised by or about feminist criticism. Again, the Unit aims to enable you to be aware of the further work that is possible. However you may find the following topics useful in thinking about your work on the Unit now and at a later date.

1   The Unit is about alert and attentive reading, i.e. about the nuances and implications of specific pieces of language. You should be able yourself now to give an account of the set texts and extracts which you have read in the Unit.

2   Such skills are not applicable to these particular texts alone, and so you should be able to demonstrate your understanding of the methods we have used by analysing other texts — particularly texts by women.

3   The Unit has also emphasized the importance of approaching women writers 'though the fact of their sex'. You should now be able to describe the implications that being a woman has had for the writers discussed in this Unit. Again, the questions raised in the Unit are not only applicable to the writers discussed; you should be able to demonstrate your understanding of them in relation to other writers. You should be able to recognize points where being a woman has had a determining effect on other women writers.

4   The Unit has also considered how being a woman may affect the reading of a text. Again you should be able to demonstrate your understanding of these issues by identifying points in the set texts and in your other reading where a man might read a text differently from a woman, or where a particular text might have a different effect on a man or on a woman because of their sex.

5   The Unit has concentrated particularly on Agnes Smedley's *Daughter of Earth.* After the work on Parts 1, 5, and 6, you should be able to give similar descriptions of other Parts of the novel.

6   Finally the Unit has emphasized throughout how sex differences are involved at all points of the literary process. You should be able to give definitions of the phrases 'reading a text', 'the literary process', ' the literary canon', and 'feminist criticism'.

Answers to Revision Exercise

Check your answers to the questions in Section 9.4 against the following list.

1   Some act of criticism of evaluation. Such an act is at least as much related to the values of a particular society as it is to standards of 'absolute' quality.

2   A literary canon is a list of works that conform to some definition of excellence. More than one of these definitions may exist in a society at a particular time, but one of these will be dominant, reflecting the values considered most excellent, for example, by universities, patrons of the arts, etc.

3   Since a feminist critic is likely to have a critical and questioning attitude towards the organization of society, she will also have a critical attitude towards the dominant literary canon. She may also wish to suggest an alternative canon.

4   Section 4 discusses briefly how women have been important as writers and readers in the development of the modern publishing system. Look back particularly at p.9 if you are still uncertain about this.

5   The writer, the text, and the reader. You might also have thought of including, for example — education, the publishing process, or social class and gender — all of which have an important part in the process.

6 Both girls and boys can be enchanted by the magic of the story, but *Snow White* seems to offer a harsher lesson to girls. They must, it seems, choose between the contrasting stereotypes of evil stepmother and virtuous, but more or less helpless, wife. Girls see men in the story as benevolent. Boys may read the story as telling how, in marriage, they may do good by guiding and protecting women in the family and the home.

7 My reaction is that it is a brilliantly constructed piece, which combines a realism of detail with a wit and fantasy of conception. Bathing a baby is the most normal part of a woman's routine — how often might she be entranced by the romantic delight of the occasion and how often tempted to more mischievous thoughts?

8 Obviously I cannot provide you with a specimen answer to this question, but I hope it enabled you to reflect on the story and illuminated your thoughts on the particular literary process you experienced in reading the story.

Appendix 1 'The broken fragment'

The image of the broken vase pulls together ideas about sex from the book as a whole. In a general way the fracture in the vase shows the way the past reaches out to disrupt the carefully constructed present life, especially if that present is built on a *complete* rejection of the past. In a more particular way, at the point at which the dream occurs, the crack refers specifically to Juan Diaz's telling Marie's Indian Conference colleagues that he has had sex with her (the incident happens when she is protecting Talvar Singh and is described on pp.192−8). Anand's reaction to the story destroys Marie's most stable relationship with a man. Nobody is to blame, Marie thinks, because she has herself colluded with Diaz. Looking back at the earlier incident, you might also see the crack as symbolizing the eruption of more physical and less controlled sex into Marie's relations with Anand, which hitherto have been quite close to the pure friendship Smedley describes in 'Glimpses from the Past'.

But for Marie the most disturbing thing about Juan Diaz's seduction is the sight of his coloured belt as his body moved towards her:

> . . . I forgot the question, for the firelight had caught his glistening belt buckle and my eyes became fastened upon it. Where had I sat just like this before and seen that belt buckle! Above was his face, so strangely familiar, the high forehead, the broad shoulders, bent forward. There was a faint trace of scent about him — or was it from the pine knots in the fire? (p.194)

The reader is plainly challenged to answer the question that seems to elude Marie. Smedley's writing proves her own understanding:

> Even the way he wore his clothing distinguished him: there was his broad belt of many colours, with its buckle of silver. He had bought it in St. Joe, he said. Any other man would have been ashamed to wear such colour. But my father was a colourful man who dared what no one else dared. (p.15)

> As he turned I saw the shining buckle of his many-coloured belt (p.22)

It is hard to believe that in introducing the dream into her novel Smedley, as well as being true to her memories, was not also aware of the antique and beautiful golden bowl in Henry James's novel, *The Golden Bowl,* published 1904. That too shatters, symbolizing a fatal sexual flaw at the heart of perfect, reasonable and friendly relations. But Smedley's linking of the bowl to the claustrophobic and threatening vision of the man's belt, and to Juan Diaz and her father gives her image an additional powerful and physical urgency.

Bibliography and further reading

The following books are quoted in the text of this Unit:

AUSTEN, J. (1972) *Northanger Abbey,* Penguin.

*BERNIKOW, L. (ed.) (1979) *The World Split Open: Four Centuries of Women Poets in England and America 1552–1950,* Women's Press.

BETTELHEIM, B. (1976) *The Uses of Enchantment,* Thames and Hudson.

BRONTE, C. (1966) *Jane Eyre,* Penguin.

CARTER, A. (1981) *The Bloody Chamber and Other Stories,* Penguin.

FAIRBAIRNS, Z. (1979) *Benefits,* Virago.

FAIRBAIRNS, Z. (1981) 'On Writing Benefits'. See Feminist Anthology Collective

DICK, K. (1972) 'Thinking about Stevie', See Smith, S. (1972).

*FELL, A. (ed.) (1979) *Hard Feelings,* Women's Press.

FEMINIST ANTHOLOGY COLLECTIVE (eds) (1981) *No Turning Back,* Women's Press.

GILBERT, S. M. and GUBAR, S. (1979) *The Madwoman in the Attic: The Woman Writer and the Nineteenth Century Literary Imagination,* Yale University Press.

GRIMM BROTHERS (1896) *Grimms' Household Stories,* Routledge.

GÉRIN, W. (1967) *Charlotte Brontë,* Oxford.

LESSING, D. (1964) *African Stories,* Cape.

LESSING, D. (1975) 'My Father' in P. Schueter (ed.) *A Small Personal Voice,* Pantheon.

LESSING, D. (1979) 'Woman on a Roof' in D. Lessing Collected Stories Vol. 1: *To Room Nineteen,* Granada.

MEW, C. (1953) *Collected Poems,* introd. by A. Munro, Duckworth.

MEW, C. (1981) *Collected Prose and Poems,* Virago.

MICHAELIS-JENA, R. (1970) *The Brothers Grimm,* Routledge.

*MOERS, E. (1978) *Literary Women,* Women's Press.

*OLSEN, T. (1980) *Silences,* Virago.

PERRAULT, C. (1977) *The Fairy Tales of Charles Perrault,* translated by Angela Carter, Gollancz.

*SHOWALTER, E. (1977) *A Literature of Their Own,* Virago.

SMEDLEY, A. (1944) *Battle Hymn of China,* Gollancz.

SMEDLEY, A. (1977) *Daughter of Earth,* Virago. (Set Book).

SMITH, S. (1972) *Novel on Yellow Paper,* Penguin.

SMITH, S. (1978) *Selected Poems,* Penguin

WARD, M. A. (1888) *Robert Elsmere,* Smith and Elder.

WOOLF, V. (1967) *A Room of One's Own,* Penguin.

*All the books marked with an asterisk in the list above deal with issues raised in the Unit. The works by Moers, Olsen, Showalter and Gilbert and Gubar offer excellent introductions to feminist criticism. The anthologies indicated with an asterisk offer selections of women's writing particularly relevant to this Unit. But, as with many areas of Women's Studies, new books of women's writing or about women's writing are being published all the time so the above selections can only be a very incomplete list.

THE OPEN UNIVERSITY
A Second Level Course

The changing experience of women

Unit 6

Femininity and women's magazines: a case study of Woman's Own –'First in Britain for women'

Prepared for the Course Team by Janice Winship

The Open University Press

Contents

Study Guide

This Unit is oriented towards your doing practical work on women's magazines. It is concerned with how women's magazines are produced and how they are read by their readers.

To study this Unit you need the Main Text which you are now reading, the copy of *Woman's Own* you have been sent with the Unit, and the associated hour-long cassette. There is no other reading or TV programme associated with the Unit.

The Main Text discusses women's magazines generally but pays special attention to *Woman's Own*. The cassette deals more particularly with *your* copy of *Woman's Own*.

At certain points you will be asked to study your copy of *Woman's Own* in detail. You may, however, find it helpful to browse through the magazine — reading bits and pieces as you *might* if you had actually bought it, or picked it up in someone's house — before you continue any further with the Unit.

The Unit comprises four main Sections and an Introduction (Section 1):

Section 2   Women's magazines for sale

Section 3   Ideologies of femininity

Section 4   Social readings and reading for pleasure

Section 5   The short story

To study each Section, you will need all three components of the Unit: this Main Text, *Woman's Own,* and the cassette.

The Main Text

You will find that the Sections of the Unit differ in terms of the number of activities you are required to do, and in the difficulties of those activities. They also vary in terms of the number and difficulty of concepts to which they introduce you. The Sections will, therefore, take you different lengths of time to complete.

In Sections 2.1 to 2.3 — which analyse the covers, contents, visual and verbal forms and styles used in women's magazines — there are many activities that you need to work through and digest in detail. Section 2.4 — which examines women, consumption and magazines — is more descriptive and there is less for you to do. Do not spend too long on Section 2 as a whole.

Section 3 is fairly abstract. It introduces several difficult concepts such as ideology. Though it is important that you have some understanding of these concepts, it is more germane that you do the suggested activities. Some of these require concentrated thought. Do not spend too much time on this section initially but return to it after you have completed the rest of the Unit. In total, it may take you longer than any of the other Sections.

In Section 4 — on reading and the pleasure to be derived from reading women's magazines — there is little activity for you to do. It is also a more descriptive Section which you should find more straightforward conceptually than Section 3. You should spend much less time completing it.

Section 5 provides a brief resumé of the general method of *cultural studies* that the Unit has been adopting. It also introduces you to a method and concepts for analysing the short story, and asks you to consider closely the text of one story. Your analysis of the story will allow you to bring together many of the dimensions of women's magazines that the Unit has been considering. Spend about as much time on this Section as you did on Section 2.

At the end of the main Sections 2 to 4, I shall be referring you to the cassette. Drawing on the work you will have done in each Section, I shall be asking you to examine certain features in your copy of *Woman's Own*. I shall then discuss the analysis you might have made and some of the issues that arise from such an examination.

On the cassette, in addition to providing supplementary information on each Section I shall be discussing *Woman's Own* — with particular reference to your issue — with some of the people who produce the magazine.

Though it would be better to do the cassette work at the end of each Section, you may prefer to leave it until you have completed the Main Text. Listening to the cassette and carrying out the related activities should take you no more than three hours.

Introduction: Why bother about women's magazines?

To begin the Unit, think briefly about the relevance of women's magazines to women's changing experience of social life in contemporary Britain.

● On the basis of what you already know about women's magazines what is your opinion of them? Do you find them:
(a) interesting and useful;
(b) obsessed with selling a feminine image, and an affront to women's position in society;
(c) entertaining and a good read, but not to be taken seriously?

I have asked you these questions, half expecting that many of you will respond — especially in the context of an intellectual pursuit like doing this Open University course — with answers (b) or (c) rather than (a). Many of you will dismiss women's magazines as at best superficial and trivial publications, at worst a commercial con to sell women all and sundry. Even those of you — presumably mainly women* — who find them both useful and pleasurable may hesitate to admit so much, lest you be scorned. Moreover, that such ephemeral publications should be the subject for serious discussion and take up a whole Unit of this Course may seem to some of you at least odd, if not a complete waste of valuable time. So why bother with women's magazines? There are two reasons pertinent to this Course.

First, women's magazines provide a long-standing public record of women's lives and experiences. They have an extended history well documented by Cynthia White in her book *Women's Magazines 1693–1968* (White, 1970). As she reports, the first women's magazines were diaries and almanacs addressed mainly to women. Women's magazines proper, directed at a small upper-class readership, and intending to 'amuse and improve the minds' of women, began in the second half of the eighteenth century. By the middle of the nineteenth century, one Samuel Beeton (husband of that doyen of cookery Mrs Beeton) recognized the financial possibilities of a cheaper publication aimed at the newly forming middle classes. These wives and daughters were increasingly devoting their energies to the home and domestic management. (Catherine Hall discusses their move into the home in her article in the Reader, 'The butcher, the baker, the candlestick maker', which you will be reading later on in the Course.)

Beeton's *The Englishwoman's Domestic Magazine* (to which his wife contributed 'Notes on Cookery and Fashion') catered to their interests. According to Beeton, it was intended to provide 'a fund of practical information and advice tending to promote habits of industry and usefulness, without which no happy home can be rendered virtuous or happy' (cited in White, 1970, p.44).

The forerunner of today's mass weeklies, like *Woman's Own, Woman*, and *Woman's Weekly* were launched at the beginning of this century. Magazines with the more informal and friendly titles of *Home Notes, Home Chat* and *My Weekly* (the latter is still is circulation, the former two are not) were the first to provide that 'fund of practical information and advice' to make a happy home for a lower middle-class and working-class readership.

Checked only by the financial restrictions imposed by two World Wars, the women's magazine industry steadily expanded, producing magazines that were read by increasing numbers of women of all ages and from all classes. Sales peaked in the second half of the 1950s and early 1960s, when it was estimated that 'five out of six women saw at least one women's magazine every week' (W.D. McClelland, IPC's Research Director. Quoted in White, 1970, p.216).

* At points in the unit you may notice that I address only women, as both the readers of women's magazines *and* the readers of the Unit. Though I am well aware that many men do read women's magazines, and that some of you studying this Unit are men, women's magazines are, nevertheless, primarily directed at women. They assume a woman readership and therefore the problems and questions they raise and which are discussed in this Unit are ones pertinent to women rather than to men. It is for these reasons that I have adopted the convention of sometimes using 'she' not 'he' (or the cumbersome 'she and he'), and the 'you' I am referring to is often assumed to be a woman.

Section 2.4 will examine the economic and social implications of this trend for women and discuss the issue of the subsequent decline of the magazine industry in the latter part of the 1960s. The point to emphasize here is that, in so far as this Course is examining the changing experience of women, women's magazines perhaps provide an unparalleled popular or mass documentation of that changing experience.

However, this documentation in the pages of women's magazines has always been a highly selective one, focusing particularly on women as the creators of that 'virtuous and happy' home mentioned by Beeton. Women's magazines provide what can be described as 'mirror images' for women, i.e. public images of femininity against which women measure themselves, men judge women, and which are, therefore, formative in actually *shaping* women's experiences. If those images are ones that many of us may dislike or reject, they are none the less powerfully pervasive.

The massive numbers of women's magazines which (despite the 1960s decline in the industry) are still sold and read, their taken-for-granted presence within British culture, like the national habit of eating fish and chips, establishes them as part of every woman's life: at the forefront in defining those 'mirror images', and in *moulding women's experiences*. This then, is the second reason they are worthy of serious analysis.

But why have I selected *Woman's Own* as the prime magazine to study? There are three related reasons for this choice.

First, *Woman's Own* has vied with *Woman's Weekly* and *Woman* — all owned by the International Publications Corporation (IPC), part of Reed International — as the top-selling women's magazine in Britain since the mid-1970s. For July 1980 – June 1981, its weekly circulation was 1 401 032; *Woman's Weekly's* circulation for the same period was 1 487 245; and *Woman's* 1 340 652 (figures from the Audit Bureau of Circulation). However, the magazine proprietors reckon that because, like other magazines, each copy is passed from one woman to another and may end up in a doctor's surgery or in a hairdressers, the magazine is in fact read by at least three times the circulation figure.

Second — and this marks *Woman's Own* off from the very traditional feminine world on offer to an increasingly older readership in *Woman's Weekly* — it has introduced a wider perspective which moves beyond the domestic sphere of women's lives. More than any other mass service weekly throughout the 1970s, under the resourceful editorship of Jane Reed and then Iris Burton, it has concerned itself with a discussion of the problems, debates and campaigns initiated or inspired by the women's movement. For example, in 1979 the magazine commissioned a survey from Gallup Poll focusing on the child-care problems of women in paid-work, and followed it up with the campaign 'Fair care for children and a fair deal for Mum'. It was this feminist edge — especially evident after the legitimation given to feminist issues by the implementation of the Sex Discrimination and Equal Pay Acts in 1975 — which constituted the magazine's winning appeal in the 1970s. However, this feminist edge was, and still is, diluted amongst the more traditional fare of the magazine.

Third, and as a result of this success (if success is measured on the basis of sales), *Woman's Own* has influenced the contents of other weeklies with which it is in competition. It is notable that at the time of writing (1982) *Woman,* the long-term rival of *Woman's Own* — which remarkably topped the weekly charts for the whole period from the Second World War to the mid-1970s — is adopting a more outspoken and feminist stance on some issues of pertinence to women. Significantly it is again Jane Reed whom IPC has wheeled in as editor-in-chief to orchestrate the new style *Woman* magazine. It will be interesting to see whether such a magazine will again attract proportionately more sales to *Woman.* In my view, it is this kind of magazine, rather than the conservative variety like *Woman's Weekly.* that *will* win sales in the future.

This Unit will examine women's magazines as *cultural forms,* i.e. as objects that are part and parcel of a feminine culture in Britain. In particular it will consider their *cultural representations* of femininity. Culture here, clearly, does not refer to the Great Works of English Literature or to Sadler's Wells Ballet — Culture with a big 'C', or The Arts, as it is more customarily referred to in Britain — but to a wider corpus which includes the most mundane and everyday-life expressions of a group's social existence. What is distinctive about a *cultural studies approach* is, first, that it takes all experiences, all cultural expressions and forms, as not only proper foci for cultural analysis, but necessary to that analysis. It is only possible to understand how a culture is put together, how it operates, by examining its most familiar and taken-for-granted forms, as well as its so-called creative cultural forms, for example, the kinds of activities supported and financed by the Arts Council.

The approach also tries to understand the underlying social activities in which classes and groups are involved which produce these cultural forms. In the case of women's magazines, then, we shall be looking at what it is about the lives of women and about mass publishing that contributes to the shape women's magazines take.

Women's magazines for sale

This Section begins to make explicit the representations of femininity to be found in women's magazines, and to explore the various constraints on the production of those representations. In particular, as the title of the Section implies, it considers the *economic* conditions that have shaped women's magazines, and indeed shaped women's own experiences of femininity.

The analysis opens with an examination of the *covers* of a cross-section of English-language magazines available in British newsagents. It is the cover which has the greatest public visibility, and it is the part of any magazine to which your eyes are first directed. Though this exercise might initially seem curious to you, I hope it will make clear the *extent* of the coded, cultural meanings to be read off the kind of everyday representations to which you usually may not pay much conscious attention.

2.1 The cover 'advertisement'

Whether or not magazines depend on advertising for revenue they all need to sell sufficient copies to keep in business. At the newsagents or on the station bookstall about a hundred magazines compete with each other to attract our eye and our purse. The overriding purpose of any cover in this context is to aid the sale of the magazine in question: it serves as the magazine's advertisement.

With this aim in mind, the cover must firstly allow us, the prospective purchasers, to assess at a quick glance the *category* of magazine being sold — women's magazine, magazine of social and political comment, or men's special interest magazine, for example. We want to know immediately if we are interested in that *kind* of magazine before we pursue its detailed selling points. To this end, the cover also tries to tell us something about the audience for whom the magazine is intended.

Second, for those of us who are regular purchasers, any cover must bear the hallmark or stamp which differentiates one magazine from another, competitively nestling along-side it, in order that we can pick it out from the mass with relative ease.

Finally, as we home in on any one magazine, the cover strives to entice us to buy what is suggestively promised as unique and special in *that* issue, of *that* magazine.

But how exactly do magazine proprietors and editors put together a cover to convey this complicated 'sales talk' to us? How, particularly, are women's magazines marked off from other sorts of periodical? And how do we come to recognise *Woman's Own* as a certain type of women's magazine?

To tackle these questions we shall look at a cross-section of magazine covers from a range of periodicals, and then at the narrower spectrum of women's magazines. Before continuing with the written text, it might be helpful to look quickly at the two sets of magazine covers (Figures 1 – 6, pp. 9 and 10, and Figures 7 – 12, pp. 13 and 15) and that of your copy of *Woman's Own*. In so far as the reproductions here are in black and white, you would also find it helpful if you were to gather together your own copies of these magazines.

The Introduction stressed that a cultural studies approach to a cultural form was concerned with the production of *cultural meanings*. What also needs emphasizing is that those cultural meanings are structured, patterned or coded. That is they are produced by putting together certain cultural elements according to specific conventions or codes which can be discovered by the analysis of the cultural form. The type of analysis that we shall be making — to discover the variable elements with which different covers may be produced — may be described as one of *deconstruction* and *decoding*.

By deconstruction and decoding I mean that the analysis is concerned to *break down* the complete image, which we gloss over in an everyday reading, to discover *the different elements which constitute* that image, and to understand the *pattern* or find the *key* to how those elements are *arranged or put together*. As in decoding any code (like Morse or the Highway Code) the analysis attempts to understand the *meanings* attached to those elements. But what is significant about the cultural codes in operation on the cover of women's magazines is that — unlike Morse, perhaps — you are, if you are a reader of such magazines, already familiar with them. What the analysis has to do, then, is to *make explicit* the cultural codes which are generally taken for granted as you read and gaze at the cover.

The first and most basic element to consider is the *paper* used for the covers. If the magazines themselves are at hand, the type and quality of paper tell us much about the category of magazine we are looking at. We soon learn that in our culture it is conventional (and not wholly related to cost) for *monthly* magazines to use glossy, fairly thick paper for their covers. In our selection, they are represented by *Motor Sport, Practical Computing,* and *Men Only* (Figures 3–5). At the other extreme, we soon learn that the roughest paper, similar to that used for newspapers, is used for the covers (and inside pages) of weekly news magazines like the *New Statesman* (Figure 1). Other weekly magazines, associated more with entertainment, use a paper whose texture lies somewhere in between: smooth but not glossy, flimsy rather than substantial. This includes the *Observer* supplement (Figure 2) and *Woman's Own.*

● Try feeling the textures of different magazines. If you have a selection of magazines in the house, gather them together with your copy of *Woman's Own* and feel what discriminations you can make by shutting your eyes and relying on your fingers. (Otherwise steel yourself to look slightly silly at your local newsagents carrying out the same test!) Can you pick out the monthlies from the weeklies?

With a little practice, then, if we shut our eyes, and pick up a copy of *Woman's Own,* we know, merely from its feel, that it is some sort of weekly entertainment magazine. That knowledge is also given to us if we key into the visual clues of the cover: the different types of magazines carry different styles of visual.

● Look at the sample of covers illustrated here and try to describe, briefly, the differences in visual style between the covers of the *New Statesman* and the *Observer* supplement. (Since these are black-and-white reproductions, you would find the following exercises easier if you were to look for similar covers yourself.)

The *New Statesman* has the typical style of the newsphoto on its cover — the grainy, black-and-white, and deeply shadowed photo, showing the public figure not posed for the camera, but at work. We are left in no doubt of its serious news quality. The other covers all employ colour photography; none the less, their styles and colour tones are distinguishable. We recognize in the subtle, sombre tones of the *Observer* cover the documentary but romanticizing eye of the camera which produces the photographically and artistically excellent photo typical of the topnotch Sunday supplements. In contrast we soon come to know that covers of women's magazines, and men's so-called girlie magazines, tend to be less artistically subtle, more colourful, using the posed female model who is evenly lit, to eliminate any atmosphere, character or individuality from both the photo and, by association, from the nearly-always, young, smiling (white) woman represented there.

● Look for a moment at your copy of *Woman's Own* and see whether you agree with my description of the photographic style.

It is not just the style of visual which brands a magazine: so too does *layout.* Look at the visual on the *Motor Sport* cover.

● What do you think are the signs — apart from its verbal indication, 'Founded in the year nineteen twenty-four' — which indicate its long-standing reputation? Briefly list the elements of the visual that contribute to that reading.

FIGURE 1

FIGURE 2

FIGURE 3

FIGURE 4

FIGURE 5

FIGURE 6

It is the cover's old-fashioned style — the kind of lettering, the (dull moss green-and-white) striped background, the ungimmicky, simple photo and its uncluttered look which all point to that reading.

The title of the magazine is the element of the whole cover image that has the most constancy from issue to issue: its print type, size, position on the cover, and colour are generally invariable. In this way the other elements of the cover may change without the identity of the magazine being lost. For example, the sloping capitals of *Woman's Own* and the small letters of *Woman* have long been part of their respective hallmarks.

Thus, the visual, though it contributes to the magazine's identity by conforming to the generic pattern of images pertaining to that magazine, also has some degree of flexibility. For example, *Men Only* magazine always flaunts a (different) partly clad female on its cover. *Woman's Own*, like many other women's magazines, generally carries a close-up of a (different) woman's face.

What I refer to as the feature leads or *trailers* — the verbal captions on any cover — are the third main element making up the cover's image. They serve to conjure up the *particular* contents of any issue, and hence are unique to that issue. Even so they usually fit in with the magazines general style, whether it be the sentence structure they adopt or the type and colour of lettering.

● Look at the *Woman's Own* illustrated in Figure 6; notice how the trailers *invite* you, the reader — to 'Embroider a work of art', 'Clown around with our fun kit'. They also ask you *questions* — 'Can you really contact the dead?' which are presumably answered inside. They *titillate you by a partial revelation* — 'Brando. The wife who waited for revenge' . . . Examine the cover of your copy of *Woman's Own*. Do the trailers follow a similar style?

Trailers are, in fact, double edged: they're intended to *grab* their audience with their suggestion of better things inside; but they also have to affirm who that audience is. To take one example, *Practical Computing* (Figure 4) manifestly addresses those who-already-know-about computers: 'byte' and 'virtual memory' are not yet household terms for many of us. The trailers as a whole back up the magazine's claim to practical computing: its audience would seem to be less the boffin at his desk, more the technologist putting science to use, and the amateur who likes to play around with this new toy. The cover grabs its audience with a *riddle* posed by the trailer — 'Baby's first byte' — in conjunction with the visual — the tampered old-master painting of Madonna/ Christ, Mother/child — in which the baby chews on a component of computer hardware. By implication, computer technology is the work of the 'new masters'; in time it will also claim classic status. As readers of this cover, we might guess what the article 'Baby's first byte' is about, but the riddle is not really solved for us until we turn to the inside pages. (It is actually about a mother teaching her young child to play with a computer.)

From this example we can see how the cover of a magazine, and particularly its trailers, are *addressing* you-the-reader-in-your-many-guises. We shall be returning to the question of how the reader is addressed throughout the Unit; the point to emphasize here is that this address is one of the ways that representations ensnare us, catch us in their meanings, without us having a chance to make a choice about that engagement.

● Now turn to the covers of women's magazines (Figure 7—12, pp. 13 and 15), and examine how each cover sells a different package. Look at how each cover points to a different contents, and addresses a different woman reader. In particular try to discover how *Woman's Own* marks itself off from the rest.

Focus first on the titles, visuals and layout. Answering the following questions about the covers should help you to focus on these three elements:

Do the titles differ in their lettering styles?

What image of the home or women does each title convey?

How do the various female models shown on the covers differ?

And what do the visuals which do not use women suggest of their magazines?

What is distinctive about any of the layouts?

One of the features you should have noticed about the titles is that each uses a wholly different type of print with which to name itself. The profile of each magazine also begins to be spelt out by their respective titles. *Woman's Weekly* sounds cosy and homely. *Ideal Home,* on the other hand, has an out-of-this-world ring to it; *Company* plays on the ambiguity of social companionship and company referring to work and industry; and the wry, jokey, title of *Spare Rib* leaves us in no doubt that it is somehow different from other magazines.

One pronounced characteristic of the visuals is their *similarity.* With the exception of *Ideal Home* and *Spare Rib,* they all carry the softly lit woman's face already referred to. Nevertheless, they variously inflect that image. For example, in our selection here, the *Company* model is black, a *bold* gesture since models are invariably white. She's also young, stylish and, with her bare shoulders, has a definite seductive appeal. *Woman's Weekly* — in displaying more than just a head and shoulders, and shot so that you can really see the model's knitted cardigan — highlights its knitting emphasis.

The two anomalous covers in this set — *Ideal Home* and *Spare Rib* — mark themselves as on the periphery of the category women's magazines. *Ideal Home* makes explicit its major concern in desirable decor for the home, on a grand and not always achievable scale, rather than any wider womanly interests. The cover of *Spare Rib,* with its two-toned, deeply shadowed photo of Bernadette Devlin McAliskey, whose gaze is off centre, has much in common with the *New Statesman* photo of Rupert Murdock. It suggests a news/comment emphasis to the magazine.

In terms of layout you may have noticed that *Woman's Weekly* stands out with its *framed* visual and, if you could see the colours, its old-fashioned pink and blue letterhead. Some other magazines, you may have noted, run their visuals right to the edges, like *Woman* and *Woman's Own* and superimpose the title.

The *trailers,* on the other hand, aim to specify quite precisely the contents of a particular issue and the audience to whom it is addressed, as well as the style and tone of the magazine as a whole.

● Table 1 lists some categories into which the content pointed to by the trailers might be slotted. Try filling them in with ticks and crosses as I have done for *Woman's Weekly.*

TABLE 1

	Women's Weekly	*Company*	*Spare Rib*	*Ideal Home*	*Woman*	*Woman's Own*
Home	✓					
Beauty	✓					
Personal relationships	✗					
Paid work	✗					
Offers/ competitions	✓					
Social issues	✗					

● In Table 2 consider the woman reader who is addressed by the trailers, in terms of age and social class. The social class of readers to which the magazines are appealing is difficult to pin down from the covers, not least because the signs of class in British culture are often subtle. Use a simple classification of upper, middle and working class, based on *lifestyle* — like the kind of goods on offer, suggested house decor or menus — to classify these magazines.

TABLE 2

	Woman's Weekly	*Company*	*Spare Rib*	*Ideal Home*	*Woman*	*Woman's Own*
Age	middle age					
Class	middle class					

Check your results with mine on p. 72. Then compare your findings about age and class readership with Tables 3 and 4, taken from the *National Readership Survey* (NRS) carried out on behalf of the Institute of Practitioners in Advertising. It gives the results of a sample survey of the newspapers and magazines read by the adult population. The percentages in both Tables refer to women and women readers only.

The National Readership Survey distributes readers according to a definition of class based on the occupation of the *head* of household. Thus, unless a woman is the head of the household, which is unusual, it is her husband's or father's job, *not her own*, which defines her class position. (This issue of women's dependent class position will be discussed further in Units 10 and 11 on women and employment.) It is, clearly, not a

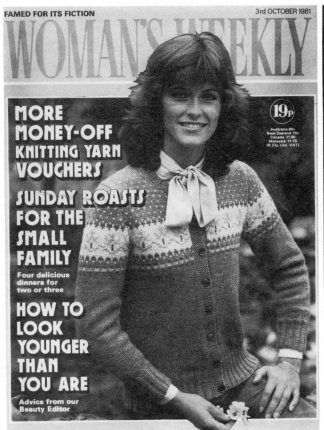

FIGURE 7

FIGURE 8

FIGURE 9

FIGURE 10

wholly satisfactory definition of women's class position. Nevertheless, for our purposes, in so far as head-of-household occupation is linked in part to household income and lifestyle of the marital home, there is likely to be some agreement with the definition of class based on lifestyle that you have used above.

TABLE 3

	Upper* middle class	Middle class	Lower middle class	Skilled working class	Working class	Those at lowest level of subsistence
	%					
National distribution of population	3	13	23	29	19	13
Woman's Weekly	2	13	24	30	20	11
Company	6	20	35	25	14	1
Ideal Home	8	21	29	26	12	4
Woman	3	14	27	31	18	8
Woman's Own	3	13	26	31	19	8

*The occupational breakdown into classes that the NRS uses is elaborated on Table 7, p. 72.

Adapted from the *National Readership Survey*, 1981.

TABLE 4

Age	15–24	25–34	35–44	44–54	55–64	65+
	%					
National distribution of population	19	17	14	14	14	22
Woman's Weekly	14	15	14	16	17	24
Company	58	21	10	6	4	1
Ideal Home	19	22	18	18	11	12
Woman	26	20	14	14	13	14
Woman's Own	25	19	15	13	13	16

Adapted from the *National Readership Survey*, 1981.

● Ring the two highest percentages for each magazine in order to make it easier to interpret the results.

There are two things you should notice in particular. First, that all the magazines, without exception, have the highest proportion of their readers in what are described as the 'lower middle class' and 'skilled working class', though the weightings towards one or other of these varies. This is not surprising since, as the national distribution of women shows, a larger proportion of women are in those classes. Still there must be other factors about the magazines themselves which contribute to women of those classes deciding to buy them.

Second, with the exception of *Woman's Weekly,* which has a greater proportion of readers 65+, all the rest have most readers in the first two age groups: 15–24/25–34. Again, this partly relates to the national distribution of women according to age. There are more women aged 15–34 and 65+ than there are between those ages. But, again, there must be other factors persuading women of those age groups to buy women's magazines.

Woman's Own you will notice has very much the *same* class range as both *Woman's Weekly* and *Woman,* but only the same *age* range as *Woman.* Interestingly, it is *Woman's Weekly* whose distribution seems most closely to follow the national distribution of the female population according to class and age.

FIGURE 11   FIGURE 12

● Finally, think about the style and tone suggested by the trailers in terms of the criteria listed in Table 3, and tick or cross appropriately in Table 5. Check with my answers on p. 72.

TABLE 5

	Woman's Weekly	Company	Spare Rib	Ideal Home	Woman	Woman's Own
Matter-of-fact	✔					
Racy	✘					
Investigative *and* serious	✘					

There are several general characteristics you may already have deduced from the information somewhat roughly entered in Tables 1, 2 and 5.

1   With the exception of *Spare Rib*, all the magazines are concerned to interest their readers in a *sale*, in something the magazine has on offer, or which readers could win.

2   The areas of paid work and social issues are of very minor interest compared with the heavy emphasis on home, beauty, and personal relationships.

3   The address to women readers — again with the exception of *Spare Rib*, and notwithstanding the black model on the cover of *Company* — is wholly to a white audience. There are no signs either of an address to an older woman readership, despite the fact that *Woman's Weekly* clearly sells to an older audience.

4   Similarly, there are only very slight indications of an address to a working-class readership. The magazines seem overwhelmingly to address a middle-class to upper-class readership. Yet the magazines are *mainly* bought by women who are likely to think of themselves as working-class.

5   The tone of the magazines (excepting *Spare Rib* and *Ideal Home)* is either matter-of-fact or racy, or some combination of both. Their style, this suggests, is intended both to *inform* and importantly, to *entertain*.

15

These are pertinent findings whose significance the Unit goes on to explore. I have briefly spelt out from these Tables the individual profiles of two magazines.

● As you read them, consider whether you agree with me.

Woman's Weekly It refers in a matter-of-fact way to knitting, the family's Sunday roast and trying to look younger and, in doing so, makes clear that it is addressed to a readership that is no longer young, and who are family women in a traditional and conservative style. The offer of money off knitting yarns suggests a not-too-well-off readership at the lower end of the middle class. The trailers have an eminently sensible and unspectacular tone, and imply that the contents will be likewise: practical and informative but not exciting.

Spare Rib The trailers here are notably different from other magazines in their social range — from motherhood to race and the disabled — in one issue, and in their investigative and serious stress. Thus the news/social comment style I noted from the visual is corroborated by the trailers. The magazine's address to the reader is somewhat different too: it does not assume a universal 'you' (except that she's a woman) but points to distinctive groups of women — Asian, disabled, mothers. It suggests also that its class readership might be more wide ranging than most women's magazines.

● Now briefly sketch the profile of *Woman's Own* (Figure 11) from its cover.

Its cover embraces a concern with beauty, 'Do you think your face is really clean?'; a possible pleasurable side of domesticity, 'Embroider a work of art', for which there are appropriate commodities on sale, 'Special offer craft kit', to aid this pursuit. This everyday life stands alongside the intrigue of another world, 'Can you really contact the dead?', and that romantic and entertaining other world of the rich and the famous, with its gossip of how the other half lives, and more crucially, loves (and hates).These trailers suggest that the magazine seeks to inform, provide practical advice and to entertain — as do other women's magazines.

The areas of interest pointed to are middle-of-the-road: neither outrageous nor conservative, neither solely for a very young readership, nor for an older readership, neither over-domestic nor lacking completely in homely pursuits. The model is young, but not *that* young. She looks 'smart' but would not appear to be concerned about up-to-the-minute fashion: hair, blouse, earrings are not ultrafashionable (in 1982). There is no suggestion about the marital status of readers.

As far as class is concerned, we are given few clear signs. The notion of 'embroidering a work of art' with a kit, hints perhaps at the lower half of the class spectrum; the model with her classic pearl earrings also plays safely in the hazy middle of the British classes. Similarly, there are no signs of richness, but neither is there any indication of poorness.

At this point, jumping a little in the analysis, read an editorial — the 'Our World' slot in *Woman's Own* — in which Iris Burton defends the magazine against its critics. She provides a useful, if very general, view of whom *the magazine* thinks are its readers:

Our World
'What is a Woman's Own woman?' I'm often asked, and I suppose I do have a very definite image of her, but she is awfully difficult to describe. Statistics can tell me her socioeconomic group (class and income to put it baldly), age and interests but, since there are so many of you, you're spread across a wide spectrum. In age alone you range from 15 to 70 plus. But there is one thing that most of you share. You are that bit more curious about what's going on around you. You are that bit more likely to take up outside interests, be more adventurous with cooking, or get your noses into a good book. And it's that 'bit more', borne out by figures, that makes a Woman's Own woman and helps all of us here feel we know you. I am often irritated to see or hear people who know very little about the magazine or its readers take it upon themselves to describe one or all of you in unrecognisable terms. It's happened twice recently, in a TV play and in a newspaper article, where Woman's Own has been used rather dismissively to sum up women preoccupied with trivia ... (Iris Burton, *Woman's Own*, 6 March 1982)

● Do you think her image of the reader and the magazines coincide with what we have discovered so far from the cover of *Woman's Own?*

I think, her image is more 'progressive' — women who are that 'bit more' as she puts it — than the one we have come up with. Bear her view in mind for comparison as we delve into the serious heart of the magazine. You will be asked to study it again at a later stage in the Unit.

We have devoted a long Section to the covers of women's magazines for two reasons. First, the Unit has been introducing you step by step to the relatively unfamiliar territory and tools of a cultural studies approach as applied to verbal and visual representations. If you have grasped how to begin to analyse a cover for its cultural meanings, you should also be able to tackle the rest of the magazine. Second, the cover of women's magazines represents a condensed summation of what you will find on the inside pages. Thus, if you know your covers, you are well on the way to decoding and deconstructing the whole of the magazine for its cultural meanings.

2.2 The contents page: ingredients for a woman's magazine

From each cover we have gained knowledge about the category of the magazine: about some of its general characteristics and how any issue attempts to entice us to buy and read the magazine by the suggestion of some special and spicy items inside. But, like most advertisements, the cover is very *selective* about what it represents. Like many advertisements it persuades the reader that she will be *edified* by buying the magazine: she will be handed out sound practical advice and be *entertained*. The world beyond that cover is above all a pleasurable one: it is a world of rose blooms without their thorns.

The contents page, on the other hand, begins to fill in the more mundane ingredients of a magazine as they are labelled by the magazine editors and proprietors. That list of ingredients begins to define any magazine more precisely but we require *more* than just a knowledge of *which* contents in order to do that. We also need to know how the content is arranged, and classfied, and which items are stressed . To illustrate what I mean, examine the contents columns of the three magazines shown in Figures 13—15.

● Run down the list of articles and features, and fill in Table 6(a), putting in ticks if you find any items fitting the category. (Disregard those which do not fit any category.)

TABLE 6

Category	(a)			(b)		
	Ideal Home	*Woman*	*Sunday Times*	*Ideal Home*	*Woman*	*Sunday Times*
Home						
Cookery/ food						
Beauty/ make-up						
Fashion						
Personal relationships						
People 'ordinary' 'celebrities'						
Paid work						
Consumer items						
Offers/ competitions						
Fiction						
Holidays/ travel						

• When you have completed that, repeat the exercise in Table 6(b), but this time consider only the *main headings* (marked by arrows) by which the magazine differentiates its groups of items. Check your results with mine on p. 73.

IDEAL HOME

OCTOBER 1981 VOLUME 122 No. 4 ISSN 0019-1361
KING'S REACH TOWER, STAMFORD STREET, LONDON SE1 9LS

▶	**HOUSES**	
	RESTYLED FOR THE 80s An Edwardian semi brought right up to date	3
	AT HOME WITH ROBERT POWELL	8
	ON SHOW Designers' talents transform the once humble show house	14
▶	**REGULAR FEATURES**	
	SHOPPING	41
	BENNY GREEN Discovering there's more to Wodehouse than Wooster	48
	CONSUMER AFFAIRS Eliminate tarnish with varnish or other metal cleaners	50
	MONEY IN YOUR LIFE The legendary fast buck—and how to make it	61
	THE WAY WE LIVE NOW	118
	TECHNICALLY SPEAKING Bill Eykyn cuts the overheads of re-roofing	141
	LETTERS	144
	HOLIDAYS Sun and fun on an autumn break	169
	FAMILY CAR TEST Fiat 127 1050 Comfort	177
	MOTORING NEWS	179
	BOOKS	225
	AT HOME WITH THE LAW The rights of the mortgagor to sell	229
	LEADERGRAM	232
	ADDRESS BOOK	234
▶	**SPECIAL FEATURES**	
	THE CHOICE IS YOURS Choosing your ideal home	22
	LIVING COLOUR Create a mood of interest for your living-room	30
	FLOOR SHOW From rugs to riches	37
	KATE McKENZIE'S PRACTICAL KNOW-HOW Tap your resources—plumb it yourself	79
	ECOLOGICAL TIP FOR THE FUTURE? The controversial Vale of Belvoir	108
	COUNTER ATTACK Linda Gillard's view from both sides of the counter	148
	YOUR IDEAL COOKER What you told us, and what we've done about it	185
	A LOVESOME THING, GOD WOT! Michael Aspel hides in the long grass	220
▶	**JUST TALKING** about people, places and events	97
▶	**HOME DEPARTMENT REPORT**	
	VACUUM CLEANERS The low-down on a clean sweep	52
	FUEL FOR THOUGHT Gas and electricity board services	57
▶	**HOME IMPROVEMENTS SECTION** Bathroom planning	69
▶	**GARDENING**	
	ORNAMENTAL OUTLOOK Finishing touches to transform your garden	156
	GARDENING HOW-TO Ornamental stone features	160
	SPECIALLY SELECTED Gardener's shopping guide	163
	GARDENER'S DIARY	166
▶	**COOKERY**	
	RISING TO THE OCCASION The secrets of successful yeast cookery	198
	PLANNING AHEAD Bake now for Christmas	206
	TRIED AND TESTED New ideas for the discerning cook	209
	PERSONAL CHOICE Haute cuisine at Heathrow	210
	WINE Not all sherries come from Spain	213
▶	**SPECIAL OFFERS**	
	SELECTION FOR AUTUMN SHOPPERS Bargains galore	87
	IDEAL HOME WINE OFFER	214
	IF YOU WANT MY ADVICE	125
	YOUR DECORATING QUESTIONS ANSWERED	133
	KITCHEN PLANNING SERVICE	138
	FREE MAIL-AWAY SERVICE TO ADVERTISERS	247
	COMING NEXT MONTH	248

FIGURE 13

woman

WHO WE ARE

EDITOR IN CHIEF	Jane Reed
ASSISTANT EDITORS	Billie Figg George Cannon
ART EDITOR	Nick Overhead
MANAGING EDITOR	Betty Hale
SENIOR EDITOR	Gaythorne Silvester
FEATURES EDITOR	Dee Nolan
FASHION	Geraldine Gobby
BEAUTY	Arline Usden
HOME	Jane Graining
KNITTING	Lesley Stanfield
COOKERY	Frances Naldrett
FICTION	Rose Wild
TRAVEL & MOTORING	Jean Barratt
YOU & US	Kate Mahony
PICTURES	Barbara Peevor
CHIEF SUB-EDITOR	Linda Belcher
READERS' SERVICE	Terry Austin

WHAT'S IN IT FOR YOU

FASHION

54 **Why Pay More?**—sensational style at sensible prices

HOME

12 **Boxing Clever**—make the most of the littlest room

59 **Don't Keep Your Cool**—hot tips for insulation

KNITTING

34 **Indian Summer**—super knits for the surprise season

COOKERY

30 **Give It A Whirl**—with a food processor it's a piece of cake

56 **What Do You Do For Dinner Parties?**

FEATURES

8 **The Secret Side Of Johnny Mathis**—we meet the singer on his home ground

21 **Partners**—a look at today's most common partner problems and how to solve them

33 **Behind The Gossip**—secrets of snooping cameras

40 **Would You Leave Your Handicapped Baby To Die?**

63 **Hangovers—A Survival Guide**

ACTIONWOMAN

16 **"Waiter, Waiter, What's This In My Soup?"**

FICTION

46 **The Long Masquerade**—serial

TRAVEL

28 **South Of France**—for two wonderful weeks

SUPERSAVERS

14 **This Is Glamour**—leisure suit

51 **Woman Cost Clippers**—all from Woolworth

REGULARS

66 **Star Guide**—Jillie Collings

70 **Problem Page**—Virginia Ironside

Cover—picture of Isabelle Adjani and Thierry Lhermitte by Dominique Issermann/Sigma

WHERE WE ARE

KING'S REACH TOWER
STAMFORD STREET, LONDON SE1 9LS.
TEL: 01-261 5413.
Advertising inquiries: 01-261 6770.
Editorial Offers: Medway (0634) 407380
VOLUME 89 NUMBER 2293
Prices—including VAT at current rate—quoted in this issue are correct at time of going to press. © IPC Magazines Ltd., 1981.

FIGURE 14

What Table 6 should reveal is that if the contents list is taken item by item, the three magazines appear to have much in common with each other. Many items are presented across the board. But when the *classification* of the contents, rather than the contents itself, is considered, the differences become more apparent.

Thus we can conclude that it is the *organization* or mix of the content, as much as the content itself, that contributes to the identity of a magazine and makes it recognizable *as* a woman's magazine. Table 6 begins to reveal the limits to a woman's magazine. Fiction, for instance, which is carried neither by *Ideal Home* nor the *Sunday Times* magazine, stands out as an important component in the constitution of a woman's magazine. However, neither the category of 'woman's magazine' nor the divisions within it are, in fact, unproblematic.

As Cynthia White discussed in her submission to the Royal Commission on the Press, even the trade papers for such magazines 'use different classifications systems, and are idiosyncratic in the way they distribute titles between them' (White, 1977, p.30). She herself defines the women's magazine market in terms of four broad editorial categories, of which the first is the largest: 'General service and entertainment', 'Fiction', 'Fashion', and 'Special service'. All these categories are produced primarily for women, and *addressed* to them, though they may have a considerable male readership (*Woman* reckons it has about one million male readers).

The difficulty with this categorization is that magazines do not fit the label very neatly. Most are to some degree 'general service and entertainment'. Indeed, it can be argued that this combination is one of the most important characteristics of women's magazines. The other three labels on the other hand, point to an *emphasis* in any magazine rather than a total preoccupation with that label.

The problems of this categorization are well illustrated by reference to *Ideal Home*. It is altogether outside White's category of women's magazines. Yet, on the magazine stand at W.H. Smith's, it appears alongside *Good Housekeeping* and *Home and Gardens* under the shelf label of 'Woman's World' magazines. The magazine proprietors class it alongside the above magazines as 'Leisure and Home' interest magazines mainly addressed to women. And, clearly, from Table 6, its contents are not definitively marked off from women's magazines proper as defined by White. Certainly it *could* be described as 'general service and entertainment'. In fact *Ideal Home* has about 40 per cent male readership — *Good Housekeeping* only 19 per cent.

In labelling magazines like *Woman* and *Woman's Own* as 'general service and entertainment', let us consider now the exact combination White has in mind. Certainly it is a combination that the editors themselves seem to recognize. Iris Burton the editor of *Woman's Own* (in 1982) assures her readers in one issue that it is packed 'full of interest, information and entertainment' (2 January, 1982). On another occasion, she proudly boasts that 'Obviously it's the balance of features that has made us good value for money' (19 September, 1981).

● Examine the contents list of *Woman* (Figure 14) in order to spell out more precisely 'service' and 'entertainment'. Attempt, quickly, to slot the items into either service or entertainment. You may find it difficult!

You have probably found that some items fall neatly into those categories, others just do not. But, overall, they seem to be *balanced* between service and entertainment. Let us consider now *what* the service is and what constitutes entertainment.

The first six items listed can fairly reasonably be described as service items. What is clear, too, is that each involves, first and fundamentally, *purchases*. That is, each of them provides information and gives advice on what women can buy to aid various aspects of their femininity. (Note that if we include commercial advertising, notably missing from contents lists, this function of magazines would seem overwhelming.)

Second, however, they are concerned with what should be *done,* or with the work women should do *after* they have bought certain goods. They should, for example, arrange them in some appropriate way. Here that would be respectively to work at being 'stylish'. This work I shall describe as the feminine *work of beauty*. There is also the work involved in 'making the most of a little room'. This kind of work I shall describe as the feminine *work of domesticity*. But notice how, although I am referring to these activities *as work*, that idea is manifestly absent from the contents list.

THE SUNDAY TIMES *magazine*

Contents, June 28, 1981
Cover: fashion photograph by Sacha; champagne photograph, Tony Stone Associates

MAIN FEATURES ◄

18
Strange sisters
The case of the Chaplin twins, who think and talk as one and whose obsession with a man led them to prison.

28
The outsize shirt
A versatile new fashion for summer ideal for the beach or the Ritz.

32
Eye on the Earth
Dramatic satellite pictures from America's Landsat 1 give surveyors a view they have never enjoyed before.

36
Knight life on screen
A look at John Boorman's new film based on the Arthurian legend.

LIFESPAN ◄

48
Design
For the high-rise household, stools which stack. And bins, bowls, jars . . .

51
Environment
The house that Mr Pym doesn't want.
Art
Brian Clarke on show.

52
Folk remedies that work
Marigold, for cuts and bruises.

Wine club offer
All that sparkles isn't champagne. We explain the champagne method and offer two cases : one of champagne, one of the best of 'the rest'.

55
Claire Bretécher

START HERE ◄

56
Photo competition
Calling all young photographers. There is £500-worth of photographic equipment to be won. Prizes include a 35mm single lens reflex camera with motor drive and the most sophisticated instant camera available.

57
White House model
What does the home of America's President look like inside ? Artist John Zweifel has made a perfect replica.

59
Games
Bridge and Chess.

62
A Life in the Day of
Roy Plomley.

FIGURE 15

Moving further down the contents list, there is another sort of 'service' item typified in the item 'Partners — a look at today's most common partner problems and how to solve them'; but it is best known and most important in the discretely mentioned 'Problem Page'. The problem page in most women's magazines is arguably the one page that attracts more readers than any other, and which is read *first* by more readers — despite, as Peggy Makins (Evelyn Home), *Woman's* erstwhile and well-known Agony Aunt put it — its position in the 'hinterland' of the magazine.

The popularity of the problem page says something about the pertinence of this kind of 'service' item for women, which does not deal in the currency of commodities but in that of *relationships*, in people's personal and emotional lives. In particular, and hinted at in this contents list, it is women's relation to men as potential or actual sexual partners, and to children, which provide the central topics for advice and information.

Moreover, the importance of relationships can be further gauged by the extent to which *even* those items you might have unhesitatingly judged as 'entertainment', like 'Fiction' or 'The Secret Side of Johnny Mathis', *also* deal with the terrain of personal relationships. Indeed, the category 'entertainment' is related less to the content than to *how* certain items are dealt with. If you look again at the titles of the articles, this will become apparent: 'Boxing Clever', 'Don't Keep Your Cool', 'Give It A Whirl'. Each *sounds* like entertainment, yet their substance is 'service'.

● Turn to your copy of *Woman's Own* for a moment and check that its contents fall into these slots of 'beauty work', 'domestic work', the 'work of relationships', each framed by entertainment.

This Section has tried to suggest that if we 'go behind' or delve underneath the contents list and the description of 'general service and entertainment' magazine for women, we discover a hidden mix of *women's work:* with respect to commodities in the area of beauty and domesticity, and with respect to personal relationships. And those two areas are bound within a framework that seeks to entertain and provide women with pleasure. What it is important to highlight here is that, though there are individual differences between them, *all* women's magazines have this balance in common.

2.3 Visual and verbal forms and styles

From its contents list you have probably gained some idea as to the tone of any article, whether serious or lighthearted, investigative or gossipy. But you cannot know its pitch entirely until you *read* and *look* at the article in question. What you will find then is that varying *visual* and *verbal forms* and *styles* are used for different kind of articles. And, if a good journalist learns to write any piece in the correct form and style, you and I as readers not only come to recognize and expect those forms and styles, but also to understand their *cultural meanings* in the magazine. Thus the bare content of any magazine is worked up through these forms and styles to give it a particular character.

2.3.1 Visual forms and styles

In women's magazines, visual forms are either artists' impressions or photographs. Each of these forms can be reproduced either in black and white or colour. The most marked shift since the Second World War has been that towards photography beginning in the 1950s. In contrast, in the first decade after the Second World War, most women's magazines still relied heavily on artists' impressions, with colour photography, especially, minimally in evidence. Today (1982) magazines rely predominantly on the reproduction of photographic prints, and no magazine could possibly do without colour photography. Be that as it may, artists' impressions *are* still used, though in very particular ways. Likewise black-and-white as well as colour photography have their specific places and deployments in the magazines.

In addition, each of these forms can be used in a different *style* of visual, as you began to see when we were looking at magazine covers: the difference between the artistic photo of the *Observer* supplement and the news photo of the *New Statesman*. Other possible photographic styles are the family snapshot or professionally posed and photographed shot, whereas artists' impressions may be reproductions of cartoons, line drawings, water colours or oils.

The form and style used in any article reflects how, as readers, we read and understand the article or, to put it another way, the visuals themselves have a cultural meaning that supports and clarifies the verbal intentions. For instance, the colour photography of most advertising material in the magazine and of many editorial features has the associations in our culture of leisure, pleasure and lavish spending. Seemingly, in itself, colour reproductions of carefully staged sets tell of a world that is excessive and on the edge of fantasy, but that money might buy. Though, unfortunately, not reproduced in colour here, Figures 16 to 18 give some indication of this excess and fantasy.

FIGURE 16 *(top right)* from an article, 'Pencil Power', demonstrating cosmetic pencils, *Woman's Own,* 5 September 1981.

FIGURE 17 *(bottom left)* From a cookery article, 'Filled with delight', which provides recipes for stuffings, *Woman's Own,* 5 September 1981.

FIGURE 18 *(bottom right)* An advertisement from the same issue as the two previous examples.

Black-and-white reproductions, in contrast, convey a hard, real quality to us as readers, like the news photo on the cover of *New Statesman*. But they also suggest the mundane, everyday life in all its ordinariness. In women's magazines black-and-white reproduction is used, on the one hand, for serious investigative journalism; the black-and-white photo marks the feature as serious and the reader recognizes it as such (Figure 19). And, on the other hand, it is used to accompany the article featuring a purported ordinary family (Figure 20), or a not-so-ordinary family which the magazine is striving to present as ordinary (Figure 21). Figures 20 and 21 adopt the family snapshot style, which may be authentic, (i.e. they are the family's own photos) or which may be professional look-alikes (both appear in the Figures). As readers we tend to respond to and understand the snapshot as an invitation to identify with the people concerned: they are ordinary folks just like us, as in Figure 20.

Distinctively different from any of these photos is the artist's impression, which is unfailingly used to accompany fiction in the magazine (Figure 22). It is usually a soft, hazy water colour of a scene or people, though more recently has shown signs of bolder, more riotous colour. But whatever the exact painting style and use of colour, the visual means for the reader in a cultural sense — an entry into a fictional world of romance, introversion and reverie, or of exciting but dreamlike and distant fantasy — the scenes and people are abstracted from history, dateless and classless.

A small artist's drawing, in a somewhat different style, frequently accompanies Polly Graham's 'Me and Mine' feature, and also provides the humourous light relief on the 'Your World' page in *Woman's Own*. Indeed, the style of these visuals implies that what is being discussed should *not* be taken too seriously.

The differential use and uneven distribution of these forms and styles in the magazine suggests that there is some kind of balance between features on every day life and those reaching into the realms of fantasy or humour.

● Before you go on, stop and briefly look at your copy of *Woman's Own*, to see whether you can recognize some of the different forms and styles that I have been discussing.

2.3.2 Verbal forms and styles

Verbal forms and styles also contribute to how any article is put together and to the cultural meaning which we as readers take from any article. For our purposes here, we can think of verbal forms as defined by their *mode of address*. If you recall the discussion of the covers, you will remember how the trailers addressed the woman reader (p.11). This is just one mode of address, the direct address to *you* the reader. Here is another example:

For budding poets . . .

As we know so many of you enjoy writing poetry, we thought you'd like to know about the Outposts Poetry Competition 1981, which is organized by the publishers of Outposts, the quarterly poetry magazine . . . *(Woman's Own,* 3 October 1981)

A second mode of address is to write in the *first person* as in this feature:

A day in the world of . . .

The day begins at 7.15 when I share my breakfast toast with Tina, before dashing through our small bungalow with Hoover and duster . . . (*Woman's Own,* 3 October, 1981)

Another possibility is the detached-third-person mode, as in this extract from a feature on Ursula Andress:

They have just finished shooting for the day and Ursula Andress is distinctly unhappy. Her hands are on her hips and she's tut-tutting in sheer frustration. But her agitation is, for the most part, private and quiet — none of the public tantrums that she might have thrown in earlier days . . . (*Woman's Own,* 3 October 1981)

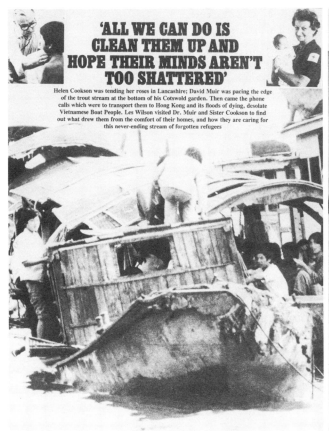

FIGURE 19   From an article on caring for refugees in Hong Kong, *Woman's Own*, 3 October 1981.

FIGURE 20   From an article, 'My husband's gone! Won't somebody find him?', *Woman's Own*, 10 October 1981.

FIGURE 21   From an article on Twiggy, 'Like Eliza said: "I really *am* a good girl"', in which she discusses her family life and her role as Eliza in the play Pygmalion, *Woman's Own*, 26 September 1981.

FIGURE 22   This black-and-white illustration accompanies a short story, 'First Flight', by Vicky Martin, *Woman's Own*, 5 September 1981.

Each of these modes can, however, be used within a different *style* of writing. You will probably already appreciate that there is a world of difference between the dry, unemotional, factual report that any witness of an accident has to give to the police or insurance company, and the confessional letter about personal feelings and relationships on *Woman's Own's* problem page. Yet both are written in the first person.

In newspapers it is traditionally the editorial that represents 'the voice' of the paper, and that consequently tells us something not only about the views of the paper, but also about its style of addressing its readership in the newspaper as a whole. For example, here are two extracts from newspaper editorials:

Well done, Ted

Ted Heath is reported to be lined up for a plum job
He is to be boss of a world-wide intelligence network at a salary of £50,000 . . .
If the report is correct we say: 'Well done, Ted . . . '

'Black Sunshine'

As Mrs Thatcher and her team get down to charting the course the Government intends to take economically and financially, they might spare a glance at the theories of Professor Edgar Feige, who believes the statistics upon which Ministers rely may have some short comings . . .
The professor finds a substantial disparity: that no less than £28,000 million of business may be conducted in Britain every year that never enters the books.

You should not find it too difficult to recognize these respective styles: one is of a popular tabloid, in fact the *Sun* (27 October 1981), and one of the so-called quality newspapers, the *Daily Telegraph* of the same date. The first uses what amounts to a conversational style, as if the newspaper is actually having a personal familiar chat with its readers. The second has all the marks of the well-informed, well-argued, but rather dry, lecture, to an audience which may be known professionally but certainly not personally. If you were to look through other sections of each of these papers, you would find the repetition of these respective styles.

Similarly the editorials of women's magazines set the overall style of address to their readership. What is specific about that address in all women's magazines is its friendly conversational style of *one woman to another*. The magazine speaks with some degree of intimacy as the concerned *friend* of women readers. Or as *Woman's Own* puts it each week: 'Woman's Own — the magazine that cares'.

If you read the two editorials (Extracts 1 and 2), 'The Week That Was!' from 'Your Editress' taken from *My Weekly* and Maggie Goodman's 'Inside Story' from *Company*, this friendly tone and intimate address to 'you' is apparent, though it is somewhat more directive and paternalistic in *My Weekly*. In *Company*, the businesslike report suggested by 'Inside Story' is undercut by the personal revelations with which Maggie Goodman regales the reader. In response to this friendly approach, readers write back in the same personal style. Read 'Your Views' in *Company* (Extract 2). In many women's magazines, including *Woman's Own*, the personal address achieved verbally is reinforced visually with photos of the editor, usually smiling. Likewise readers frequently send back snapshots of themselves.

Extract 2 is on p.27.

● Check your copy of *Woman's Own* for such photos.

Above all, this apparently intimate communication between editors and readers contributes to the sense for the reader of entering a 'woman's world' common to the editor and herself alike. The friendly editorial voice also resonates with a lulling re-assurance that this is a friend you the reader can rely on and trust. The latter tone is repeated throughout the magazine but is particularly evident in the regular slot, 'Dr. Michael Smith's Surgery'. Here the doctor reassuringly answers readers' worried enquiries on health matters. It is also the tone of the better-known 'Angela Willans Problem Page'. Readers make intimate confessions to the 'friend', who is also the authoritative expert. The letters are neatly edited for grammar and to eliminate any incoherence resulting from the emotion the writer is experiencing at the time. For example:

> Lately I seem to have lost all interest in sex. I love my husband very much but he doesn't seem to turn me on any more. We both work very hard as we are saving to start a family in about three years time. We don't have any problems — so what's happened? *(Woman's Own,* 3 October 1981)

The 'Auntie' couches her instructive reply in the style of the concerned but perhaps older and wiser, friend writing a letter.

The Week That Was!

WHEN did we start giving years a name? It seems quite normal now for each year to have a specific aim in mind — Women's Year, Year Of The Child, and this Year Of The Disabled.

There's a lot to be said for carrying this idea closer to home, but instead with a week devoted to a special cause, rather than a year. I don't mean the usual "Next week I'll do Christmas shopping," or "It's spring cleaning next week."

No, I'm thinking of something more beneficial and longer lasting.

For instance, now that winter is upon us, and we have the temptation of huddling close to home and fireside, perhaps a Sports Week would be a good idea.

Instead of taking the car, all the family would walk whenever possible, try to go to the swimming pool, squash courts and bowling alleys. It would be a whole week of fitness and activity. And, like these International Years, the effect is long lasting — I might even develop a real liking for skittles!

I'm thinking of having a Healthy Week, an Economical Week, and a Family Week.

Along the same lines, why wait till the New Year before starting something new? Lately I've found that I've been doing all sorts of favours for friends and relatives! I feel that a Think Of Myself Week would do me — and them — an awful lot of good! I'm not intending to turn into a self-centred egoist, simply planning to please myself for a while!

Similarly, it's all too easy to shilly-shally about things — to not make decisions. A Be Decisive Week, or even a Have An Opinion Week would give life so much more purpose and direction!

And how about a Doing Everything I Usually Put Off Till Tomorrow Week? Perhaps the week after next?

Have a nice week!

Your Editress.

Extract 1 From *My Weekly,* 3 October 1981.

● Consider such a reply in your copy of *Woman's Own* . In addition, you might like to note in your copy of *Woman's Own* that, like the 'Our World — Your World' editorial page, both 'Dr. Michael Smith's Surgery' and 'Angela Willans Problem Page' signal their intimate communication with readers. They do so not only with *Woman's Own* personal epigram: 'Woman's Own — the magazine that cares', but also with accompanying photos of Dr. Smith and Angela Willans: they *look* as if they are people you could talk to and trust.

This trustworthiness of women's magazines is something we shall return to in Section 2.4.1 on women as consumers: women's belief in the magazines' credibility has made magazines influential in, among other areas, the field of consumer advice. Any departures from it are more apparent than real. For instance, in an item of 'third person' reporting, conversational bits are introduced as an exchange between journalist and interviewees wherever it is feasible. Or, in the lead up to cookery and home features, 'sales talk', which transparently adopts a conversational style, is often adopted, as in this feature:

> The dishes are delicious, light and nutritious — creamy shellfish pancakes, tuna and potato gratin, smoked mussel and leek soup . . . And all the fish comes from a can, so just open your store cupboard, get out the tin opener, and you're off to a marvellous start, says our Cookery Editor Alex Barker   (*Woman's Own,* 3 October 1981)

Section 2.3 has examined how the visual and verbal forms and styles of a magazine make a distinctive contribution to the component parts of the magazine. They thus contribute to the shaping or character of the magazine as a whole, making it one particular cultural form — a women's magazine.

With respect to visual forms and styles, we noted the differential use of styles to suggest 'fantasy' and 'real life'. With respect to verbal forms, we discussed specifically the conversational style by which women's magazines set themselves up as 'every woman's friend', and construct a 'world for women'.

This combination of visual and verbal styles has undoubtedly won readers for the women's magazines, and contributed to their success. Section 2.4 discusses the wider basis for the economic prosperity of women's magazines in Britain in the period after the Second World War.

2.4 Women, consumption and women's magazines

That women's magazines are in the business of selling themselves and a variety of other commodities has already probably become abundantly clear to you.

● Just to confirm the importance of selling commodities in the magazine, count up the number of whole-page advertisements in your copy of *Woman's Own,* and work out the rough proportion of the whole magazine which that represents.

On any measure, the proportion of advertisements is considerable; even more so since that count does not include the sales advice proffered in editorial features. Implicitly what this weighting also emphasizes is women's role as buyers of those commodities, i.e. as *consumers*.

This Section will consider:

(a) the developments in Britain since the Second World War by which women have become major consumers, and some of the contradictions for women that this has thrown up;

(b) how these same developments have shaped women's magazines, which, in turn, have confirmed women in their relation to commodities and consumption.

2.4.1 Women as consumers

In the 1930s Margery Spring Rice recorded the lives of some working-class women. A Health Visitor had reported of one woman in Newcastle, with husband and six children living in a three-room tenement, that the woman had: 'no wash-house, and coal house is downstairs; clothes are boiled on kitchen fire . . . The woman has never been to a Picture House; she does all the washing and bread-making at home' (Spring Rice, *Working Class Wives,* 1981, p.115).

In 1982 the numbers of women and their families who are living below the breadline may be increasing, yet their domestic lives will most definitely *not* include boiling clothes on a kitchen fire, and are unlikely to include bread-making. For, in the intervening forty odd years, a diverse range of *commodities,* goods that can be bought, has changed the shape of domestic life, especially for women.

COMPANY REPORTS

INSIDE STORY //////////////////////////////////////

When I was nineteen and newly up from the country, London was Mecca. It was where you had to be, not just for the best jobs but for the quality of life. Only in the metropolis, I figured arrogantly, could you find people to empathise with, conversations to get high on, places and happenings that would plug you in to the main generator. And, judging by the hordes of provincial arrivistes who drank my foul coffee, this view was widely shared. I'm still beguiled by London but can easily understand the increasing disenchantment. Dirt, crime, high prices, inadequate transport and bad housing have tarnished the golden pavements, and latest census figures show declining populations not only in the capital but in big cities throughout the UK. And it's not merely the drop-outs and alternative life-stylers who are escaping the urban blues; a far wider cross-section are yearning for fresh fields. On page 32, Madeleine Kingsley investigates the rush to the country, talking to couples, families and singles who have made the radical decision; if you're also thinking of swapping the smoke for the trees, you need to read every word. The reality is nothing like the home-grown-vegetable fantasy, and even those who've successfully adjusted have many reservations. This is an important subject and we'd love to hear more firsthand reports from ex-townies.

Is there any reason to apologise for not wanting children? It's surprising to me that this is still an issue in 1981 but, according to Jeremy Pascall and his wife Susan, the pressure is alive and well and not even particularly subtle. Admittedly, *most* couples want children, but not siding with the majority surely doesn't turn you into a freak or an undesirable. In his article on page 78, Jeremy explains his reasons for being child-free (as opposed to childless,

which is not necessarily voluntary) and obviously thousands of people will have a counter-argument for every point he makes. (Just as well if the world is going to continue.) Fine – you make sacrifices if you have kids, you miss out if you don't and, thank heavens, unlike the situation in China (where, apparently, mandatory abortions are carried out), we have a choice.

Don't shrink from the word etiquette (page 85). Just because many of the old-fashioned rules are better broken doesn't mean you can survive without guidelines. New situations demand new treatments to avoid embarrassment and insecurity, and although our Etiquette For The Eighties is not intended to be a rigid diktat, it could keep you out of trouble. Ever wondered how to treat your husband's ex-wife? How to score as a single hostess? What to tell the bank manager? Read on.

We have extracts from two books in this issue. Hazel O'Connor's autobiography (page 40) is refreshingly honest as well as vastly entertaining. And Nicki Household's guide to getting started as a model (page 72) is so practical and down to earth that it should short-circuit a lot of disappointment. British models have acquired a record for unprofessionalism in the last few years – here's hoping the tide will turn.

The Shape Of Work To Come is the title of our special careers In-Fact, intended to help you think positively about the future instead of bewailing the present gloom. Lateral thinking will be as important as relevant qualifications – we talk about both. We also have valuable research on interview techniques, from both sides of the desk.

Our Panda car competition has an extra bonus. Every entrant will be making a contribution to the World Wildlife Fund which has the interests of the beautiful panda animal very much at heart. Help save a four-legged panda and you might win a four-wheeled Panda. How can you resist?   *MAGGIE GOODMAN*

YOUR VIEWS //

SELFISH SENSE

While I agree with much of what Jane Walmsley says in The Importance Of Being Selfish (*September*), I am not sure that 'selfish' is the right word. Looking after Number One is just commonsense; unless you have self-respect you are unlikely to respect others. It may be necessary to struggle for those top positions but just because men are greedy, insensitive and selfish doesn't mean that these qualities are necessary or even desirable. By all means *assert* yourself – but isn't there too much selfishness around already? *G T, Winchester*

LIBERATING THE SLAG

Who are these 'we' Rosie Boycott (Liberating The Slag, *September*) says believe that the quantity of a man's sexual activity makes him more interesting and fanciful? I'd rather sleep with a man for one reason only: if I were so overwhelmingly interested in him that sex became essential.

Also, if we need a male equivalent for 'slag', I have a suggestion; tripod, ie, one who cannot stand on his own two feet but needs his penis for support.   *R T, York*

After reading Liberating The Slag I wish more women would realise that by entering into any relationship purely to get rid of loneliness makes them vulnerable and loses them the respect of those on whom they try to lean.

Women cannot behave as if they are dependent on men, and then expect equality and respect. Sex discrimination on every level will not end if women treat themselves as second-class citizens.   *H W, Glasgow*

THE PRICE OF PASSION. . .

I enjoyed Is The Price Of Passion Too High? (*August*) but on reflection feel it had a very one-sided approach. With the exception of some of the books and films mentioned (which are fiction), almost every example given to portray these unusual behaviour patterns concerned a woman. The inference can be made, therefore, that it is only we who act in an unbalanced fashion 'in the name of love'. Surely men are capable of acting irrationally and irresponsibly when it comes to passion; they, too, have been known to wreck their careers, commit murder, abandon their families and even give up a crown for 'love'.   *R W, Shetland*

. . . AND THE PRICE OF BEAUTY

I had a hilarious half hour reading Rosemary Mills's School For Beauty (*August*). After all that hard work in order to 'catch a man' I would have been too exhausted to try – nor would I have been able to find £89 for all the preparations!   *C W, London*

MANILOW MANIA

Although I was interested to read Anthony Denselow's article on Manilow Mania (Despatches, *August*), I wonder why, in

common with other journalists, Mr Denselow seems to find Manilow's popularity so surprising.

Many people are too eager to dismiss him as a pleasant singer who found his way to the top by having his hair blow-waved and peddling romance. But Manilow received a classical music education, and is a skilled jazz pianist, an arranger, conductor and producer. Above all, he is one of the finest songwriters of his generation.

OK, so there's no political statement, no message attempting to change the world, but in these dark days there is a place for escapism, too.   *J M, Sutton Coldfield*

IT'S NO BETTER IN BED

I would love to take Sarah Meysey-Thompson's advice and just stay in bed (It's Better In Bed, *September*) – that is, if I had a gorgeous bedroom like Mary Vango's with its luxurious bed and an expensive stereo. But whenever I stay in bed the sheets crease, the blankets crawl onto the floor and, if I want to listen to music, I have to get up to put it on, get up to turn it over and get up to turn it off. In the end, I just give up and get up!   *R L, Crowborough*

Please send your letters to Your Views, Company, National Magazine House, 72 Broadwick Street, London W1V 2BP. A cheque for £5 will be sent to the writers of each letter which is published on this page. We reserve the right to shorten and edit letters.

Extract 2 From *Company*, November 1981.

Think back over your own life for a moment and see if you can recall any highlighted moments when you, your family or friends purchased some brand-new commodity for the home, whether a so-called labour-saving device like a washing machine or vacuum cleaner, or a leisure item like a wireless (later a transistor), a gramophone (later a stereo or music centre), or a television (first black-and-white and then colour).

What you remember will depend partly on your age, partly on your class background. I remember very vividly the occasion in the mid-sixties, when my parents at last bought a washing machine, about six years later than all the neighbours in our lower middle-class area. I was relieved that my mother no longer had to spend a whole day in a steamy kitchen (boiling up the gas copper), arduously wringing out clothes.

For those of you who were born from the late 1950s onwards, and into middle-class homes, washing machines may be something you take for granted, as you do also paper hankies, frozen foods, polythene bags, cling film and non-stick frying pans. Indeed, for any domestic task you can think of whether it is bathing and looking after baby (or the family pet!), cleaning various parts of the home, maintaining a car, or simply cooking, or washing your hair there are a whole host of commodities you can choose from, which certainly help you in your task, but which also suggest other tasks to be done on your home, or car, or whatever. Yet, though in 1982 these may be commonplace items, even in very poor homes, they have all appeared on the market in the years since the Second World War. This production and purchase of new commodities for use both in the home and on our person, has been gradual but spectacular, and has continued, even during periods of economic recession (like the 1970s). Thus all of us — though we are likely to be more implicated if we are well-off — are caught in a process of *continuous consumption.* Whatever our commodity needs ten years ago, they are likely to have moved on today.

This process of economic expansion and diversification of commodities for the home (and leisure) by capitalist industry began in the nineteenth century. It is part and parcel of capitalist industry's tendency constantly to win or penetrate into new and different markets in order to gain a competitive edge over a rival firm. Catherine Hall in her article in the Reader, 'The butcher, the baker, the candlestick maker', discusses the expansion of retailing in the early nineteenth century, and its effect on the lives of the shopkeeper's family. She mentions the increasing sale to the middle classes of a wide range of goods from cocoa to dress and furnishing fabrics and trimmings, and metal goods like candlesticks.

What is significant about the period since the Second World War is both the acceleration of this process and the availability of products of capitalist industry at relatively cheap prices *across classes*. If the processes have affected everyone's life, it is *women* who have been primarily been urged to desire, to need and to buy goods in two important areas: household goods and foods; clothes and beauty preparations. Sheila Rowbotham's evocative description of this invasion of the home and person by commodities as an 'imperial onslaught' on everyday life and sexuality (Rowbotham (1973), *Woman's Consciousness Man's World,* Penguin, p.109) gives some indication of the profound impact it has had on women's lives. That 'onslaught' continues, notwithstanding economic recessions, but its distinctive features, which tied women to consumption in particular ways, were defined in the 1950s and 1960s. It was during those years that women became the 'Big Spenders', even if more often than not it was not their own money which they were spending. The rest of this Section will primarily be considering women and women's magazines in those years.

After the devastation of the Second World War, the post-war reconstruction took place on many fronts, not least the economic. But, as James Drawbell (a retired newspaper editor who became editor of *Woman's Own* in 1946 and continued through the 1950s) wrote, regarding 1946, in his autobiography:

The war was over, peace was here but the longed-for-era of 'plenty' had not come. The world of women was at its lowest ebb.

It was a drab and dreary let-down after our high expectations Rationing was still with us, more severe in some things than it had been during the war. We were down to 2 ounces of butter a week each person, one egg, 2½ pints of milk, 14d worth of meat; and if you wanted to make a complete wreck of you figure you had 4 ounces of chocolate and sweets to do it with. A woman had 24 clothing coupons a year. If she needed a coat or mack, which took away 18 coupons, she had 6 left to twist in her tortured fingers as she contemplated the purchase of a corset (3 coupons), a skirt (4), a dressing-gown (8) ...There was little scope for gracious living of any sort . . . (Drawbell, 1968, p.45)

The Labour Government's immediate concern after the 1945 General Election was to harness industry to exports and the dollar drive in order to place the country's finances on a sounder footing. The country had to win and come through its 'economic Dunkirk' before the era of 'plenty' could be heralded in. When it seemed as if this battle was being won, the Korean war, in 1950, once more voraciously drained the country's resources. Some rationing continued until 1954, by which time, stoical as the population was in the face of more than ten years of penury, it had had more than enough.

After the Conservative Party came to power in 1951, the needs of the home market were gradually acceded to. Though this was welcomed by many, some on the left of the political spectrum were critical of its effect on long-term trade and economic expansion. Nevertheless — with rationing finally abandoned, industrial restrictions lifted and R.A. Butler's 1953 'New Look' budget (as the press called it, comparing it to Christian Dior's extravagant 'New Look' in fashion) cutting income tax and purchase tax — the consumer boom, as it was referred to, swung into the High Street. And domestic commodities were swallowed by an eager and insatiable market.

People *were* able to buy, and wanted to buy for several reasons apart from general feelings of deprivation. One vital development after the war was a replacement of the housing stock destroyed or damaged by bombs. It was one of the Labour Party's political priorities in 1945 and was continued in the Conservative administration. The latter claimed that by 1964 no less than one in four families was living in a house built while they had been in office. One upshot of such a programme was the demand for goods with which to furnish those homes in an appropriately *contemporary* style (the term coined at the Festival of Britain in 1951).

As importantly, many people were increasingly able to *afford* to buy these goods. A relative greater affluence, especially for working-class people, was the outcome of the combined effect of the new social security and unemployment benefit system provided by the post-war Welfare State, and relative full employment. Full employment brought in its wake, not only greater trade union bargaining power, and hence higher wages for many manual workers, but also work for immigrants *and* part-time work for married women, because the Welfare State and expanding service sector demanded more labour than could be found among the male population. Women's contribution to the family's pay packet was often spent on goods for the home or things for the children. These factors led Harold Macmillan, the Conservative Prime Minister of the day, to declare to the nation in 1959, 'You've never had it so good'.

A commentator writing in the 1960s also saw the consumer boom of the 1950s in rosy light.

> A great new urban, white-collar population now arose which went to work in private cars, dressed better than ever before, and spent considerable sums of money on food, kitchen and household appliances, holidays and entertainment. A 33 year old wife . . . said 'We've got everything we want now. I've a fridge, a washer, and a TV set and that's all I want in life'. She was speaking for the masses of the British people during the fifties. (John Montgomery, 1965, p.268)

This new-found affluence was by no means the leveller of class differences that some Conservative *and* Labour pundits set it up to be. It represented less a redistribution of wealth from the rich to the poor than a general increase in the standard of living across the board. As Michael Pinto–Duschinsky (1970) suggests, even allowing for inflated costs between 1951 and 1964, the standard of living rose over 30 per cent.

More tangible, perhaps, is the measure of this in terms of consumer items. According to the market researcher Mark Abrams, between 1955–65 the proportion of families owning cars, TVs, vacuum cleaners or washing machines doubled, while the rise in food consumption showed a shift towards 'frozen vegetables, processed meats and instant coffee'. The purchases of children's clothes and cosmetics were up by 50 per cent; there was a much greater expenditure on women's clothes, but no comparable leap in the purchase of men's clothes (1966, p.9).

If such a welter of purchase was made — to make no mention of the thousand-and-one small items from curtain hooks to lavatory brushes and potato peelers needed to equip and furnish the post-war home — it is pertinent to ask, who chose and bought them, and who used or arranged them in the home? In the main, and unsurprisingly, it was *women*.

● You might at this point like to cast back, in your own memory, or ask women friends or relatives whether life in the decade 1955–65 *was* experienced as one of affluence when compared either with the years before or with those after. If the answer is largely no, bear in mind the reasons they give and consider whether there are connections with what is discussed in the next few pages.

What is surprising, looking back from 1982, is not that women's role dovetailed so neatly around consumption, but that this could have been seen as a 'New Deal' for women, consolidating the 'equality' with men they had so admirably demonstrated during the war. The educationalist John Newsom maintained that: 'Woman as purchaser holds the future standard of living of this country in her hands . . . If she buys in ignorance then our national standards will degenerate' (Newsom, 1948, p. 103). And Mark Abrams proposed that: 'Since now home has become the centre of his activity and most of his earnings are spent on or in the home his wife becomes the chooser and spender and gains a new status and control — her taste forms his life' (Abrams, 1959, p. 914).

Thus, together with the availability of more and new goods for the home, went a whole new era of *knowledge* and *work* to be done by women. The occupation housewife was upgraded in two ways: some of the manual arduousness of her chores was supposedly relieved by her access to so-called labour-saving devices; simultaneously, she was elevated to be the expert in what I shall describe as *consumption work*. As Evelyn Home put it when replying to a reader whose fiancé had twice jilted her: 'To almost every woman her work comes first too — the work of homemaking and husband tending. He is interfering with your career as a wife and I advise you to tell him so' (*Woman,* 13 January 1951).

Her description of women's work makes clear that the sexual division of labour between husband and wife was regarded as a *complementary* sharing of power and responsibility. Woman were regarded as equal but different from men.

I have discussed these ideas about women, domesticity and consumption in the 1950s in some detail because they are still evident in the 1980s, most particularly in the service magazines like *Woman's Own.* Moreover, though feminism has charged that a sexual division of labour organized around equal but different roles *cannot* be an equal one for women, it is a notion that continues to prevail. In Section 3, we shall be examining the relations between domesticity and consumption in *Woman's Own* in the 1980s.

But if women's magazines came of age on the back of domestic consumption, there was a further contributory component of consumption which became increasingly significant as the 1950s moved into the 1960s. It is also a constituent of femininity in the 1980s: The consumption of women's clothes, cosmetic and toilet preparation — goods I refer to as beauty commodities.

In 1947 the fashion leaders of Paris had shocked a war-sullied Britain by the extravagance and flippancy of their 'New Look' for women: full skirts, 'wasped' waists, and emphasized bust and hip lines, marked a post-war return to a feminine look. Women were indeed to be women again. And, as chain stores like Marks and Spencer and British Home Stores expanded, and the availability of relatively cheap but well-made garments increased, the sales of women's clothes rose rapidly.

Women were as concerned about their appearance as their homes; both — fitted out stylishly and with care in the appropriate commodities — were signs of success for women and their families, especially for working-class women. A 'nice house' and a 'smart wife' were signs not only of an upward mobility for men, when measured against the pre-war standards, but also of successful womanhood. The 'contemporary' wife could look after home and children, possibly do a part-time job, *and* look nice: she was not going to 'let herself go', as these figures given by Harry Hopkins in his book *The New Look* (1963) suggest, 'In 1954 total production in Britain was 4.2 million brassieres and 5.6 million foundation garments. The comparative figures for 1959 were 20 millions and 35 millions respectively' (p.232).

But it was young, especially unmarried, working-class women, earning relatively high wages, who at the end of the 1950s were recognized by market researchers as potentially large spenders whose commodity 'needs' were not yet tapped. It was for them that the fashion trade expanded. Small boutiques selling ever shorter skirts sprang up like wild flowers, while the cosmetic industry multiplied its brand names, and proliferated a colourful array of products: fibre mascara, waterproof mascara, block mascara, mascara for sensitive eyes; eye shadow as cream, powder, in tube or palette, shiny, dull, or sparkly; cleaners, toners, moisturizers for oily, dry, allergic, spot-prone skins; false eyelashes and nails, hair pieces and hair removers — and so on.

The avid consumption in the 1960s of (to the older generation at least) indecently short minis, almost childish clothes, and a battery of 'beauty aids', which young women used to mask any natural facial expression, was as double edged as the purchase of vacuum cleaners and the ideology of domesticity in the 1950s. On the one hand, it broke the staid and strict fashion protocol of the 1950s: fashion was meant to be fun, it was intended to shock and to be sexually provocative. It spoke of individuality and freedom for women. In her book, *Say I'm Sorry to Mother*, Carol Dix and three of her old school friends recall their lives in the 1960s. One of them, Georgina, has this to say about clothes:

> I remember very clearly the day I suddenly realized it was all right to show my body off . . . I came home one day wearing Ellie's too-small, very tight pair of corduroy jeans which wound their way round my curves, and with them a tiny jumper. I knew my bottom stuck out a mile — but I already knew that men fancied it and I wanted to be proud of it . . . any girl who raised her skirts inch by inch to the point of no return knows what I mean when I say there was nothing more liberating than the feel of the wind, the air, rushing up between your legs, fanning your fanny. It was a childlike, innocent sense of freedom, I reckon. A freedom from restraint I felt as I skipped along in my dolly, baby-doll clothes, knowing that men could look up my skirt when I climbed to the top deck of the bus, or bent over to pick something up. (Dix, 1978, p.58)

On the other hand, the pressure on women to achieve the right sexy look, as described above, fed into their insecurity and uncertainty about their bodies and their sexuality. Georgina may have felt good about her stuck-out bottom. Many others did not. As in the area of domesticity, the consumption work attached to beauty commodities was enormous. Girls, alone or with friends, spent many a vicariously pleasurable hour (as many still do in the 1980s) 'improving' their hair, skin and figures. Though commodities were being used to assert an individuality and sexuality, as Georgina describes above, they also tended to reduce women to nothing more than just the summation of those commodities. It was the photographic advertising image which perfected this sleight of capitalism's hand: women as the commodity who herself could be consumed. As Juliet Mitchell writing in 1970 put it:

> . . . having been offered all possibilities for self-glorification, having produced the sexually radiant you, the commercial dimension of capitalism can re-use you; this time you, yourself, will do to sell the drabber products: cars, washing machines, life-insurance. No city in the world boasts such a density of 'sexual objectification' on its bill boards and subways ads, as does London. (Mitchell, 1971, p.141)

You might recall that this was one of the extracts on the subject of advertising which was discussed in Unit 1, p. 27.

Section 3 will examine the 'sexual objectification' of women that Mitchell discusses as it is represented in recent magazines.

● For the moment, however, turn to your copy of *Woman's Own*. Make a rough measurement of the relative importance of domestic and beauty commodities to femininity by counting up the page space devoted to them.

2.4.2 Women's magazines become big business

Returning to the post-war history, I would argue that women's magazines alone were not the initiators of women's intimate relation with consumption, but their rise to become big business most definitely leant on that relation. As Cynthia White (1970) comments: 'The boom in women's periodicals has in fact paralleled the boom in domestic consumption and the vast expansion in advertising which has accompanied it' (p.201). As already indicated, it also paralleled the boom in clothes and cosmetics.

But the roots of the magazines post-war success lay in their achievements during the war. They had rallied women to the war effort on all fronts: they provided helpful advice for managing on grossly insufficient food and clothing coupons, and generally boosted morale. The limited supplies of each flimsy issue were well thumbed and well loved.

By the time ration books were joyfully abandoned and print restrictions were no longer in operation in the early 1950s, *Woman's Own* and *Woman* in particular (launched respectively in 1932 and 1937), had each built up a sound reputation and a core of loyal readers. These two magazines had one vital advantage over their rivals — colour. It was produced by a print process called photogravure, which enabled large numbers of colourful magazines to be produced cheaply, and this they were able to capitalize on further as the 1950s progressed. James Drawbell (1968) had firm ideas of of how to use colour, and high ideals of what his post-war redesigned and modernized magazine was going to look like:

> Very simply I wanted to produce cheap magazines which would look anything but cheap, and which would provide colour, entertainment, escape (yes escape!), and *understanding and reassurance to women*, with contents of a higher literary and artistic quality than had been offered to them before in this medium. (p.45, my emphasis)

Mary Grieve, who edited *Woman* throughout the war and up until 1963, was more explicit about the areas in which 'understanding and reassurance to women' was needed. As she put it retrospectively:

> A very great part of woman's life is spent choosing, buying and preparing goods for her own and her family's consumption — be it food, clothes or home requirements. An immense amount of her personality is engaged in her function as the selector of goods, and in this she endures many anxieties, many fears . . . Because she has this preoccupation with, and responsibility for, material living, she feels the need for what is virtually a trade press. *It is because women of all ages hold in common this consumer-concern that a vast, profitable press has grown up to service them.* (1964, p.138, my emphasis)

Thus both editors recognized the ambiguous edge to consumer concerns for women: women needed and wanted to know how to select goods, but this also caused them 'many anxieties, many fears'. What both editors saw their magazines as doing was catering to this: providing a 'trade press' but also 'understanding and reassurance to women' about their feminine role. James Drawbell also stresses how he wanted *Woman's Own* to be entertaining for women.

Without the recognition by manufacturers and their advertisers of the potential readership to be gained by women's magazines, the latter could not have become so profitable. In the magazine world, large sums are made not just from selling a lot of copies but by selling space to advertisers. As far as *Woman's Own* and *Woman* were concerned, advertisers not only spotted the increasing circulation figures, but also the advantage to be gained from their facility for colour gravure. By the end of the 1950s, the colour James Drawbell had wanted to see seemed likely to provide a dubious pleasure for women since it weighed heavily on the side of advertising. In 1955 about equal numbers of colour pages were devoted to advertisements and to editorial. By 1959 proportionally twice as much was given over the advertising.

The financial power of the advertisers weighed in other ways too. Cynthia White goes so far as to say that by the 1960s it directly curtailed editorial freedom, 'Features which cannot be used to sell goods are wasted space as far as advertisers are concerned, and Editors are forced to keep them to a minimum' (1970, p.203). Readers were not so satisfied, and the circulation figures of many magazines did fall in the 1960s.

Mary Grieve denies such power but, nevertheless, admits at least one compromise. In 1956 she agreed *not* to carry a feature on natural fibres when British Nylon booked *Woman's* first double-page spread in four colours (for the then princely sum of £7 000). This she remarks 'seemed reasonable' (1964, p.105).

You might think that if the top-selling magazines had circulations which were rising as fast as those of *Woman's Own* and *Woman* they could afford to set terms to suit themselves rather than the advertisers. (In 1946 their sales were respectively ½ million and 1 million; in 1950 1½ million and 2 million; in 1958 2½ million and 3½ million.) However, as production costs also rose in the 1950s, the magazines became *more* dependent on advertising in order to subsidize what they considered a necessarily low cover price.

Yet the business ventures of women's magazines were not just with the advertising. Features on the home, fashion and cosmetics increasingly discussed the various brands and available stockists. Moreover, on top of this consumer advice most magazines in 1950s began to carry special offers which readers could buy. These would be carefully designed for the magazine as to quality and price, and the sales were enormous. Mary Grieve describes the wool jersey cut-out suit offered by *Woman* in 1962: they sold 107 746 at a cost to the readers of £269 853. Here, too, was 'big business'.

The magazines' rise to 'big business' was not, however, without its setbacks. If, in the 1950s, women were eager to be 'educated' on the consumer front, by the 1960s, such an emphasis, together with the dominance of advertising, was beginning to be a stale read. Without articles of general interest to women on the subjects that were preoccupying them — like part-time work for married women, changing morals among the young, contraception and so on — the magazines were a less attractive proposition to readers. Except for *Woman's Weekly*, the circulation figures of all the mass service weeklies, as well as many of the monthlies, fell, and some old stalwarts like *Woman's Illustrated* and *Everywoman* folded altogether, or were merged. Nor were the efforts to check those falls entirely successful: the circulation figures have never regained their peak of the late 1950s. Though this is not to say that women's magazines have not reaped enormous profits.

In 1964, IPC commissioned Ernest Dichter, an American psychologist who had worked for advertisers, to report on *Woman's Own*. His recommendations to up-date women's magazines in terms of style of presentation and content were far-reaching within the industry. *Nova*, proclaimed in 1965 as 'The New Magazine for the New Kind of Woman', was a direct product of his report. But when *Woman's Own* adopted his suggestions, they found they had to tread more carefully and not put forward ideas that were too far ahead of their readers if they were to maintain their sales.

The main strategy the industry adopted, which Dichter had proposed, was to rationalize the magazine market. Magazines were geared to particular interests and consumer markets rather than to a certain age or class of women. In this way, neither their readership nor their advertising, on which they were heavily dependent for revenue, overlapped. Magazines began to be tailor-made to the specification of the market researchers on particular commodity buying. For example, *Honey* was launched in 1960 to capture the 'young woman' market of cosmetics and clothes discussed earlier. *Family Circle* (1964) and *Living* (1966) were clear attempts to capture 'the young housewife with a full-time interest in homemaking' (White, 1970, p.150), and the corresponding food and household goods advertisement market. *Annabel* (1966) was for 'young mum' — buying prams, pedal cars and beauty products; *19* was for the 'younger sister' of *Honey* readers, who had less money to spend on make-up. And so on. Each of these magazines carries general articles, but a particular emphasis on consumption also comes across both in advertisements and in editorial features.

In 1982 the new magazine *Options* was described in the publicity for advertisers as being aimed at the woman who:

> . . . is an entirely new breed of consumer. She sees herself as the kind who should have a calculator in her handbag, a stereo in her car, a note recorder at her office. She is the generation for whom video and telecom were made. Busy women with open minds who will take advantage of every technological advantage to make work more efficient and play more fun. The first generation of women for whom freezers, dishwashers and microwave ovens are not luxuries but essentials.

Around the same time, IPC also launched the first British magazine (as it proudly boasted) for black women, *Black hair and beauty*, costing an exorbitant one pound. It is, however, more a sales vehicle for items of make-up and hair styles, than it is a women's magazine. It certainly was not given the one-million pound multi-media campaign that *Options* had received to advertise it!

Rationalization, however, has also taken place in a way characteristic of capitalist industry as a whole. Since the evident commercial success of women's magazines, from the late 1950s there have been mergers and take-overs within the publishing world, a fierce fight which the *Economist* in 1959 called 'The Petticoat Battleground'. The outcome has been that by 1982, IPC heavily dominates the market. It owns the top four weeklies — which in the 1950s were owned by three different companies — and many of the monthlies. Such large international concerns are well able to survive temporary storms in one area, are able to experiment without severe financial loss, and to switch around resources in order to maintain their magazine profit as a whole. But it is also inevitable, despite some degree of autonomy given to various editorial staffs, that all the magazines are somewhat similar. The identical size, type of paper, colour reproduction (to say nothing of the contents) of *Woman's Own* and *Woman* — the two arch rivals from the 1950s — is a case in point. Whether this lessens the chances of either magazine providing the readers with the kind of magazine they would like is arguable. What is certain, though, is that the chances of an innovating outsider breaking the monopoly of the weekly market, especially, are very slim: this particular big business is just too expensive and initially risky for any but the largest company to venture into it.

In 1972 IPC introduced a new weekly *Candida*, which had what seems, retrospectively, to be much the same philosophy as *Options* a decade later. Its formula and timing were clearly not right, and the magazine failed abysmally; IPC ventured on, of course.

Those monthly magazines that are run independently, like *Spare Rib* and the long-established *The Lady* (founded in 1885 and renowned for its classified ads) have much lower circulations than the more commercially oriented magazines. They are often in financial straits too. *Over 21,* which was initially an independent enterprise launched in the early 1970s by Audrey Slaughter, who had successfully edited *Honey* throughout the 1960s, was taken over within eighteen months by a public company. In 1982 *Over 21* is owned by MS Publishing, a subsidiary of Morgan-Grampian, itself a subsidiary of Fleet Holdings.

As far as the editorial content of the more commercial magazines is concerned, what I finally want to stress is that although economic priorities have undoubtedly compromised it, it is *by no means* wholly bound by those restrictions.

2.4.3 Summary

Section 2 has examined some of the features contributing to women's changing experience of consumption, particularly in the 1950s and 1960s. It has suggested how important domestic and beauty commodities became to ideas about femininity, and how, in advertising especially, the image of woman as a commodity became exchangeable with other commodities. Woman became defined as consumer, and her image, one that could be consumed. That definition has continued into the 1980s.

The growth of women's magazines into the realms of big business was then discussed. This growth leant on the expansion of consumption for women. Women's magazines provided the solutions for women on what and how to consume; they, therefore, fed into definitions of women as consumers.

Section 3 will return to a detailed visual and verbal analysis of *how* those definitions of femininity are represented in women's magazines, and how they *address* and implicate women readers. However, those definitions of women — as consumers and that which can be consumed — do not exhaust the definitions of femininity. Some of the other components that make up femininity will also be explored. These components will be called *ideologies* of femininity.

● Before you move on to the next Section turn to the cassette. On it I discuss with people who work on *Woman's Own* some of the editorial questions around, for example, the choice of cover image and visuals generally. I also ask you to do some exercises related to your copy of *Woman's Own*.

---

3 Ideologies of femininity

3.1 Introduction

So far this Unit has discussed the ideas and definitions of femininity to be found in the pages of women's magazines. In this Section, you will be asked to consider these various strands of femininity in terms of *ideologies* of femininity. The term is also an important concept and analytical tool in cultural studies. It emphasizes that, for example, the ideas and definitions of femininity have ramifications beyond their representation in women's magazines; it is central to the concept of ideology that women's experiences are also caught up in those ideas and definitions of femininity. In Unit 1, if you remember, you were briefly introduced to the term ideology as an important one in a Marxist feminist framework (p. 48). In putting forward these two characteristics of ideologies, I am drawing on a particular definition originating in the work of Karl Marx. You should be aware, however, that the concept of ideology has a complicated history, and has been, and still is used to mean a lot of different things.

For the purposes of this Course and the analysis of women's magazines, the term ideology will be used to refer to sets of *common-sense knowledges,* which are *also practical knowledges.* In other words, these knowledges define and explain the social world and our social place within it, and also shape our everyday feelings, thoughts and actions. They can be written, visualized, spoken and acted out. But the knowledge they offer is always a *partial* or *selective,* and sometimes *contradictory,* description and explanation of the social world. Ideologies construct certain aspects of this social world as *natural* and *universal,* and these latter characteristics are particularly true for the prevailing or dominant ideologies within any culture.

Let us look at this definition of ideology more closely with reference to ideologies of femininity. By *sets* of knowledges I mean that one ideology — like the dominant ideology of femininity that we have recognized in the pages of women's magazines — may be made up of a series of ideologies, each referring to and organizing discrete, if sometimes overlapping, domains of social life. Each ideology will draw on a repertoire of elements that may intersect or crosscut with that of another component ideology of femininity *or* with other, different, ideologies. For example, this Unit has been concerned generally with the dominant ideology of femininity represented in women's magazines. Within that umbrella ideology, the ideologies of domesticity and beauty have been isolated. Though I have shown how these two ideologies organize two different areas of life for women, they both rely to some extent on the need to encourage the consumption of commodities. Further, although consumption is linked to this dominant ideology of femininity, it also refers to social-class differences in patterns of consumption.

Thus, through the element of consumption, the ideologies of femininity *and* of social-class position coincide, intersect or crosscut each other.

By *common-sense knowledges,* which are also *practical* knowledges, explaining and shaping that world, I mean two things:

1 Ideologies have developed out of, and deal with, the concrete circumstances of our lives (i.e. that we are women or men, rich or poor, work and have families, grow old, etc.) and the knowledge they provide about those aspects of our lives seems self-evident. For example, within the ideology of domesticity of the 1950s, it seemed only commonsense that women, and not men, should be houseworkers, i.e. housewives.

2 Ideologies also discuss and deal with those circumstances in a practical way, i.e. ideologies set the terms within which we can act by offering explanations of how social life is, and of how it works. Thus, having prescribed that women should *be* housewives, an ideology of domesticity then sets the terms for *how* women should act out their position as housewives.

By suggesting that ideologies offer only a *partial or selective,* and sometimes *contradictory knowledge* and explanation, I mean, for example, that the ideology of domesticity of the 1950s covered up the fact, and its consequences, that housewives were unpaid whereas husbands were in paid work. It could, therefore, suggest contradictorily that the division of labour between wife and husband was a complementary one, *and* an 'equal' one.

By suggesting that ideologies construct certain aspects of the social world as *natural* and *universal*, I mean that they deny that these aspects of the social world are *produced* by certain social groups. In other words, ideologies are *social constructions* and not natural phenomena. For example, the ideology of domesticity begs the question of *why* it should be women who do the housework and cooking and shopping, and *where* those ideas came from. It encourages us to think that 'it is only natural', 'it is only common-sense', 'it has always been so' — for all groups within the culture — that women do housework and men are the breadwinners. And in so far as women and men continue to behave in the ways that the ideology predicts, the ideology appears to be even more true. Yet, despite this 'naturalizing' tendency of ideologies, they are not static systems of knowledge and explanation.

A dominant ideology is more easily able to present its ideas as natural and universal because it is produced and reproduced by those in positions of power. In other words a dominant ideology is closely tied into the interests of those social groups who are economically and politically dominant. For example, the dominant ideology of femininity found in women's magazines has the capacity to present itself as natural and universal, only so long as the social positions of men and women are those of relative economic and political power, on the one hand, and powerlessness, on the other. However, in so far as ideologies depend on the relations and activities between social groups, they are constantly reworked and transformed as part of the historical process of changing social relations and personal experiences. Thus, when the pattern of relations between women and men changes, or the class or racial structure changes, the ideologies which the dominant class or sex or race produce to justify and legitimate that pattern of relations also change. This process does not, however, indicate that there is a simple causal relationship: ideologies often lag behind social or economic changes.

It should be clear from this relation between ideologies and social groups that ideological shifts are inseparable from issues of power and, therefore, of politics in its widest sense. Thus, the ideology of femininity found in women's magazines is not just a cultural issue, it is also a political issue. Indeed, the reworking of ideologies also tends to be triggered by the effects of oppositional ideologies, produced by subordinate and oppressed groups, such as women, or black people. For example, feminism, which is a political response to women's changing social and personal experience, has markedly influenced the dominant ideology of femininity, even though the latter may not have been radically overhauled in the last forty years. We shall be looking more closely at the impact of feminism on the dominant ideology of femininity as we work through the copy of *Woman's Own.*

These then are the characteristics of ideology that I have outlined:

Ideology is made up of a *set* of *common-sense knowledges,* which are also *practical* knowledges.

Ideology offers only a *partial* or *selective,* and sometimes *contradictory,* knowledge.

Ideology presents a world that is *natural* and *universal.*

Ideology hides the fact that it is a *social construction* produced by certain social groups.

Ideology changes *historically* and can be *opposed* by social groups.

● Go back over these five characteristics, and read the previous pages again, if necessary. Then try to write down those characteristics of ideology in your own words.

We shall now consider three further aspects of ideology that are particularly pertinent to the analysis of the visual and verbal images of femininity of the kind that we are considering in women's magazines.

First, you might at this stage be wondering at the use of the two terms *culture* and *ideology.* Why make the distinction? The answer lies in the fact that although ideologies are produced from culture (they start, if you like, with the culture as it already is), they can, in turn, affect that culture. Thus culture can be thought of as 'the complex of ideologies that are actually adopted' (Johnson, 1979, p.234). This complex of ideologies will vary from class to class, so that we can talk of a middle-class culture, or a working-class culture. It will also vary from one cultural form to another. Thus, in any one cultural form, like a magazine, or in television, there will be a range of ideologies in play, each of which will not be discretely organized and labelled for us to recognize. Rather, in practice, one ideology will overlap, merge, and crosscut with others to produce this complex. What our analysis of the cultural form attempts to do is to begin to disentangle these different ideological strands. So, for example, I distinguished between the ideology of femininity and the ideology of social class in women's magazines.

The second important distinction to be made is between *cultural sites* and *ideologies.* The latter are to be found throughout society in different cultural sites such as the family, the work place, schools and the mass media. The same ideology can take different forms in each of these sites. What this implies about women's magazines, as one such site of cultural production, is that the ideologies produced by and represented in such magazines will also be found in different forms *outside,* in other cultural sites. We should expect to find, therefore, the dominant ideology of femininity represented in family relations, work relations, in schools, etc.

The third reason for the distinction between culture and ideology relates to the very important point made at the outset of this discussion of ideology. If you look back to p. 35 you will find that ideology was characterized as a set of ideas, definitions and knowledges represented verbally and visually in, for example, the pages of a woman's magazine. And yet ideology was also characterized as practical knowledge which is acted upon and, therefore, experienced by women. The first was called *common-sense* knowledge and the second *practical* knowledge. Underlying this definition is a distinction between ideology as representation and as experience — a distinction that is largely an analytical one. An adequate analysis of any cultural site, such as those mentioned above, would involve looking at both these aspects of ideology. Nevertheless, in the analysis of women's magazines as one cultural site, the discussion has mainly focused on the first aspect, i.e. on the nature of ideology as representation. We should not forget, that in practice (and this begins to explain the importance of women's magazines) the process of reading those representations of women involves those ideologies of femininity that we have identified as being *understood* in terms of women's actual experiences of the world. Further, such ideologies of femininity are *fed into* women's experiences. Thus these ideologies of femininity might have their counterparts in other written and visualized forms such as television, as argued above. But they also have their counterparts in the actual lives of women, as they experience them.

3.2 *Woman's Own* — finding ideological solutions

In Section 2 we examined *Woman's Own* as a woman's magazine. We recognized the formal aspects of the cover — paper, print, and visuals — that place it in the category of a weekly woman's magazine. We narrowed down the magazine's concerns by attention to the trailers on the cover and the list of contents, and we found that it concerned itself with what was referred to as two areas of women's work, one which involved the use of commodities, domestic work and beauty work, and the other, the sphere of their lives involving personal relationships. In addition we noted the added ingredient of something larger than life, epitomized in the 'lives and loves of the rich and famous'. By studying the contents page and editorials we also gained some insight into how this content is presented to us: the style of one woman friend to another, and with the aim of providing advice, reassurance, and entertainment.

These are very general characteristics, which are also attributable to other women's magazines. But we also began to spell out *Woman's Own's* specific shaping of those characteristics. From its cover (p.11), but more particularly from its editorial, we began to recognize the 'progressive' edge to its middle-of-the-road profile, in terms of its contents and the women readers it seemed to be addressing.

In building up this picture of women's magazines, and *Woman's Own* especially, we were in fact beginning to spell out key ideological concerns in their construction of a 'woman's world'. Magazines trade selectively in some ideologies and not in others; the weighting and emphasis of ideologies and how they are represented varies from one magazine to another (as well as historically). And the interest and pleasure of any magazine for its readership is partly generated by the particular way it defines, represents and *finds solutions* to the problems thrown up by ideologies.

There is, then, an overall *ideological pattern* to the way in which women's magazines put together their features and articles; and this pattern delivers a *series of ideological solutions* for the reader. It is this pattern and these solutions in *Woman's Own* that we shall now explore in more detail.

We discussed earlier how editorials of women's magazines were a good guide to the voice of a magazine, setting its style and tone and address to the reader (p. 24). They are also likely to set out the ideologies with which a magazine is operating. Similarly the readers' letters that are selected for publication are likely to highlight the ideological issues the magazine thinks are the concern of many of its readers, and especially is that so in the *lead letter,* usually rewarded with a larger sum of money!

● Read again the *My Weekly* and *Company* editorials on p.25 and 27 respectively. Then consider the following comments.

My Weekly moves off fairly squarely from a base of home and family, with you, the reader, addressed as wife and mother. But notice how the editorial draws on wider, more worldly, issues, which it brings into the terrain of home. The same rules or conventions as are used in the outside world are being advised as solutions for inside the home. In this way the magazine is asserting the importance of the home; there are echoes here of the ideology of the 1950s of complementarity between the sexes.

But there is also an indication of the personal tensions around domesticity for women: that, in working and caring for others, women tend to neglect themselves (hence a 'Think of Myself Week') and lose themselves and their individuality (hence a 'Have an Opinion Week'). In the need for a 'Healthy Week', an 'Economical Week' and a 'Family Week', there is the suggestion of the difficulties involved in maintaining a balanced household and family when women are so dependent on their husbands' income and favours.

In contrast, *Company's* domestic and familial concerns are more peripheral to the focus on the young, paid, working woman, carving out her own life in her own way. She is a woman who, above all else, is going to express her *individuality*. But notice how that individuality, the choices — which are yours the readers', like choosing to move to the country — are not wholly feminine concerns. 'Inside story' illustrates what I described as the crosscutting of ideologies in this case, of femininity and individuality.

There appear to be contradictory pressures for women between those two ideologies: between conformity and traditionalism — living in town, having children, doing a run-of-the-mill job; and breaking away — moving to the country, not having children, taking up an unusual job.

● Now read the *Woman's Own* editorial (Extract 3, p.39). Bear in mind what Iris Burton said on p. 16 about the readers of *Woman's Own* as you read her discussion of women and beauty. She describes three views or three sets of knowledge (i.e. three ideologies) about women's relation to their bodies and beauty. Try to outline them.

The three views are:

1 To encourage women to concern themselves with their bodies and attempt to thwart the ageing process is to trivialize their role as women. Woman should be comfortable the way they are naturally and, in that way, their lives will be personally more rewarding, and their status as women will grow accordingly. This view is a caricatured version of feminist ideas about beauty.

2 Youth and beauty equal happiness for women. Iris Burton implies that this is the traditional view of women's attitudes to their bodies. However, she believes it is not a belief that is still held.

3 Iris Burton's view: For over a decade, women's magazines have been encouraging the view that happiness for women comes from self-knowledge, self-honesty and a positive approach to life. 'Getting to grips with oneself physically as well as mentally is part of that . . . women should have the opportunity of looking their best if they wish to.'

Woman's Own – the magazine that cares

Our World

Omar Sharif is very definitely in the "love him or hate him" category. I happen to be a fan, not because he's my type or because I especially admire his acting but because I met him once and, like **Shirley Flack**, writer of this week's lead feature, found him genuinely charming and likeable. Shirley's story, on page 8, is a surprisingly sad one of an ageing superstar.

Do we, I wonder, have the right to encourage women to look Thinner, Fitter, Younger? (see page 12). I have one correspondent who thinks not. Enraged by recent beauty advice on how to thwart the ageing process, she accuses me of trivialising the role of women. Be totally comfortable the way you are naturally, she advocates, and not only will life be more personally rewarding but the general status of women will grow accordingly. I don't entirely disagree, but life is never that simple. I honestly don't believe that any woman still thinks youth and beauty equal happiness. For over a decade now women's magazines have successfully pushed the message that happiness comes from self-knowledge, self-honesty and a positive approach to life rather than the traditionally negative one of "taking what comes." Getting to grips with oneself physically as well as mentally is part of that. Of course, it can be overdone but, unlike my critic, I feel women should have the opportunity of looking their best if they wish to.

Most people, especially uncultured Sassenachs, visibly wince at the sound of bagpipes wheezing and skirling away. Not so the crowd of holidaymakers who were on The Scottish Spectacular coach trip we describe on page 37. When piper **Johnny MacKinnon** played in the lounge after dinner at the Hotel Morar everyone was visibly moved by the sad notes of old favourites like Loch Lomond and Over The Sea To Skye. But when the reels began the mood changed completely. Hitherto sedate people jumped up to join in and the room was full of whoops, cheers and laughter. Quite a few drams were drunk that night and when Johnny MacKinnon promised to pipe them off in the morning, few believed him. But like a true Scot he was there, piping away in the early morning mists. There weren't too many merrymakers dancing that time, though.

Iris Burton

EDITOR

Your World

How to free the kitchen slaves

We pay £10 each week for the lead letter

When everyone came home at different times I seemed to be perpetually cooking meals, keeping food hot and washing up. Early comers started on the biscuits, then left their dinner, and there was always something someone didn't like, so that catering for my family of six became a nightmare. Now they all cook for themselves as and when they want it. I provide a list of things in store with some serving suggestions, and we eat only when hungry. Not only is it proving more economical, it is also slimming. We are all learning to know our own body timetables; they differ so greatly that I wonder if our traditional three-meals-a-day are the cause of much of today's obesity. One can train bodies to expect meals even when they don't need them. The youngsters are developing their own potential as cooks and personal tastes are catered for. Next problem is how to get them to wash up and keep the kitchen floor clean.—Gwen Barnes, Longfield, Dartford.

pictures in their family album I would be grateful if I could borrow them briefly and have copies made. No harm would come to the original.—Gertrude Buckman, London W8.

Readers should mark envelopes "Gertrude Buckman," and send to address on page 6 for forwarding.

That's the limit

The little boy next door announced: "I know why Mum and Dad aren't having any more children." Cautiously I asked: "Why's that, Ben?" only to be told: "Because we've just got a new dining room suite and there are only four chairs!"—Mrs. A. Stock, Deal, Kent.

Quality not quantity

Cuts in education needn't lower teaching standards as Miss Dempster (November 7) says. Newly qualified teachers are being employed at a slower rate

Home truths

Standing in the bus queue I overheard two men discussing

childhood chums. Even so, my feelings were mixed when she wrote that every time she saw a donkey

Extract 3 From *Woman's Own*, 6 February 1982.

Notice how this latter view combines aspects of the 'feminist' and 'traditional' views. It insists on the importance of self-knowledge and self-honesty for women's happiness, but *includes* the appraisal of their looks and their bodies within that. It is alleged that, at least in part, happiness can come from 'women looking their best'. You should note too, how it stresses women's *individual* choice and control over decision making in this area: 'women should have the opportunity of looking their best *if they wish to*' (my emphasis).

● Now read the lead letter from Gwen Barnes in 'Your World', just below the editorial (Extract 3).

What are the two versions of domesticity for women which she recounts?

1 Domesticity as a nightmare for mum, who has a perpetual round of cooking, keeping meals hot, watching food being *not* eaten, and washing-up as various members drift in around the clock.

2 Domesticity as less oppressive, less time-consuming for mum, who has organized her family each to get their own meals.

You might note though how *she* provides a list of what is in store and serving suggestions, and still washes up and cleans after them!

In getting you to spell out these different views on women's relation to beauty and domesticity, I hoped that the ideological pattern particular to *Woman's Own* would become clearer to you. The magazine voices the problems thrown up by ideologies of femininity for women. It tries to tackle them head on and has a bold stab at 'solutions'. These solutions tend to be ones proposed for individual women.

It is this kind of definition, representation and finding of solutions to the problems thrown up by ideologies which it seems to me Iris Burton is referring to when she talks about *Woman's Own* readers and the magazine as that 'bit more' in the editorial reproduced on p.16 of the Unit.

We shall now attempt to fill out that ideological pattern and those solutions by looking at three ideologies of femininity in *Woman's Own*: sexuality, paid work and domesticity.

3.2.1 Sexuality

Look once more at the cover images of women's magazines, but this time think about that woman's smiling face *in a context wider than* that of women's magazines.

I want to suggest two things about this smiling image of women. First, it is an image that presents itself as the normal and natural representation of womanhood, of the feminine woman, in our culture. It does that even though most readers of the image recognize that many, if not most, women for most of the time do *not* look like that. Second, I suggest that this natural representation of women is a *sexualised* one, even though as readers we do not necessarily consciously recognize its sexual appeal.

Let us investigate the basis of this sexual appeal and ask *how* sexuality is built into the image.

● Look carefully at the cover image of your copy of *Woman's Own,* and at the one shown in Figure 23. At whom does the model seem to be gazing?

The model seems to be *gazing at a man.* She is doing that despite the likelihood of the actual object of the gaze being a woman.

● Are there any other signs of sexuality?

In Figure 23, the arrangement of the model's hair — seductively over one shoulder — can plausibly be read as a sign of sexuality. In addressing *men*, the image of femininity is one which presupposes masculinity: masculinity is heavily present as the imagined voyeur, though it is actually absent from the visual itself.

This type of image is not just generic to the cover of women's magazines or even just to images directed at women. It is also the typical representation of *The Sun's* page-three pin-up, of soft-porn magazines, and it is often deployed in magazines like the Sunday supplements or in men's specialist magazines. It is also prevalent in advertising addressed to women and men.

● Look at the visual images shown in Figures 23 to 27. Consider for each of them: whether you like the picture, and if so why? If you don't like it, why not? Then take a sheet of paper and place it over the body from the shoulders downwards of Figure 26. Look at the face for a few moments and then transfer the paper to cover the face only. Ask the above questions of each of these two views of Figure 26. Then turn back to Figures 23 to 27. Do you respond to them any differently this time around? Consider what the signs of sexuality are in the images.

What I hope the exercise of looking at the two views of Figure 26 made manifest to you is the potential sexuality behind all these smiling faces. In comparison with the body-without-the-face — which I, for one, respond to as patently sexual and indecent— the facial images in the first four examples seem fairly innocuous. We can conclude, then, that the *face suggests* the sexual body, even when the latter is not present.

Let us now look at the sexual signs we can note in those five images, apart from the gaze directed at men, which is common to all of them.

Figure 23 Her lifted arm, ruffling her hair, makes her sexually vulnerable. The plunging, slightly gaping neckline sexually reveals a nipple and breast, and we can see the shape of her body through the flimsy material of her dress. Yet the style of the photo and its appearance on the cover of this 'respectable' Sunday magazine makes it easy to overlook these aspects. The make-up mirror, held too high for her actually to use, indicates, perhaps, her own concern about, and pleasure in, her appearance.

Figure 24 The black woman and the white woman have *full, red* lips, very slightly *open*. These features are sexual signs, which the extravagant roses pinned below the ear corroborate. Their dresses are off one shoulder, flimsy, almost see through.

FIGURE 23

FIGURE 24   From women's monthly magazines, 1982.

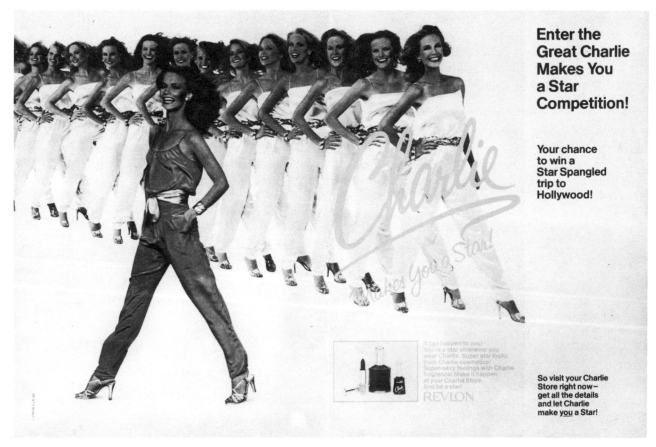

FIGURE 25   From women's monthly magazines, 1980.

Figure 25   A combination of windswept (mostly blonde) hair, arched neck and bare shoulders, silky white material and one-hand-on-hip indicates not only glamour and style, but potential stardom redolent with sexual overtones.

What I want to emphasize about these signs of sexuality is that they *do not intrinsically* mean sexuality-for-men. That is culturally how sexuality has come to be coded, and consequently those repetitive signs seem *naturally* and inevitably to suggest sexuality for men.

Representationally the most striking factor about the images in the *Daily Star* and on the cover of *Woman's Own* is their similarity; one woman is fairly indistinguishable from the other. (Yet any cover of *Woman's Own* is marked as a particular issue by a *different* women — in the *same* image.)

● Look at the Charlie ad again (Figure 25). It addresses 'you' as if 'you' were an individual: 'it *can* happen to you!' Only 'you' — and, yet to *each* of 'you'. Visually, however, the women are not individuals. Clothes, posture, figure, hair, facial expression are virtually similar and women are being judged, so the ad suggests, on the basis of *how they look.*

I have gone into the characteristics of the imagery in fine detail because this measurement of women by their looks is perhaps one of the most central constructions of femininity. It is the way in which men *and women* see and judge women. And it is markedly different from how men are seen and judged. John Berger has put it very well:

> *Men act* and *women appear:* Men look at women. Women watch themselves being looked at. This determines not only most relations between men and women but also the relation of women to themselves. The surveyor of women in herself is male: the surveyed female. Thus she turns herself into an object — and most particularly an object of vision: a sight.   (Berger, 1972, p.47)

FIGURE 26   From *Daily Star*, Tuesday, 17 August 1982.

Jo Spence, a photographer has examined the photos she has taken and those of herself in terms of this same phenomenon, which she describes as 'the Look' for women'.

> I . . . became aware of 'the Look' the media has created for women — the full-faced come-on, a full frontal attack. You don't see many active images of woman around; it's your face that represents you. And the eyes say 'I'm available'. Wearing glasses is tantamount to wearing a mask; it cuts off 'The Look' . . . that's why I'm glad now I wear them.
>
> It only recently occurred to me that all my early photographs were about 'come-on'. We are supposed to spend all our time, energy and money trying to look perfect. When we've achieved that 'peak' we have to worry about 'keeping our looks'. But life's not like that. We are constantly changing. The mirror image shown to working women is totally static. It represents an ageless, classless view of people with different lifestyles and values. (Spence, 1978, pp.7—8)

She shows some of the photos of herself (Figure 27) in which she is striving to achieve
'the look'.

FIGURE 27   From Jo Spence, 'Facing up to myself', *Spare Rib*, No. 68., March 1978.

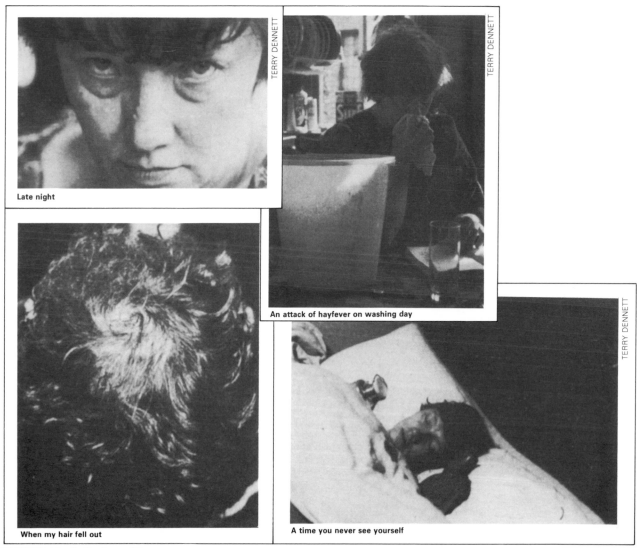

FIGURE 28   As for figure 27.

● See if you can find similar ones of yourself or a woman friend or relation. Do you like them?

She contrasts these with more recent photos of herself (Figure 28), the kind of photo you don't want to be shown publicly and you may often destroy. She is not glamorous but, at her most ordinary, as she is in everyday life.

● See if you can find such pictures of yourself or a woman friend or relatives. Do you dislike them?

As Jo Spence comments, some of this second set of pictures could well have been 'used to raise money for charities!' It's not surprising then that 'nobody in their right mind preserves pictures of themselves looking like that because of the connotations with failure'.

The pressures on women to conform to what Jo Spence describes as 'The Look' do not simply occur when women are being photographed. They are a consistent pressure of women's daily life: from the irritating comments of workmen who make such remarks (especially if you are young) as 'Give us a smile luv' or 'The world's not that bad is it?', if you happen not to smile pleasantly in their direction, to concerned enquiries — by family, friends or work colleagues, when you happen to look 'less-than-turned-out' as usual — of 'Are you all right?', 'You're not ill (or upset), are you?'. Large numbers of women in paid work are partly paid to look nice and to make themselves pleasing to men: secretaries, receptionists, air hostesses all have to collude with these ideas of femininity. In psychiatric hospitals and prisons, one of the signs that women patients or inmates are 'improving' is if they begin to take an interest in their appearance. It is a pressure which results in women, on the one hand, endlessly dieting, spending vast sums on clothes and beauty preparations and, on the other, constantly being self-conscious and dissatisfied with their appearance and their bodies and afraid of growing old and 'ugly'. It is this tension on which women's magazines ambiguously thrive, and *Woman's Own* is no exception. Bearing in mind this characteristic of femininity, it becomes less surprising that a magazine geared to older women, like *Woman's Weekly,* has a *young* woman on its cover.

As the *Daily Star* pin-up made clear, the face is commonly accepted as a respectable aspect of an often more hidden sexuality of women. But women's sexuality concerns not only their looks; it also concerns their desires and actions. If women are caught up in striving to appear as men supposedly want them to look, sexually or otherwise, they are also caught up in being as men sexually desire them and want them to behave. And there are the same anxieties for women over their sexual desires and actions as there are about their looks. The problem page in a woman's magazine indicates that only too well: its existence is an explicit acknowledgement by the magazines that all is not well in the 'woman's world', especially on the sexual front.

The page itself represents only the tip of a large mailbag from readers, each of whose letters will be answered by the magazine staff. In 1982, as in the 1950s, the letters are largely concerned with personal relationships, either familial relationships or relationships with men. In the next exercise, we focus primarily on relationships with men.

● First, read through the 1956 problem page (Extract 4, p.47). Then try to answer the following questions in order to begin to find out how the ideology of sexuality might have changed in thirty years. (We have numbered the Letters 1 to 13.)

What are the words used for sex?

What might the implications of that vocabulary be?

What differences are mentioned between women's and men's sexuality?

What opinions are expressed about premarital sex, pregnancy outside of marriage, and abortion?

What opinions are expressed about extramarital sex?

The avoidance of the word 'sex' is striking. It does not appear once. Various words are used by the authors of the letters to suggest sex (though remember that readers' letters are edited and that these substitutes may be ones that the magazine thinks are appropriate). For example, sex for a married couple is 'love-making'; for an unmarried couple, 'love-making' which has gone 'too far'. An extramarital relationship is described as 'something between them'. The absence of sex within marriage is referenced by 'a wife in name only' and living as 'brother and sister'. Mary Grant's reply to a married woman mentions 'a right to normal life' and 'your natural desire'.

These euphemisms, alongside Mary Grant's sensitively worded invitation to readers — 'Write to me on any problems on which you hesitate to seek the advice of your friends' — indicate the delicacy and embarrassment for women of discussing and reading about matters of sex. The letters also reveal that sexuality is not a topic that is easily discussed between couples, even when they are married (see Letters 1 and 8).

There are some contradictions in the ways that the differences between women's and men's sexualities are seen and represented. In Letter 8 there is a sense of *male activity* implying, at least, female passivity: he 'makes passionate love to me'. In Letter 12 there is a reference to a boy being 'fast', suggesting an active and easily aroused sexuality. Mary Grant considers men 'naturally less romantic (Letter 6), and more likely to experience sexual frustration' (that is the 'emotional strain' of Letter 8). In Letter 11 she insists that men are able to love their wives but still 'yield to temptation'. Men are seen as having sexual urges that must and need to be satisfied; and these are normal and natural.

On the other hand, in Letter 1, Mary Grant encourages the woman writing to believe that *her* sexual desires are 'natural', that she has a right to a 'normal life' and that to be sexual as a *married* woman is not 'disgusting'. None the less, the problem has arisen for her because her husband has *failed* in his masculine sexual role: he does not express any wish to make love to me'. Natural male sexuality is again envisaged as active. These differences between an active male sexuality and a passive female sexuality are part of what Sonja Ruehl describes in Unit 4 as the *double standard* of sexuality between men and women.

You can see in these examples how the ideology of sexuality 'naturalizes' the different sexualities of women and men in the way described on p. 36. Though there is not quite an explicit drawing on biology, the use of the term 'natural' by Mary Grant seems both to imply a normality which is morally prescribed and to suggest something which is biologically determined. If you remember back to Unit 2 (pp. 7 and 8), Lynda Birke discussed these different meanings of the term 'natural' in some detail. And, in Unit 4, Sonja Ruehl discussed the *natural* view of sexuality, which posits sexuality as primarily a biological phenomenon. In particular, the biological definition hinges on seeing an inevitable relation between *reproduction* and sexuality.

Premarital sex, pregnancy, abortion and extramarital sex are all frowned upon by Mary Grant. She is, however, more adamant about abortion, which, unlike the others, was illegal in 1956. In both cases of premarital sex resulting in pregnancy (Letters 2 and 7), Mary Grant advises the writers to think of the future of the expected child. Marriage, when at all possible in these circumstances, is seen as the 'best solution'; it is what the woman should 'obviously' do. The woman's own feelings, and even the man's, seem to take a back seat to what is considered the *moral* action and the 'entitlement' of the coming *child*.

Contraception receives only a veiled reference in Letter 13, and only in the context of marriage; it is not mentioned in relation to any of the problems of courtship (for example, Letter 9).

As far as extramarital sexuality is concerned, Mary Grant responds to the woman who is having an affair with a man thirty years her junior with sheer disbelief (Letter 4). Implicitly, this says something about what is regarded as 'normal'. In Letter 11 she shows extreme tolerance for the husband's actions. You might like to consider what her replies to each of these letters might have been if the gender roles had been reversed in each case. Note that in all these letters and their replies there is an assumption of heterosexuality. The question of lesbianism simply does not appear.

In the last thirty years, however, the ideology of sexuality, and how it is represented in women's magazines, has changed. From what you have learnt (in Unit 4 especially), or will learn in other Units, you may be able to offer some explanations — not least the introduction of the contraceptive pill — as to why and how precisely this ideology has changed. Nevertheless, some elements of the ideology that we have seen at work in the 1956 problem page have been more resistant to transformation and are still in evidence in the pages of *Woman's Own* in 1982.

Extract 4   From *Woman's Own*, 2 February 1956.

★ Write to me about any problems on which you hesitate to seek the advice of your friends. However difficult, however simple, I shall be very pleased to help you

Mary Grant's PROBLEM PAGE

HOW CAN I SAVE MY MARRIAGE?

1

I HAVE been married for three months, and am still a wife only in name. I loved my husband when I married him, but he has become irritable and over-bearing, and now sometimes I feel I almost hate him. He never shows me any affection or expresses any wish to make love to me. I did once try to broach the subject, but he made me feel I had suggested something disgusting. We can't go on like this—what should I do?

● *This distressing situation is made even more difficult by your husband's refusal to discuss it. I agree that you can't go on like this, and I can only advise you to tell him so frankly. You have a right to a normal life, and it is quite wrong that your husband should make you feel that your natural desire for this is disgusting. As things are you would be entitled to apply to have your marriage annulled, but I hope this will not be necessary. What you write suggests that he is as worried as you are. Try not to let him feel he has failed you, but persuade him to seek medical advice.*

2   **Ours is a tragic triangle**

When I returned from leave a few months ago I was told my fiancé had been going out with another girl. I loved him so much that I forgave him and forgot. Now she is to have his baby, and wants him to marry her. We had planned to marry very soon and all the arrangements are made. I love him, but hate to think of her being in such a predicament.

● *It is very difficult for me to advise you without knowing more of the situation. I appreciate your generosity in considering the other girl—but you must bear in mind that she showed no thought for you when she allowed your fiancé to make love to her. I should be more inclined to consider the future of the baby she is expecting. If your fiancé is willing to marry her, and if they both feel that their marriage would be successful, there is no doubt that this would be the best solution. But, if they have no feeling for each other, then it would be adding another mistake to one already made.*

3   **He puts his religion first**

I have been going out with the most wonderful boy for some months. We love each other dearly, but as we are of different religions he says we could never find happiness together. He says his religion means more to him than anything else and I know this to be so, as he always puts it first.

● *Feeling as he does, I think he is right in saying that he could not be happy with someone who held different religious views from his own. Therefore there are only two choices: either you must give up seeing him and hope that in time you will forget each other—or, if you can do so sincerely, adopt his faith.*

4   **I know she was unfaithful**

My wife and I have been happily married for nearly 30 years. Now I know that she has been unfaithful to me with a young man some 30 years her junior. At the time I didn't want to cause a scandal, but have gone through so much since that I wish I had taken proceedings. She cannot know that I know about the affair, because she is always condemning immorality—which proves to me that she is a liar and a hypocrite.

● *As your wife does not know of your suspicions, you apparently never found her in compromising circumstances, so how can you be so sure that she has been unfaithful? It strikes me as being very unlikely that she was, not only because you have been happy together for so long, but also because of the very big age difference. If you cannot overcome your suspicions, I can only suggest that you tell your wife of them; I'm sure she will laugh you out of them.*

5   **He talks about his lost love**

I have been engaged for 18 months to a man I love very much. When I first met him his fiancée had just broken their engagement, leaving him terribly depressed. He says he loves me, and behaves as though he does—but will insist on talking about her. She seems to have been so perfect that I am getting an inferiority complex.

● *It seems that he loves you, but I think it is he who has the inferiority complex. Probably the breaking of his engagement not only depressed him, but left him feeling insecure. He wants to be sure of you, and perhaps hopes to achieve this by talking about his ex-fiancée to make you feel unsure of yourself. I don't think you need worry, but it is not fair that you should be made unhappy like this. Tell him that his previous engagement belongs to the past, and ask him to stop talking about it.*

6   **Have I disappointed him?**

I have been married for only three weeks, and feel rather disappointed with married life. My husband is not affectionate as he was before marriage, already forgets 'the little things that means so much,' and we often quarrel. I am 19, and very homesick too. Do you think I have disappointed him?

● *Most people do find great happiness in marriage, but it does not come automatically, and it rarely comes at once; normally it builds up over the years. I don't expect your husband is in the least disappointed in you, but as he is a man he is naturally less romantic than you are. I'm afraid that most men tend to develop into settled-down husbands very soon after the honeymoon is over. I think you should talk things over frankly and try to find out in which ways you can help each other to find happiness.*

7   **I don't want this child**

I am 20 and look after my widowed father. I am in love with a man who is now abroad, and the night before he went away we let our love-making go too far. Now I think I am going to have a baby. Although the man will be home before it is born I don't want the child. Is it legally possible for anything to be done to ensure that the child is not born?

● *No, it definitely is not, and I am sure that such an idea would never have occurred to you if you were not so distraught. Do be sensible. You love your baby's father, and I assume that you always intended to marry one day. What you should obviously do is to marry immediately he returns and give the child the home and the love to which he is entitled.*

8   **Are we being foolish?**

My boy friend makes passionate love to me, and although we've never done anything wrong, I can't help wondering if it's wise. We've been going out together for three years. Do you think he means to marry me?

● *Passionate love-making before marriage is unwise, because it usually involves great emotional strain for the two people concerned—especially the man. It certainly seems to me that you must love each other, and I don't think he would have taken you out regularly for so long if he did not intend to marry you.*

9   **I'd be afraid to marry him**

For ten years I have been in love with a man. The last two years however, there has been a change and I can truly say that he is to blame. We quarrel often and he says all sorts of hateful things—then comes back next day as if nothing at all had happened. He has often asked me to marry him, but I'm afraid of what he would be like after marriage.

● *Don't you think the quarrels may be due to the strain of your exceptionally long courtship? I don't for a moment suppose he means the 'hateful things' he says—under emotional strain people tend to say things they do not mean. I feel the problem would not exist if you married him.*

10   **I hope to reform him**

I am 21 and engaged to a boy of the same age. My parents dislike him, and my brother says that when he did his National Service he was a perfect nuisance to the officers. He smokes and drinks and I'm afraid he tells lies, but I hope to make him give up his bad habits. I pay for us both when we go out, and have spent quite a lot of money on him. I love him so, and he even writes out poems to make me see how much he loves me. I'm unhappy at my home, but he says I can come and live at his. I couldn't do that—his family are very common. Should I go into lodgings?

● *I must say your family seem to have ample reason for disapproving of your fiancé. Unless he makes a real effort to give up his bad habits, you will not be able to make him do so. Such an effort would be a much more convincing proof of love than writing out poems! Don't marry him at any rate until he shows signs of developing a sense of responsibility. As for leaving home, I think you would be wiser not to do so.*

11   **How could he do such a thing?**

About a year ago I was in hospital, and a neighbour looked after my husband. When I returned I had a feeling that there had been something between them, though at first he denied it. Now he has admitted that I am right, but says that he never loved anyone but me and that it 'just happened.' I don't think I can ever forgive him, and shall never understand how he could do such a thing.

● *You can only hope to find happiness again if you dismiss the incident (for that is all it was) as something unfortunate but not really important. I don't doubt at all that your husband was truthful when he said he never ceased to love you. Few women can understand that it is possible for a man to love his wife and yet give way to temptation; but it is a fact and you must try to accept it.*

12   **They say he's 'fast'**

I am 17 and have been asked out for my first date. The girls in the office have warned me against the man—they say he is 'fast.' I like him and would like to go out with him.

● *Let your parents meet him before you go out with him. Why not ask if you may invite him to tea one weekend, and tell him that your parents do not like you to go out with men they have not met? And, if you do go out with him, let him see that you are not the sort of girl who goes in for casual love making.*

13   **We haven't a home for a family**

I recently had my first baby and my husband and I are thrilled with him. However, we live with my family, and if we had another baby it would be very difficult. Now we are living as brother and sister, and find it a great strain.

● *Will you write to me again, enclosing a stamped addressed envelope, so that I can send you a leaflet to help you with this problem?*

Write to: Mary Grant, WOMAN'S OWN, Tower House, Southampton Street, Strand, London, W.C.2, enclosing a stamped addressed envelope for her reply.

Thus, today in the pages of *Woman's Own*, though sexuality is no longer morally bound to the marital bedroom, and women's active sexuality is recognized, and adequate contraception and knowledge about it are regarded as musts, and abortion is certainly deemed a possibility after careful thought, *still* the question of lesbianism has scarcely gained visibility. When the latter does surface, it is usually as quickly dismissed. For example, the reader who, married, writes to say she has fallen in love with her best woman friend, is advised by Angela Willans to put her husband and family first: 'The ache you occasionally feel about your friend is nothing to the losses sustained by everyone concerned if you're silly enough to think you can have everything' (*Woman's Own*, May 1982).

Despite this negative attitude towards lesbianism, which Willans views as a kind of childish aberration and selfish indulgence, feminist ideas about sexuality have had a profound influence on the representation of sexuality in the pages of *Woman's Own* (and in other progressive magazines, like *Cosmopolitan* and *Company*). Since the early 1970s feminism's impact in this area has become more apparent.

Rather than discuss *Woman's Own's* representation of sexuality in 1982 in this Main Text, I shall be looking at its particular representation and comparing it with the 1950s, in your copy of *Woman's Own* on the cassette. I shall be referring you to the cassette at the end of Section 3. For the moment, turn to another area of ideological concern — also influenced by feminism — paid work.

3.2.2 Paid work

It is quite revealing that *Woman's Own* and even *Cosmopolitan* have found it easier and more acceptable to their readership to introduce more sustained and feminist-inspired treatment around sexuality — including discussions of rape, sexual violence, prostitution and pornography — than of the (for them) more profane issues around paid work for women. Thus it is not just accidental that, in the Unit so far, we have scarcely touched on the topic of paid work. Issues of sexuality, whatever way they are discussed, slot neatly into the category of 'personal relations' with which readers are familiar. More importantly, perhaps, the ideology of sexuality in our culture is still such that there is always an avid desire to read and know more about it. Reading about it provides not just information but entertainment — a vital element in the magazine's make-up.

Paid work does *not* have that kind of interest for readers; even though women's sexual gains of the last twenty years undoubtedly owe as much to women's increasing participation in paid work and their consequent greater economic and personal independence — at least for some women — as they do to changes in the field of sexuality. Rather, paid work is marked as serious, if not boring, so that it has never quite been an integral part of women's magazines in the same way that domesticity, beauty and personal relations have. Still, there have been periods, as in the Second World War and up to 1949, in which paid work featured regularly in women's weeklies. But at that time married women's labour was seen as a national necessity to aid the country through an *exceptional* crisis.

In 1982, then, there is still not a regular slot allocated to paid work in *Woman's Own*. In contrast, in the United States, there is now a magazine called *Working Woman*. In Britain the space devoted to paid work has gradually increased since the mid-1970s with the passing of the Equal Pay and Sex Discrimination legislation, and the wider currency of feminist ideas. And, despite increasing unemployment among women, that trend is continuing. To this extent feminism has made its mark; women increasingly believe in women's right to work.

But paid work *is* still a difficult area for a magazine like *Woman's Own* to tackle, and not just because it does not have the entertainment (or vicariously voyeuristic) value of sexuality. It remains a *sensitive* issue for many women. Though I have maintained that women increasingly believe in their right to work, the dominant ideology still maintains a critical stance to married women with young children working — a group which includes many of *Woman's Own* readers. For the women in this group, not least because there are inadequate nursery facilities, paid work is not yet considered to be a wholly acceptable component of their lives.

In its discussion and representations of paid work, *Woman's Own* tends to *harmonize* paid work with domestic life. The magazine selectively *omits* what are, in its terms, the seedier aspects of paid work, like industrial conflicts or the ensuing marital and familial problems that women sometimes experience. Characteristically, the only slot in the magazine which deals with paid work regularly is the reader's feature 'A day in the world of . . . ', but the paid work is generally set within and overshadowed by the domesticity of family life. To give some indication of the uneven way in which the magazine takes up the issues, the 18 July 1981 number carried two articles on different sorts of paid work for women, as well as the start of a new serial, 'Women's Work', described as 'Ann Tolstoi Wallach's glamourous novel of a Manhattan advertising agency'. For the following two months, with the exception of 'A day in the world of . . . ', there was no feature at all. Since many casual readers would not bother with the serial, they would be left with the impression that paid work was not an issue the magazine dealt with. But the serial, though in flamboyant style, did take on some of the thorny problems for women in paid work. As the extravagant blurb to the first episode put it.

> Madison Avenue: it was all there — the glamour, the money, the office in-fighting and after-hours love-affairs . . . This was the world Domina Drexler had chosen — a world full of false illusions, where women had to use every feminine wile to get to the top . . . and even then would always meet a man one step ahead, determined to keep things that way.

It was about the problems of successfully combining femininity with a masculine-type career as an advertising executive. It focused on discrimination against women in the work place and at the difficulties raised in (hetero-) sexual relationships if women insist on the primacy of their career. Significantly, the heroine was also a mother, divorced, who had struggled to bring up her children alone while continuing with her career. Significantly, too, the career was likely to be outside the range of possibilities for most *Women's Own* readers: it therefore represented a fantasy world. In this vein, the trailer on the magazine's cover made no reference to paid work: 'Starts today. Glamour, passion, intrigue — they're all there in our latest novel'. Thus it insisted on the entertainment value of the story, not on its seriousness.

We shall now consider a number of examples that illustrate well the ambiguity of *Woman's Own's* treatment of paid work.

● Extract 5 to 9 are from five other, different, kinds of article in which paid work features. Study them carefully, initially thinking about the ambiguity and tension between the *entertainment* value and *seriousness* of the issue of paid work, and between *domesticity* and *paid work*.   The Extracts are on pp.50—3.

First, as in 'A day in the world of . . .' (Extract 5), the magazine makes very clear the angle from which it tackles paid work: it deals with women's *personal experiences,* and it tends to deal with those only in so far as they are *successful.* 'Successful' means both that the work itself is enjoyed, or is satisfying, and (for married women with children) that it slots (eventually) with relative ease and harmony alongside their domestic and familial commitments, with no costs either to the family or to women themselves. In Extract 5, for example, the reader is given only hints of potential difficulties, in the caption to the photo: 'Daphne's firefighting duties mean she's on 24-hour call. *Luckily her family prefer simple meals'* (my emphasis).

Second, the magazine constructs works as if it were only a matter of *choosing* what you want to do and going ahead and doing it. Claire Rayner (Extract 6): '. . . if you are 15 today, you have a marvellous prospect in front of you — once you know what you want out of life'. Home-making and paid work tend to be represented as choices of equal value, ones equally worth doing. In Twiggy's success story (Extract 7) you can see how the magazine strives to impress on the reader her harmonious management of motherhood and paid work. The former is represented to be as important as the latter to Twiggy.

This ideology of paid work is highly selective. Paid work as dirty, boring unsatisfying, extremely badly paid — the kind of work women do on a factory production line or as a cleaner, i.e. working-class jobs for women — rarely (if ever) appears in *Woman's Own.* Nor is it often that the reader is given much sense of women doing paid work, any kind of paid work, largely for financial reward rather than for the intrinsic satisfaction it offers. If some of the particular problems of paid work for women (combining family and work, descrimination in the work place) *do* get an airing, much is also left

Extract 5   From *Woman's Own*, 7 November 1981.

A day in the world of...

... DAPHNE JORDAN, one of the first of two mothers ever to join the fire brigade in Britain. She lives with husband, Charles, and their two children, Mark, 21, and Linnet, 17, at Much Hadham, Hertfordshire

Daphne's firefighting duties mean she's on 24-hour call. Luckily her family prefer simple meals

Bleep bleep . . . bleep bleep! Charles just grunts and turns over, but I leap out of bed. It's 3 o'clock in the morning, and my emergency signal is calling me out to a fire. Perhaps a child is trapped in the upstairs room of a house. When the bleeper goes, we have to rush off —night or day.

I started the job four and a half years ago. The station was going to be closed down unless manning levels could be maintained, so I volunteered, along with Ingrid Kay, another mother, who I didn't know at the time. I felt it was a challenge. I'm only 7½ stone and 5ft. 2in. tall, but I handle all the heavy

Fire practice for Daphne, right, and Ingrid—"We don't mind getting hurt or dirty"

equipment and can even carry a man down a ladder.

I'm normally up at 6 a.m. to get breakfast. Charles, who works for the Department of the Environment, and Linnet, a groom, leave the house by 7. Mark, who works with computers, is away by 7.30.

In the morning I start my dressmaking and curtain-making. As I've lived in the village all my life everyone knows me, so I'm never short of work.

When the fire alarm calls us out in the winter it's usually to chimney fires and car accidents, but in the autumn we do get hayrick fires. Many farm fires are caused by electrical faults.

For lunch I usually make do with a quick snack so I can carry on with my sewing. Our fire station is a retained station which means nobody's on duty full-time; we just all get there if needed. For two weeks there may be no calls, then we'll get four or five in a week. So you've got to be a free agent to do this work, and mustn't mind getting dirty or hurt. Working as a team gives you confidence.

Early evening I start the family meal. We prefer simple, basic food which is just as well since if the bleeper goes I just have to switch off the cooker and take off. We get to local fires quicker than the nearest brigade in town which is why it would be terrible if the station closed.

By 6, everyone's home and we

all tuck in. Tuesday nights we have fire practice, so at 7 I change into my uniform and get to the station. Ingrid and I are not exempt from anything. Last year we helped rescue a 91-year-old lady and all her family, including the dog, from the bedroom window of a blazing pub. Fires in the home often start in the kitchen or through TV sets going up. Guy Fawkes' Night is hazardous too: people should keep an eye on bonfires, and watch which way fireworks are likely to head.

Last year two lads got trapped in a Landrover when they tried to drive down a road which gets flooded during winter. One lad waded through to alert the station and Ingrid and I were first on the scene. Imagine his amazement on being confronted by two women as he stood there stripped to his underpants.

When we girls first joined the brigade some of the men said: "No way are we going to work with women," but now we're accepted. Quite honestly they forget about us being women when we're wearing helmets, and once a chap came up to us and said: "Pity you lads don't get your hair cut, isn't it?"

Extract 6   From a feature by Claire Rayner, 'I am my own woman', which explores the stages of a woman's life and the decisions she has to make at different times, *Woman's Own*, 25 April 1981.

I AM MY OWN WOMAN

Continued from page 25

demand—shy, timid people get bullied; aggressive people get slapped down. Which brings me to the next important self-assessment —that of ability and interest. Look first at stereotyped ideas, and what effect they have had on women. And take a close look at the so-called revolution caused by the Women's Movement. It is said by some of its activists that it is the politicising of feminist groups that has changed life for modern women; that women can have a career as well as a family, and compete with men in a man's world.

In fact, all that has happened is

that a few women, the particularly energetic and organised ones, have been able to add on to their basic stereotype roles additional roles. They are a remarkable lot! They study for degrees while running the family business, rearing four children, baking their own bread—and, of course, being stunningly sexy.

But this is another tyrannical stereotype and has to be resisted most vigorously by all of us. Most of us are like most men—middle-of-the-roaders, able to cope happily with just so much. Yet we are being made to feel too often that unless we take up a highly academic career while young we are failures; that home-making and child-rearing are insignificant occupations for intelligent women. This just isn't

true. A successful woman is one who is doing what she wants to do and using her abilities as she sees best. And she is one who is flexible.

Too many women believe that a career means you have to start at the earliest possible age and beaver away for years to achieve success. This is the case sometimes—but it is equally the case that many women, and men, have more than one career. (I'm busy with my third; I may well move on to a fourth yet.) And if you are 15 today, you have a marvellous prospect in front of you—once you know what you want out of life.

How to decide that? There is a lot to be said for making lists again. A list of what you most enjoy doing. Another of what you most hate. Something like this perhaps:

LIKES	LOATHINGS
Brainwork—reading mathematics, puzzling out problems	Easy or repetitive jobs
	Boring people
Travelling	Working with my hands
Being busy	Being tied to a timetable
Competitive activities	
OR	OR
Being with people	Being under pressure
Children's company	
Working with my hands	Being answerable to a boss
Being in charge of my work	
Making things look attractive	

A girl with the first list may be no brighter academically than the girl with the second—but at the time of making out these lists it is clear she's ideal for carving a business career for herself. She certainly isn't ready for being a housewife —a job that demands flexibility, a willingness to cope with repetitive tasks as well as more artistic and creative ones (like cooking and child-care). This does not mean she won't be later. The lists you make when you're 15 won't be the same as the ones you'll make at 25, and there'll still be ample time to enjoy being a housewife and mother, and to return to career activity later on.

It does not mean to say, however, that the girl with the second list, which shows many of the qualities a successful home-maker needs, should take it for granted that a rapid marriage-and-

motherhood plan is for her. The hard facts are that people who marry too young—that is, in their teens—have a much higher incidence of marriage breakdown. Over and over again it is demonstrated that young couples end up in divorce courts much more easily than mature ones.

What such a girl needs is a sensible choice of occupation (of which more next week). The same skills that make people good home-makers make them good at any job dealing with people, from teaching and nursing (which also demand academic ability, of course) to working in cheerful offices or factories where the workforce is friendly and there is the opportunity to work with their hands (a clothing

factory, for example) or shops bustling with people. A girl I know who is now a great cook spent her first five working years in a supermarket selling food. She's very knowledgeable as a result.

Let me repeat that there is no difference in value between the business-ambitious girl of list one who opts for a competitive career and the more easy-going girl of list two who does not. Both may have the same basic IQ—but they have different interests and different personalities and needs.

So to. Guideline Number Three: don't assume that marriage makes a job interest pointless. Don't assume that a young interest in a career rules out marriage and motherhood in the

future. Don't assume you have to be an academic high flyer to enjoy a working life, either. Find out what activities you enjoy doing most and use those interests to enjoy yourself.

Which brings up the important matter of sex and love, a great source of pleasure. One of the nuisances about being women is that, like men, we're programmed by Nature to be exceedingly interested in reproduction while we're emotionally and socially young. At 15 or so our sexual appetites are likely to be as high, if not higher, than they'll ever be, and dealing with them can be tough— though in some cases, they become stronger later. We all, thank goodness, are different! It's

---

Extract 7 From an article on Twiggy, 'Like Eliza said: "I really am a good girl"', in which she discusses her family life and her work, particularly as Eliza in *Pygmalion, Woman's Own,* 26 September 1981.

TWIGGY

Continued from page 8

Continued from page 8

The scraggy schoolgirl with the Oxfam figure, whose face launched a million pairs of eyelashes, is now a slightly plumper, more conventionally attractive 31-year-old. The voice is less gorblimey, but just as vivacious, and the giggle—well, that will go on forever.

Twiggy hasn't modelled for years—"I was getting bored and it showed on my face," she explains—nor has she done much in the way of stage, film or television work. In fact, she spends most of her time at home on the outskirts of Los Angeles, knitting, sewing, looking after Carly, and doing the housework.

"We've got this lovely, old—for America—house. It's 1925 Spanish-style, not one of those Bel Air mansion things," she says with disdainful pride.

"No, ours has lovely big rooms, but we haven't got a swimming pool—no, really—just a little patio. And there's no garden, but Carly seems quite happy on the patio. I suppose she ought to go to playschool soon—but I'd miss her.

"We haven't got any expensive things—no antiques or stuff like that. There's nothing to nick. We've got some Tiffany lamps— but they're not real. The most expensive possession we have is a baby grand piano. I don't play, but it looks lovely in the window.

"Sometimes I do wish I'd been a bit better advised when I was earning a lot of money, because we aren't all that well off now. We are very money-conscious and watch the pennies like everyone else. But, obviously, life isn't hard —we can afford nice holidays in Bermuda for a start—and I have to keep reminding myself how lucky I am."

Twiggy doesn't work much in the States, preferring to stay at home with Carly and be free to travel with Michael when his work takes him away.

"Our life in L.A. is so different from what people imagine," she says. "That's the way we like it to be. I really don't know what we do to amuse ourselves, it's all very domestic and boring. We hate parties, so we don't go to them. Our friends are mostly English—

not stars or actors, more on the production side. When they come to supper they bring their kids for Carly, too.

"Michael is a very good cook, but I really don't like cooking—I wish I'd got a cook—but I will say that my chili con carne is *wonderful.* I make it the day before and serve it with a salad and fresh bread, then I don't miss any of the chat.

'I think we'll come back to England eventually'

"There's a lady who comes in once a week but I manage the rest of the housework and I do all our washing and ironing. Michael's a freak with wood and he does a lot of things around the house. So we play with Carly, or I knit while Michael potters.

"Sometimes we all go to the zoo, and I am longing to play all the games I loved as a kid when Carly is old enough—you know, Scrabble, and all that. And I can't wait to read the Famous Five books to her.

"I've never had a real nanny for her—I don't like the idea—just someone who can take the strain off if I'm working. I'm terrible at getting up in the morning and it is lovely not to have to worry about that."

But despite being so happy she "could bust," Twiggy has grave reservations about bringing Carly up in California.

"It's so easy for kids in L.A. to get all the wrong values. The only things that are important there are success, beauty and youth.

"At the moment we must stay there because that's where Michael's work is, but I think we'll be back eventually. I really do wish Michael could get a part in England. It's not easy because of the accent, but we are working on a new idea so that eventually we can set up home here.

"Michael loves England, and together here we can try to give Carly what my mum and dad gave me—love and understanding in an uncomplicated way.

"I think I'm going to be quite strict with her or she'll get the upper hand in no time; there are so many people around to spoil her. Sometimes she comes into bed with us in the morning for a cuddle and that's lovely—but

Michael has even wanted to have her in when she cries at night. He'd love that, but I know it's asking for trouble later."

When she speaks of Michael, her eyes take on the misty look of a stranger in paradise. "I love him so much," she says dreamily. And despite the well-publicised arguments of their early relationship, it seems that parenthood has tempered them both.

"We are both pretty passionate people," Twiggy admits, "and we do have some lovely rows still. But they are only over silly little things just like anyone else—and the nice part is making up."

Twiggy and Michael met in 1971 on the set of the film W, her first serious acting role. "I had to hold his hand while he looked at me. He was gorgeous and I was so *embarrassed,*" she recalls with a giggle. "I knew, too, that when he knew he'd got me for a film partner, he'd said: 'My God, not a bloody model!' "

Soon, however, Michael, whose acting career had never really hit the big time, found himself uncontrollably attracted to the world-renowned "bloody model."

As he explained later: "You can't stop yourself falling in love just because she is more famous than you."

But with Michael came the first real problem in Twiggy's charmed life. Not only was he 13 years older than her, he also had a wife —although his divorce was imminent. Then there was Justin de Villeneuve, Twiggy's mentor, manager and sweetheart, the person responsible for her metamorphosis from Neasden mod to Harpers cover girl.

"We'd been inseparable since the day he took my pictures in to the Daily Express and they called me 'the face of the Sixties'. It was great—all those places, the limousines . . . I was in a whirl.

"Gawd, they were snooty to me," she says now, remembering her days modelling for the glossy magazines. But she was not as naïve as everyone thought; nor was she without ambition. After her success in The Boy Friend, she was determined to pursue a career in films. And, understandably, when she met Michael she was anxious not to confuse her professional aspirations with her emotional needs.

"We talked it all over. We thought maybe it was the false thing of working together. It was all very intense and I was terribly confused, so I flew back to England for three months to see how we felt then.

"It would have made me ill to have two boyfriends at once," she shuddered. "I have only ever had two relationships in my life. I couldn't possibly keep my feelings from Justin, and as I missed Michael terribly, Justin suggested that, though he and I should remain business friends, I should go back to America.

"Justin had always protected me, but in the end that wasn't what I wanted. I needed to stand on my own two feet. I knew this was a very different feeling from the love I'd felt for Justin. It was real—grown up."

The Press was enraged that its little Cockney sparrow should walk out of her own fairy-tale. Despite her fame and fortune, she'd studiously avoided the excesses of the Sixties and, until then, there had been nothing but praise and admiration for the way she retained her freshness and impeccable reputation.

As her dad told me later: "It could have all gone so horribly wrong. We were desperately worried for her at the beginning. There was so much drug taking and she'd never even been abroad. But she never did take drugs, she doesn't drink much either— and she never forgot her mum and dad. We were so lucky."

'Both Michael and I are old-fashioned, moral types'

With Michael, however, the vitriol rolled. There were stories about him deserting his family— in fact, he had no children—and reports of public fights between the couple because he was jealous of her popularity.

Twiggy's parents, too, were less than ecstatic when their little girl set up home with Michael in Hampstead. "Innit funny," says Twiggy now. "There was all that hoo-ha at the time, but both Michael and I are terribly old-fashioned, moral types. I'm not a bit modern, and I'm really faithful to the people I love. Like Eliza Doolittle says: 'I really *am* a good girl!'"

unsaid. For example, Claire Rayner's recommendation to young women (Extract 6), that they don't rush into marriage, is rather more on the grounds of a risk to marriage than that there are positive gains to be made by an early entrenchment into the world of work. She says nothing about the structural disadvantages for women of either breaking off their career to have children or of not beginning a work life until after they have brought up children.

Extract 8   From an article, 'Secretaries — prospects in the Eighties', by Jan Iles, *Woman's Own,* 26 September 1981.

TEMPORARY SECRETARY OF THE YEAR

TEMPING might be a convenient way to earn money while looking for a permanent job, but there are definite challenges—and rewards—in being a professional temp.

According to Elaine Preece, 1981's Kelly Girl Temp Of The Year, a good temp must possess two qualities: adaptability and patience. "You have to be like a chameleon—but, of course, the longer you temp the better you are at assessing the situation. On Monday morning at a new job, when everyone's chatting about the weekend, the best thing you can do to make yourself useful is put the kettle on!"

Elaine, 36, trained at Hodge Hill Secretarial College in Birmingham, and her first job was with the Birmingham City Police, who allowed her to do O and A levels on day-release. She loves the challenge that her job can provide—and it's an indication of her professionalism

that she's been offered a permanent position in every company she's worked for.

She is encouraged to use her initiative and skills and has tackled jobs that have been in the junior executive league.

"In one firm I was expected to make major decisions when my boss was away, as well as having to prepare all the complicated budget sheets. It was great."

Elaine finds that temps, who are paid by the hour, are often more willing to work overtime than permanent staff.

"There are great financial rewards in temping if you are prepared to work for it. I always stay on if there's work to finish."

Elaine never finds temping boring. One week she might be working for a saint, the next a devil-double. But, as she points out: "If the job is lousy, at least you know you can soon leave."

But despite her professionalism, Elaine sounds a word of warning.

"Even if you feel you know your boss's job as well as he, never say it. You'll be demoted instantly!"

Similarly, the article on secretaries (Extract 8) adds no comment to Elaine Preece's favourable views of 'temping'. She is reported as saying that 'temps, who are paid by the hour, are often more willing to work overtime than permanent staff'. There is no mention of the fact that, in the circumstances, this is more than likely, since temps do not receive holiday pay and they jump at whatever chances there are to make more money. Notice, too, how the visual in this extract shows Elaine Preece as if she were in a position of equal power with her male boss, and yet she knows only too well how far from true that is: 'Even if you feel you know your boss's job as well as he, never say it. You'll be demoted instantly!' Elaine Preece is a 'success' in her line of work. As the article roundly insists (not in the Extract) 'a first class secretary can still be assured of a top job and good salary'. But not all women can possibly aspire to top jobs; the magazine does *not* discuss their future, of possibly dead end, exploitative jobs, or no jobs at all.

Third, paid work is romanticized in another sense. What is hidden from the reader's view is the place of work within a capitalistically organized structure. The division of labour — which tends to set boss against worker, and worker against worker, and which makes trade unions important — is not represented. There is no discussion of the fact that many people experience work as alienating and frustrating, feel like very small cogs in a big wheel that they may not understand or even care about, and that their only satisfaction is the pay packet. An old-fashioned craft method of production (by which I mean that the business is *owned* by a skill craftswoman, who sees the work through from beginning to end), as represented in 'Cooking for loot' (Extract 9), nicely obscures those problems. It presents a work environment far removed from most people's experience. The whole feature illustrates well how *Woman's Own*

Extract 9   From *Woman's Own*, 18 July 1981.

Cooking for loot

Mocha profiteroles, apricot and almond jam, lemon crunch pie, chocolates with a difference. Apart from being as delicious as they sound, all of these foods have one thing in common—they are home-made and sold commercially by women who have the talent and the time to spare. Alex Barker met them, tasted their products and passes on a selection of their recipes for you to try

Imagine making a hundred jars of marmalade a day!

At the age of 22, straight from art college, Clare Nuttall never thought she would end up cooking all day. But with encouragement from friends, she has turned her interest in organic and wholefood eating into a successful small business.

Out of curiosity she began making preserves with little or no sugar and using organically grown foods when possible. Her friends all loved them and she began selling them on a market stall in Cirencester—five jars a week. Obviously she hit the health food market with a product it sorely needed, for now, three years later, Clare is dealing with literally tons of fruit and vegetables. Everything is made by hand, and with two or three part-time helpers she can produce 100 jars of marmalade in a day.

When we visited Clare (below) in Cheltenham, her office/storeroom was stacked to the ceiling with crates of oranges and pots of preserves. In the kitchen (right) Paul Nolan, one of her part-time helpers, bottles a batch of marmalade

tackles the tension between domesticity and paid work. The women described have deployed their everyday *domestic* talent (note that overleaf are the recipes that the reader, too, can cook) to build up their own businesses. They *control* the business, which provide themselves and their customers with much satisfaction. Any potential contradiction between the demands of paid work and the talents learnt in domestic work is neatly avoided.

If the theme of Extract 9 represents a nostalgia for the past, it also holds a hope (however unreal) for the future: a world of non-alienated work, in which each woman contributes according to her ability. If nothing else, the magazine is optimistic on behalf of women; it is also *always* encouraging to *individual* women in their pursuit of paid work. In this case the magazine is advising that even if the woman reader thought she only had domestic skills, these can be put to profitable use.

This stress on women as individuals who are in a position *to choose* — whether it is paid work or merely floral curtains for the living room — is an important ideological strand in women's magazines. The appropriately named *Options* has been very explicit about this ideology: 'Options is a magazine about choice, it recognises and provides for all the different sides of her personality, and it is a magazine that is as rich and varied as her own life' (from the promotion material to potential advertisers). Clearly it is an ideology that moves beyond the terrain of paid work, yet, in meshing or crosscutting with the latter, it allows confirmation of paid work as a personal choice. It covers up the structures of work and family which militate against choice being a possibility. Claire Rayner's 'I am my own woman' can, then, only speak illusorily of 'equality' and 'independence', because it never moves beyond individual decision making to the structures in which that occurs. In such a way, responsibility is shifted wholly onto women. If women experience failure in becoming 'their own women', they do so in very personal terms: it is they, not society, who are inadequate. This onus of personal responsibility and failure for women is one of the recurring themes in women's magazines, particularly worked around in fiction. It marks the extent to which women's magazines have *not* taken up feminist frameworks for thinking about women's position.

3.2.3 Domesticity

Finally, this Section on ideology considers the area of domesticity. It is this area of women's responsibility for the home — including shopping, cooking and entertaining guests, housework or clearing up after children, making curtains or Christmas trimmings — which still constitutes the heart of *Woman's Own*.

In Section 2.4 we considered how consumption shaped domesticity for women. Here we shall consider two other elements of an ideology of domesticity that link up with consumption: (a) its class reference; (b) its construction around the poles of pleasure and work.

Differences between women and men are acknowledged in the magazine; differences between classes and between races are not — except implicitly. This is made easier by one of the characteristics of many ideologies of femininity, that they present themselves as classless and raceless. *All* women are considered to be potential mothers and housewives or sex objects, for example, and differences of other cultures and non-white races are just ignored: 'women are women the world over'. In the case of domesticity then, the kind of domestic practice and knowledge that is advocated for women presents itself as the normal and natural one. That is just how domesticity *is*.

But the act of attributing certain feminine qualities to *all* women, does not only make those qualities seem 'natural', 'normal', and 'universal' for women, it also tends to conceal the existence of class differences. The effect of this is that the magazine gives the illusion of *classlessness* in the representations of domesticity. Yet the ideology of domesticity in the magazine *is* heavily class coded. The representation of class through domesticity is an uneven combination of, on the one hand, a rather middle-class lifestyle, as in the full-colour, home and cookery features. These latter tend to show expensive furnishings in uncluttered rooms, tastefully arranged in harmonizing colour with complementary ornaments and accessories.

On the other hand, there is a representation more of a lower middle-class lifestyle and culture, as in the black-and-white documentary feature. The small suburban semi-detached, often shown in this type of feature, does not have expensive furniture or fittings; the rooms often look cluttered — but they do look lived in.

Figures 29 and 30 from *Woman's Own* give some indication of these differences. (You might also look back to the visuals accompanying the feature 'My husband's gone', Figure 20, p.23) Figure 29 is from a feature in which the designer David Hicks, who the magazine tells us has designed rooms for Prince Charles and the QE2, creates a living room for 'newly weds on a less-than-princely budget'. Figure 30 is from a feature, 'Ulster — and the women who really suffer', recounting the lives of women who have lost members of their families in the fighting in Northern Ireland.

What it is important to stress is that the room in Figure 30 is the one you-the-ordinary-reader (like Mrs Joan Beggley) are meant to adulate and aspire to. It is the middle-class room, which sets the terms of 'style' and 'good taste'. This is one of the characteristics of a lower middle-class culture: it desires to copy the class codes of the class above it. It is also in constant fear of dropping into the supposedly bad habits of a more working-class lifestyle. Not surprisingly, if working-class life is meant to be something 'to improve upon', its patterns of domesticity and, indeed, other cultural versions in Britain, like West Indian and Asian, are generally *not* shown. This absence ilustrates one of the attributes of a dominant ideology, that it can preserve itself as what

FIGURE 29   From *Woman's Own,* 25 July 1981.

FIGURE 30   From an article, 'Ulster — and the women who really suffer', *Woman's Own,*
7 November 1981.

is the *best*, the *proper* and the *normal*. In *Woman's Own* it is the normality of middle-class and white culture that is sustained, even though the magazine's readership, as we saw earlier was drawn from a lower-class grouping.

The construction of an ideology of domesticity around the poles of pleasure and work is similarly a contradictory representation: pleasure is stressed, but it is a veneer which sometimes cracks in the magazine. Then the arduousness of much domesticity surfaces. On the whole, however, the representation of domesticity recognize *some* work, but gloss over the processes of that work, to show only the pleasures of the finished item and *the pleasures of consumption*. For example, in cookery features the reader is lured into the simplicity of the production of the dish by the mouthwatering close-up of it, completed and ready to serve.

Since I have only briefly sketched out these two characteristics of an ideology of domesticity, we shall examine them in more detail on the cassette, which I shall refer you to in a moment.

3.3 Summary

This Section of the Unit, on ideology, has introduced you to the concept of ideology as common-sense and practical knowledge of the social world. It has discussed some of the general ways ideology operates and explored the ideologies of femininity, around sexuality, paid work and domesticity. The aim here was both to arrive at a more detailed picture of how ideologies work and, more particularly, to discover the ideological pattern at work in *Woman's Own*.

In discussing ideological representations, I have assumed that there is *only one way of reading them*. You may have found, however, that you disagree with my readings or interpretations. In the next part of the Unit, I shall be raising this question of readings. In making a critical reading of the ideologies at work in *Woman's Own*, I have also neglected to consider how those ideologies provide *pleasure* for women. In Section 4, I want to focus on the enjoyment women derive from reading women's magazines.

● Now turn to the cassette. On it, I shall be asking you to analyse some of the features on sexuality and domesticity in particular. I shall also be discussing the policy of *Woman's Own* on paid work and sexuality, and enquiring how feminist the magazine thinks it can be in its treatment of those issues.

---

4 Social readings and reading for pleasure

This Section will touch on how the *cultural context* in which women's magazines are read, and how the *social position* of the reader, can generate different sorts of reading and interpretations. It also considers the different possiblities for pleasure which the magazines provide.

As readers, we may be reading on the train on the way to work, while the television is on, or quietly in bed. And we may be reading with disparate *interests* in mind. Perhaps we are looking specifically for a recipe or pattern. Perhaps we just want to bury our head in something for a while and forget everything else we *should* be doing. Perhaps we are waiting anxiously at the doctor's or dentist's and are flicking idly through the pages in a futile attempt to take our minds off what is in store. Perhaps we are *pretending* to be immersed in the magazine because husband or wife, boyfriend or girlfriend or children are trying to get us to do something we are not keen to do. The possible contexts are endless, and will profoundly affect what we read in the magazine as well as *how* we read it. Moreover, *how much* we actually read, and *how often*, will also determine our overall view of the magazine. The fairly exhaustive and systematic reading that we have done for the purposes of analysis is probably unusual. Most readers will be *selective* about *what* they choose to read as well as how they read it. Indeed, women's magazines *are* ephemeral publications, which are often read with only half an eye and are only half digested before being discarded. If your *Woman's Own* has been lying where others can pick it up, you might try asking them what they remember of the magazine's contents.

As readers, we are also socially placed *before we begin* to read the magazine. We are never passive readers but bring to bear on the text knowledge of other such texts, knowledge of our culture and the experience of our social position. As was discussed in Unit 5, *Reading Women Writing,* whether you are a woman or a man will make some difference as to how you read and interpret a text. Similarly, your age, class and race, as well as your family, education, work and political experiences, and the region in which you live, will all determine what meaning you make of any feature or story. You will each have a different experience of the various topics that are written about, and you will *already* have read diversely, and gained disparate knowledge on these subjects. These factors will shape *how* you read any item.

It might seem to you at this point that, having made *just one* reading of many articles in *Woman's Own,* I am now paradoxically suggesting an infinite range of possible readings and meanings to be derived from them. It might seem that I am proposing that a reader can take from the magazine what she wants — *she can choose.* This would be to slip, however, into precisely the ideology of individuality and choice for which I criticized *Woman's Own.*

Rather, what I want to demonstrate is that although the magazine staff can write their magazine intending to convey certain meanings, they cannot guarantee that we the readers will interpret any feature in those ways. Nevertheless, a combination of cultural and ideological factors, codes of representation — with which both magazine staff and readers are familiar — together with how the magazine addresses its readers, work towards closing off many meanings. These factors make it likely that a *preferred* or *dominant* meaning will be produced about which magazine staff and many readers *will* agree. None the less, the gap or disjunction that is made between the produced text and the reading is a highly significant one: it is that space which potentially enables ideologies to be transformed.

With reference to the knitting feature illustrated in Extract 10, I shall try to make some of those propositions more concrete. The knitting pattern has been selected for this exercise on social readings on the grounds that it might seem — in so far as it is largely practical instruction — to deliver an *unambiguous* reading.

Extract 10 From *Woman's Own,* 7 November 1981.

WOMAN'S OWN—FIRST IN FASHION KNITTING

Fine feathers

The pretty and unusual motif of two lovebirds on the front of this soft, pastel-coloured mohair sweater is knitted in as you go and is not nearly as difficult to do as you might think

MATERIALS.—11 (11:12:12) balls (25 g) Jaeger Mohair Spun in pink (M.); 1 ball in each of brick, mid-blue, turquoise and pale blue (A., B., C. and D.); oddment of brown for beak, eyes and claws; a pair each 4½ mm and 5½ mm (No. 7 and No. 5) Milward Disc knitting needles.

Measurements.—To fit 81 (86:91:97) cm bust, actual size, 83 (88:93:100) cm; length, 56 (57:58:59) cm; sleeve seam, 44 cm.

Tension.—16 sts. and 21 rows to 10 cm square.

Abbreviations.—K., knit; p., purl; sts., stitches; cm., centimetre(s); alt., alternate; beg., beginning; cont., continue; dec., decrease(ing); foll., following; inc., increas(e)ing; patt., pattern; rem., remain(ing); rep., repeat; st.-st., stocking stitch; sl., slip.

Note.—Figures in brackets refer to larger sizes; where only one figure is given, this refers to all sizes.

Stockists.—For information on where to buy the yarn, write to Jaeger Hand Knitting Ltd., Alloa, Clackmannanshire, Scotland, enclosing s.a.e.

Special Note.—Use a separate ball of yarn for each colour block and twist yarns on wrong side when changing colour, to avoid a hole.

THE FRONT.—With 4½ mm (No. 7) needles and M., cast on 58 (62:66:72) sts. Work 8 cm k. 1, p. 1 rib. **Next row.**—Rib 2 (4:1:4), * inc. in next st., rib 5 (5:6:6); rep. from * to last 2 (4:2:5) sts., inc. in next st., rib to end. 68 (72:76:82) sts. Change to 5½ mm (No. 5) needles.* *

Reading chart from right to left on k. rows and left to right on p. rows, cont. in patt. thus: **1st row.**—K. 10 (11:12:14) M., 2 A., 6 (8:9:12) M., k. 1st row of chart, k. 2 (3:5:6) M. **2nd row.**—P. 2 (3:5:6) M., p. 2nd row of chart, p. 6 (8:9:12) M., 2 A., 10 (11:12:14) M.

Keeping 2 sts. in A. as placed, cont. until the 8th row of chart has been worked. **9th row.**—K. 10 (11:12:14) C., 2 A., k. to end in C. **10th row.**—With C., p. to last 12 (13:14:16) sts., p. 2 A., 10 (11:12:14) C. **11th row.**—As 9th. **12th row.**—P. 2 (3:5:6) M., p. 12th row of chart, p. 6 (8:9:12) M., 2 A., 10 (11:12:14) M.

Keeping 2 sts. in A. as placed, cont. until the 14th row of chart has been worked. **15th to 17th rows.**—With A., in st.-st. **18th row.**—P. 2 (3:5:6) M., p. 18th row of chart, p. 6 (8:9:12) M., 2 A., 10 (11:12:14) M. Keeping 2 sts. in A., cont. until the 53rd row of chart has been worked.

Next row.—With M., p. to last 12 (13:14:16) sts., p. 2 A., 10 (11:12:14) M. **Next row.**—K. 10 (11:12:14) M., 2 A., k. to end with M. Cont. as on last 2 rows until work measures 38 cm, ending after p. row.

Shape Armholes.—Cast off 3 (3:3:4) sts. at beg. of next 2 rows. Dec. 1 st. at both ends of next row and foll. alt. rows to 52 (54:58:60) sts. Cont. straight until armholes measure 11 (12:13:14) cm, ending after p. row.

Shape Neck. Next row.—K. 21 (22:23:24), turn; leave rem. sts. on spare needle. Dec. 1 st. at neck edge on every row to 15 (16:17:18) sts. Cont. straight until armhole measures 18 (19:20:21) cm, ending armhole edge.

Shape Shoulder.—Cast off 7 (8:8:9) sts. at beg. of next row. Work 1 row. Cast off rem. 8 (8:9:9) sts. With right side facing, sl. centre 10 (10:12:12) sts. on spare needle, join yarn to rem. sts. and work to match 1st side, reversing shapings.

THE BACK.—As front to * *. With M., cont. in st.-st. until work matches front to armholes, ending after p. row.

Shape Armholes.—Work as armhole shaping on front, then cont. straight until armholes match front to shoulders, ending after p. row.

Shape Shoulders.—Cast off 7 (8:8:9) sts. at beg. of next 2 rows; 8 (8:9:9) sts. at beg. of foll. 2 rows. Leave rem. 22 (22:24:24) sts. on spare needle.

THE SLEEVES.—With 4½ mm (No. 7) needles and M., cast on 30 (30:32:34) sts. Work 5 cm k. 1, p. 1 rib. **Next row.**—Rib 2 (2:3:4), (inc. in next st., rib 4) 5 times, inc. in next st., rib 2 (2:3:4). 36 (36:38:40) sts. Change to 5½ mm (No. 5) needles and cont. in st.-st., inc. 1 st. at both ends of 5th row and every foll. 12th (10th:10th:8th) row to 48 (50:52:56) sts. Cont.

straight until sleeve measures 44 cm, ending after p. row.

Shape Top.—Cast off 3 (3:3:4) sts. at beg. of next 2 rows. Dec. 1 st. at both ends of next row and foll. alt. rows to 12 sts., ending after p. row. Cast off.

THE NECKBAND.—Join right shoulder seam. With right side facing, using 4½ mm (No. 7) needles and M., pick up and k. 19 sts. down left front neck, k. centre front sts. inc. 2 sts. evenly, pick up and k. 19 sts. up right front neck, k. centre back sts. inc. 2 sts. evenly. Work 10 cm k. 1, p. 1 rib. Cast off loosely.

TO MAKE UP.—Do not press. Join left shoulder and neckband seam. Join side and sleeve seams. Sew in sleeves. Embroider birds' beaks, claws and eyes. Fold neckband in half to wrong side and slip-stitch.

Follow the chart below when working the birds motif over 48 stitches of the front. Details such as beaks, eyes and feet are embroidered on afterwards

44

It is reasonable to assume that most readers would recognize it *as* a knitting pattern and not, say, a short story. It is also likely that magazine staff and reader alike recognize that it is meant to be read by women who, in British culture, are chiefly the ones who knit. Most readers, too, will understand what knitting *is: they will have seen it being done.*

First, think about the cultural context in which a *proficient* woman knitter might read the pattern. She might, if she is flicking through the magazine (an old one) at the hairdresser's, think, 'Ah, that's nice, I wonder if I could make up something like that'. (This assumes she does not think it quite appropriate to remove the pattern — as many women are known to do!) In these circumstances, she will read the instructions *for the birds motif* particularly closely. On the other hand, if she has bought the magazine herself, she may not give the pattern more than a glance which registers that at some time-she-might-get-down-to-knitting-it. And the pattern or the magazine will be relegated to the appropriate drawer or bag. It will be read properly (though, often, it never is) at a later date when she has it in mind to knit such a jersey. Then she will be reading mainly for its size, type and colour of wools, and length of time it might take to knit.

Two different social positions, which could give rise to different readings, might be those of women and most men (but including women who were complete non-knitters). The latter are unlikely to bother with the left-hand page because they are unfamiliar with the language of knitting patterns and would not be able to read it: it would be like looking at a foreign language of which they knew the alphabet but no more. But, whereas men might look at the visual and decide they do or do not like the blonde woman with the 'come-on look', women are more likely to consider the jumper itself: whether it would suit them, the possibilities of knitting it with or without the motif, for themselves or their daughter; whether they could persuade a friend or mother or sister to knit it for them.

A girl who has just 'fallen in love', got engaged or married might wonder whether she dare wear a jumper with love birds on it. Would it be too obvious, too trite? Would her boyfriend be embarrassed? Those women who can knit, but generally do nothing more complicated than stripes in stocking stitch, will pay particular attention to the blurb, which insists that it is not as difficult to knit as it might look; they are also likely to run through the instructions to see if they can tell whether such an assertion is justified and whether, in fact, they *would not* find it tricky to knit. Someone who works in the magazine business might particularly notice the heading '*Woman's Own* — first in fashion knitting' and read into that that *Woman's Own* is carefully *not* maintaining that it is altogether first in *knitting,* a position traditionally held by *Woman's Weekly,* but in '*fashion* knitting'.

From a perspective sympathetic to black politics, a black woman might look at the visual (as indeed she might the rest of the magazine) and wonder, with some anger and frustration, why the models were always white and almost invariably blonde, and would not the jumper look stunning against a black skin. A white feminist might look at it and contemplate if it were possible to knit the birds so that it was obvious that they were two female birds and hence play politically on the idea of love birds, as love between women.

Finally, these different social readings would be followed up by different actions: some might discuss the pattern with friends, others might go out and buy the wool, yet others might assign the magazine to the dustbin.

For those who cannot read or understand the knitting pattern, there may still be *pleasure* to be derived from looking at the visual. You might think that pleasure is a highly subjective experience: one woman's pleasure is another woman's pain. It is also a social category. By that I mean that no feature or magazine, no experience *in itself,* provides pleasure. As for social readings, so too social conditions determine the experience as a pleasureable one. Moreover, we also learn the cultural codes of what is meant to be pleasurable in our culture, of how pleasure is constructed. That pleasure is a social category also implies that what might be defined as pleasure and the mechanisms by which it is generated can *change.*

Let us consider pleasure from two sides: that of the producers of the magazine, and that of the readers. In so far as women do buy and enjoy the magazine that has been produced, the pleasure as defined by these two sides must at least overlap. But this is not to suggest that they are necessarily identical.

One of the major aims of magazine proprietors is to produce magazines in a form which they regard as pleasurable commodities for women. They are meant to be commodities to *relax* with. As Jane Reed, the former editor of *Woman's Own*, described to Cynthia White in the mid-70s, she accepted that the 'weeklies are primarily used for relaxation' and she wanted 'to make her magazine provocative and funny, and "to make it a selfish purchase for women who have only 10p to spend"' (White, 1977, p.51).

To do that, Jane Reed maintained that she had to omit, for instance, features on child care. Further ommissions would presumably be the features on the nitty gritty of paid work and the arduousness of domesticity that I noted were absent in Section 3. Thus, my criticisms of the treatment of those areas are likely to be dismissed by the producers of the magazine, who will argue that I have *not understood* that women's magazines are about the provision of pleasure.

If certain kinds of feature are omitted, or kept to a low profile, others have prominence on the grounds of their contribution to this pleasure. Jane Reed cites features on 'the personal aspects of a woman's life' (as opposed to those on child care) because they allow a self-indulgence for women caught up in the routines of domesticity. Other such spots in the magazine might be the feature on a celebrity, certainly fiction, and 'Me and Mine', described as 'A refreshing, sometimes humorous, look at life from Polly Graham'.

Necessary and welcome as pleasure is to human experience, there is a worrying aspect as to how it is interpreted by *Woman's Own* (and most other women's magazines). In providing what they regard as pleasure for women, *they represent women's lives largely as pleasureable:* as rich, satisfying, and enjoyable. This is patently not true for many women, and the magazine's own problem page is witness to just that. To put it provocatively, I am suggesting that in providing pleasure in a particular way for women they also *con* women into thinking their lives are *basically all right.*

Now let us examine some of the mechanisms of pleasure for women at work in *Woman's Own.*

● Before you read the following pages, try to jot down *what* you find pleasurable about reading *Woman's Own* and *why*. If you *really* don't find pleasure in any part of it, search out a woman acquaintance who reads women's magazines and ask her. When you have read through my list of possible mechanisms, go back to what you jotted down and see whether you have enumerated similar pleasurable aspects.

Even before reading begins, there can be a pleasure associated with the act of choosing and buying the magazine. Perhaps the buying is associated with the additional pleasure, say, of going on a long journey; perhaps it is a regular event in the week to which the reader looks forward.

Similarly, the *event* of reading — perhaps on going to bed early, and the *ritual* of how the magazine is read — leaving the serials till last, can both generate pleasure. It is the pleasure both of looking forward to the event and of the reassurance of the ritual.

There are abstract and formal qualities to the magazine — its feel, its layout, the opulence of visuals, the perfection of the polished commodity — to which the reader may respond.

As she reads the features themselves, there are certain *processes* of reading that may produce pleasure. Reading magazines tends to be a private and introspective occupation: the reader becomes *absorbed* in another world. This absorption may draw her into the pleasurable 'conversation with a friend' as the magazine's voice speaks. It may involve drawing her into the narrative of the fiction so that she experiences the emotions of the problems building up and the pleasurable emotional release of their resolution.

She may find a mixed pleasure in *identifying* herself and her problems in the pages of the magazine. Or she may recognize the humorous foibles of her own and others' lives. There may be a voyeuristic pleasure, and escape from her own life, in peeping at the lives and loves of the rich and famous. There may be pleasure in the *discovery* of a design, say; *just* the style she wanted to create in her kitchen. And related to the discovery of knowledge there may be a pleasure in stimulation: she had never thought of that.

If there is a dominant mechanism of pleasure it is, I think, made up of two balancing strands which support each other: it is related to the process of *identification* — of women seeing themselves as they are, and as they might *become* in the pages of the magazine — and it is also, and as importantly, bound up with a process of escape into a world which is *not* their own.

More generally, the production of pleasure by a text and the notion of social reading both suggest how the reader is *actively* involved in the process of reading. That is, neither pleasure nor any particular reading is guaranteed by the text alone, but depends on how the reader approaches it: where she is, what mood she is in, what she wants from the magazine at the time — and so on. The magazine, through its characteristic verbal and visual representations, generates pleasure and simultaneously other, ideological effects. Thus texts do not simply produce emotional effects. In Section 3.1, on ideology, I described one of the characteristics of ideologies as being that they 'shape our everyday feelings, thoughts and actions' (p. 35), and I tried to demonstrate, when discussing the representation of 'the feminine look' for example, how that influenced women's behaviour (p. 45). Elsewhere, in the discussion of the magazine's conversational style I pointed out how the magazine addresses 'you' (p. 24). What is important to grasp here is that as a reader you are never simply a passive consumer, who can choose or choose not to digest what the text offers. You are forced, for a start, actively to engage with the text in order to make sense of it and, having done that, you are implicated in its verbal and visual representations. As a result, the text cannot fail to effect you in some way, emotionally and ideologically. When we consider the short story, we shall return to these issues.

4.1 Summary

This section has briefly highlighted, first, that although there may be a dominant or preferred reading of a text, factors of cultural context and social position allow other kinds of reading to be made. Readings have thus been referred to as social readings. Second, in considering the question of how magazines produce pleasure, the Section has been critical of their representation of women as 'happy' in order to provide pleasure for women, and it has suggested that, for *women* readers, identification and escape may be the prime mechanism of pleasure. I have proposed that these issues of social readings and pleasure raise the questions of the *activity* of the reader and the *effect* that visual and verbal forms have on the reader.

● Now turn to the cassette. On it I discuss with the editors of *Woman's Own* how important they think it is for the magazine to be enjoyable, and in what ways they conciously work to produce such a magazine. I also ask you to examine some of the 'entertaining' aspects of your copy of *Woman's Own*.

 The short story

5.1 A note on the method of cultural studies

The focus of our engagement with the cultural form of women's magazines has been on the social construction of *cultural meanings* and their patterned forms. The kind of analysis that we have been making, which attempts to arrive at these patterned cultural meanings, I have described as one which *deconstructs* or *decodes*. What has been central in this analysis is the understanding of the production of this cultural form *within the context of society as a whole*.

The first stage moved from the careful and very particular analysis of the covers and contents pages to the analysis of the more general conditions of the society in which that form is produced (the analysis of magazines as big business). Armed with that wider knowledge, the second stage moved back again to the particular cultural form. (From the history of women's magazines we moved to particular ideologies at work in the magazine.)

Thus, it is an approach that moves from the particular to the general and back again to the particular, all the time making connections between the two. This approach I have referred to as the *cultural studies* approach.

The general aim of this cultural studies analysis of women's magazines has been:

— to go beneath their familiarity, to make explicit the particular representations of femininity they put across;

— to consider the social conditions which have produced these representations in the form of a woman's magazine;

— to understand how those representations of femininity have been generated by the circumstances of women's lives beyond the pages of women's magazines;

— to understand some of the social conditions of reading, and for deriving pleasure from, women's magazines.

The cultural studies approach is a *qualitative* one, concerned with the production and reading of cultural meanings. As such it represents a departure from other approaches some of which you may be more familiar with. The focus of some approaches is *measurement* and quantification based on a statistical sample of magazines, rather than meaning (though meaning is often inappropriately inferred from this quantification). For example, a *content analysis* of women's magazines might count up column inches devoted to, say, 'domesticity', 'sexuality' and 'paid work'. It would assume these categories, rather than ask questions about their social meanings for women, and describe and judge a magazine only on the basis of how it allocated space to each.

Market research — essentially geared to selling commodities for manufacturers — might measure which magazine, or which features and pages of any magazine, were read by which social groups of women (the latter being defined, in part, by their 'buying habits').

An *audience effects* study would try to measure or to find a connection between the content of a magazine and readers' behaviour or attitudes. For example, it might attempt to discover whether women who read women's magazines were 'more domestic' than those who did not.

The cultural studies approach that we have used has not thrown measurement and quantification wholly out of court, or rejected entirely some of the questions and problems these approaches are striving to tackle. We have classified and counted up pages of content, and measured proportions; we have been concerned with the relation between women's buying habits and the magazines they buy; we have attempted to think about how the audience of women's magazines reads them. But, when we have counted and measured, we have used the results as *one* strand to begin or extend the analysis, and not useful knowledge with which to end or complete it. (For example, the quantitive analysis on p. 26 was followed up qualitatively.) We have used the knowledge so gleaned by those methods within the cultural studies framework of gaining insight into the production and reading of cultural meanings. Thus, although *overall* cultural studies is a qualitative method, it in fact draws on a diversity of methodological approaches, including quantitative ones. *Different* methods are required not only to examine the various parts and strands of the magazine, but also to study its various connections with social life. A diversity of methods is needed, then, in order to do justice to the richness of the cultural form.

Reflect on how the analysis has gone so far: we began with a simple description of *Woman's Own.* gained from the visual and verbal components of the cover, and the contents list. But we adopted several approaches to arrive at that: focusing on the formal elements of type and layout, classifying the content, and measuring the weighting of content areas. We considered the verbal address to the reader on the cover, and followed this through into various features of the magazine.

In moving out to the social context of women's magazines and the position of women in relation to them, we approached the problem historically. We looked at the economic development of women's magazines and women's economic role, particularly around consumption.

In approaching the magazine through its ideologies, we began to move back from the general social and economic context to the particularity of ideological constructions as represented in the magazine.

In looking at social readings, we were concerned with the effect of social contexts on the way people might read a particular item. We considered the pleasure derived from reading in terms of the particular mechanism at work in the magazine and women's relation to those.

What we shall do in this last Section of the Unit is explore and develop a method appropriate to the study of one aspect in the magazine — the short story.

5.2 Introducing the short story

In so far as the short story brings together many of the strands in the magazines that we have been looking at, it is an appropriate topic with which to complete this Unit. The method we shall adopt is again concerned with the production of cultural meanings, their organization into the particular form of the short story, and their interpretation by readers.

Before you proceed any further, you might like to re-read Unit 5, Section 9, on Doris Lessing's short story 'A woman on a roof'. Many of the questions Richard Allen has asked about this story are also relevant to the short stories in women's magazines. The latter, too, we can read for what they tell us about relationships between women and men in our culture. But there are some differences in the two approaches.

Richard Allen discusses the literary process in terms of three elements: the writer, the text and the reader. Each of these he considers within a social and historical context. Though short stories in women's magazines are written by individual authors — and if we had read enough of them we would be able to recognize individual styles — on the whole they tend to be written to a pattern, according to certain loosely prescribed rules or formulae that fit in with the concerns of the magazine. Authors write, though often with considerable skill of manoeuvre and negotiation, around these conventions. It is, therefore, generally *not* a useful exercise to think about the story as in any way expressing the author's views. What is more relevant is to discover what the conventions of the story are, and how they work for the readers.

The story below is actually taken from *Woman*. I have chosen it because the theme of its narrative links in well with some of the issues that we have been discussing in relation to *Woman's Own*. You might like to think about whether it does seem to corroborate the profile of *Woman's Own* that we have established so far and, when we get on to the analysis of the story in your copy of *Woman's Own*, consider whether the concerns of the latter story are dealt with differently.

As well as pleasurably rounding off our study of women's magazines, the short story also links in well to the theme of this Course: 'The Changing *Experience* of Women'. Above all, the short story concerns women's experiences; and it frequently charts the problems and the solutions to the changes that women encounter in their lives. Some commentators, however, have thought that the themes of women's magazine stories are somewhat different. Mirabel Cecil in *Heroines in Love* has maintained that:

> Reality is not what magazine stories have been for. They provide women with a world which is larger than life, more romantic, more exciting more ordered than their own world. They want to lose themselves in it for the moment and then come back satisfied, to their own familiar lives. (Cecil, 1974, p.236)

This has been seen to be unswervingly true for what is commonly thought of as the archetypal short story in women's magazines, which Mirabel Cecil is largely discussing — the romance. But, in my view, women's magazine stories are precisely *not* just about fantasy. Their backbone is the mundanity of personal relations in everyday life, but this is approached through the licence afforded them by the fictional form. That licence certainly allows leaps of fantasy, but it does not make fantasy the stories' core. Thus, they deal very explicitly with the everyday, but changing, tensions and struggles of femininity for women. And what the stories do is provide not only *fictional representations of the problems of that personal experience,* but also fictional solutions. Hence their pertinence to this Course.

It should be noted, since I do not discuss them in detail, that the serials in women's magazines, as in *Woman's Own,* are richer in their fantasy aspects. They are often thrillers or historical romances or, as in the one mentioned in the Section 3.2.2 — 'Women's Work' by Ann Tolstoi Wallach — the world that is presented and the characters that feature are glamourous, rich, often not British, and certainly do not live very ordinary lives. Even so, the emotions, the personal relationships and life crises that the female protagonist endures and works through remain those of 'the common woman'.

In looking at the visual representation of women, Jo Spence has usefully noted that there is what she calls 'a woman's narrative' in the representations, which begins in girlhood and moves on to marriage and motherhood, with 'only minimal representation of its "end" of growing old and dying (Spence, 1978, p.30). There is a similar pattern to the short stories. There are some about childhood, rarely any about old age, and they 'peak' around relationships with men, of which there are endless variations: getting a man, having got a man, relations within and outside marriage, alongside other familial relations like motherhood. If paid work for women makes an appearance, it takes a back seat to these concerns with relationships. Unsurprisingly, lesbianism never features in short stories but, perhaps more surprisingly, rarely does *friendship* between women provide the nub of the narrative. Thus, family and heterosexuality are the dominant concerns.

Though, generally, it is personal life as experienced by *women* that is the focus of the stories, there are exceptions, like the *The Daffodil Day* by Victor Canning (one of *Woman's Own* 'Big Name Fiction' stories), in which a young 'hippy' man brightens up the lives of a group of elderly people somewhat jaded by life. Nevertheless, even this story is significantly billed as 'A story of love' (*Woman's Own, 18 April 1981)*.

What is also characteristic of the 'woman's narrative', as Jo Spence describes it, is the the stereotyping of the representations of women. This, too, carries over into short stories. Indeed, many people dismiss them because they are made up of already known plots that only detail clichéd feminine and masculine behaviour. In the analysis we shall consider whether it is possible to view this stereotyping in a less negative way, and concentrate on what stereotyping might *contribute* to the story.

If the short stories are characterized in part by their trade in the problems of femininity, they are also marked by their eventual *narrative resolutions*. These are *not* always the traditional and conservative — the happy-ever-after-in-love scenario — but they *are* invariably, hopeful and optimistic. For example, this is the ending of a story by Thomaline Aguallo called 'He loves me, he loves me not'. The central figure is a mature woman who is widowed. The narrative concerns a new relationship on which she embarks and feels, eventually, very positive about: but it does not work out:

> 'Love is a gift', she said out loud. She had given hers to a man whose perceptions were not her own. Still, he had loved her; not enough or for a long enough time, but enough anyway for her to see herself as someone whole, not someone left behind.
> He had loved her for a moment. It was sweet, and she would keep it. She let it warm and comfort her until the day she was ready to give her gift again. (*Woman's Own*, 15 August 1981)

The narrative resolution suggests, then, that even though the relationship that she desired is not going to continue, he had loved her so that she could *begin to love herself again* (after the death of her husband) and, in the future, love someone else. The story ends on a high note for the woman. This is an important factor to consider in relation to the *pleasure* a reader derives from a story.

The question of pleasure and how it is produced for women as they read the pages of women's magazines, discussed in Section 4, is one of the particular aspects that I want you to consider in the short story.

5.3 A method of analysis

What the method of analysis is attempting to do is to search out both what the story is about (i.e. its ideological themes), and how it works (i.e. how it produces social meanings). It is also concerned with how these ideological themes are put together to provide pleasurable reading. The following procedure provides a guideline of what to look for in a story.

● As a preliminary, *read* the story! (Extract 11 pp.64 and 65).

THE GOOD YEARS

BY MARGARET RIDDINGTON

Reluctantly Sue threw back the covers and slid out of the warm bed. She drew back the curtains and shivered at the dark rainy morning outside as she pulled on her clothes. Robert turned in his sleep and pulled back the covers.

"It's gone seven," she told him. He raised himself slightly and peered up at her through his sleep.

"Happy birthday," he yawned, pulling her downwards for a kiss before he turned over on his other side.

"What time are you due in today?" she asked, opening the bedroom door noisily.

"Ten," came the muffled reply.

Birthdays are not important now, she thought, as she fried bacon for Julie and Sam. Even though it is my fortieth birthday, and life is supposed to begin on that all important day, it's not really very important at all. It just comes and goes like any other day, along with the weather. Nobody thinks it deserves special attention, except perhaps a woman, any woman, who reaches such a milestone.

"Time to get up," she called up the stairs to her sleeping brood.

They'll be forty one day, she thought. But perhaps then someone intelligent will have recognised the importance of a woman reaching that age and declare a day to celebrate the wonders of such a traumatic experience. Perhaps women of forty all over the land would receive a gilt-edged letter from the Queen to congratulate them.

"I've brought the post through," Julie said, handing Sue her birthday cards. Sue mindlessly dropped them on the table without opening them, before lifting the bacon from the pan and making a sandwich.

"Happy birthday," Julie said, with her first bite.

"Thanks," Sue replied, making another sandwich. "Is Sam up?"

"I could hear him moving around, he shouldn't be long." Julie gulped her coffee. "Aren't you going to open your cards?"

Sue picked up the four cards and sat down to open them.

There was one from Sam, one from Julie, one from her mother and one from her mother-in-law. The same as the last few years. Never one from Robert.

She used to protest, but as the years went flying by she accepted that to expect a card from him was folly. She would get the usual bottle of scent or a trinket, and if she made enough fuss they would go out for a meal at the end of the day. Nothing lavish or too expensive, just a meal that she hadn't had to prepare, or wash up afterwards.

"Many of 'em," Sam called noisily, as he straddled the kitchen chair. "And what madly exciting things are you going to get up to today?" He munched greedily on the sandwich. "How many cards did you get?"

She listened to him without replying. She was sure it must be very ordinary for them to know that their mother was celebrating her fortieth birthday. Sam had already told her last week that being forty was just like any other birthday. In his words, it just meant that she was "getting on a bit" but she looked young enough to him.

"You ought to go into town and treat yourself to a slap-up lunch," said Julie as she pulled on her coat.

"Won't you be in for lunch?" Sue asked with a frown.

"No, I'm going to buy myself that new home perm I was telling you about. Maybe you could help me do it tonight?" So saying, Julie crammed on her woolly hat and dashed out. Sam, at his usual leisurely pace of a morning, continued to read the paper, until he left it too late and had to make a last-minute dash to catch the bus for art school.

After they'd both gone she grimly set about washing up and clearing away. Sounds from upstairs meant that Robert was up and about. She placed the bacon under the grill, the way he liked it, and poured out some tea for herself. He liked his tea to stand for a while, so it would be just ready by the time he came down. Idly she picked up the card from Sam and wished she could laugh at it. But today, she didn't feel like laughing.

"Morning," Robert breezed as he slipped his arms round her waist from behind and lifted her in the air. Swinging her round he slapped her smartly on the hind-quarters and asked, "What's for breakfast?"

"Same as usual," she said, putting the grilled bacon and poached egg in front of him. The breakfast he never admitted he liked, but the one that would help get his figure back.

Do you ever get things back the way they used to be? Sue smiled sadly to herself. Had the days when they truly loved each other gone for ever? It hadn't mattered once that he didn't send her birthday cards. His just being there, and loving her, had been enough. Somewhere along the way, she couldn't remember when, they'd drifted apart.

No longer did she feel vital and needed by Robert. Every day came and went in the same way. Maybe she had expected too much of life and marriage. Everyone still spoke of them as having the perfect marriage, loving each other in that special sort of way that was known by few. Nowadays, when marriages were broken up and hurled aside so easily, Robert and Sue were different. Their marriage was as solid as Stonehenge.

"Doing anything exciting today?" Robert asked, picking up his briefcase, ready to be off.

"I'll think of something," she said as he kissed her nose.

"Then try smiling a bit," he said when he got to the front door. "You look as if you've just put the house-keeping money on the first horse that fell in the Grand National." He shoved on his battered hat and climbed into the car.

Sue didn't smile. Instead she wiped away the stray tear that was trickling down her nose. She didn't consider she had a lot to smile about. Robert didn't seem to notice that he wasn't paying her his attention the way he used to. He seemed unaware that something was missing.

Robert had been forty, three years ago, but it hadn't seemed to affect him. About that time he had become very figure-conscious because of the slight bulge above his belt. But it hadn't bothered him too much. He'd simply gone on a gentle diet and carried on in the same, casual way.

He told her he loved her, maybe not so often as he used to, but times were different now. Maybe he didn't love her as much. Was it unreasonable of her to think this after twenty years of being together? Twenty years with the same person. That was close to a record in itself.

As she dusted the lounge, she suddenly realised that Robert hadn't given her a birthday present. In the past, he'd always had it ready for her before he left for work.

So birthday gifts are going the same way as cards, she brooded. Even if he is falling out of love with me, he could at least have bought me something today. He wasn't bothered about being forty, but he's not a woman. Is it too much to ask that he cares, just a little?

She'd vacuumed the hall, staircase, and bedrooms, and was just about to clean the bathroom when the phone rang. At this number, she thought, as she hurried downstairs.

"Fancy going out for lunch to-day?" Robert asked.

"Lunch? Aren't you working?" Sue glanced at herself in the mirror and saw streaks of dirt where she'd rubbed her eyes, and the straggly state of her hair.

"I'm a mess," she said. "I couldn't go out looking like this."

"You've got half an hour. I'll pick you up." And he put the phone down before he could hear any more excuses.

The restaurant was bright and clean with a strong smell of pizzas which made you feel very hungry, even if you weren't. Sue thought the bottle of wine most extravagant but didn't comment when he told her that it was suitable for special occasions. It wasn't every day that you had a birthday. She smiled weakly.

She ordered lasagne, the same as Robert, and sat sipping her wine. She was conscious of Robert's glances and knew that he must be wishing she would smile, but it was taking most of her willpower to hold back tears. They'd had meals like this before. Meals where they had been unaware of their surroundings. All that had mattered was that they were together. She had been able to feel Robert's love enveloping her. He hadn't had to speak, he just had to be there.

"I love you." Robert reached across the table and took hold of her hand. His eyes said the same, and she reached out a finger to trace the smile on his lips.

"How long have you had that?" she asked, taking her finger away and looking up into his eyes.

"Had what?" he asked, taking back her hand.

"The moustache."

"About three weeks," he said, rubbing it. "Do you like it?"

Sue gripped his hand hard. "I hadn't even noticed until now," she said, her heart racing. "I'm sorry."

Robert lifted her fingers to his lips and kissed them. "No matter. Not important."

"But it is," she said, tears brimming. "I should have noticed." He handed her a handkerchief as the waiter arrived with the lasagne.

"I don't think the Italian sauce mixes well with salt water," Robert said, as he motioned her to dry her eyes. "And as it's such an important day, I didn't think you'd be crying about it."

"I'm not crying about my birthday," Sue snuffled. "I'm crying about the moustache. Your moustache. The one I didn't even notice."

"I didn't have time to buy you a birthday present."

"So what? That's not important. Your moustache was."

"When we've finished, let's go home." Robert gave her a special smile.

"It's three in the afternoon."

"Does there have to be a special time to tell a wife you love her?"

The lasagne was better than ever before and the wine reached all the parts it should have done. She would probably take Robert up on his offer of a new dress. But there again, there'd be many more birthdays for them to celebrate together, so she might just let this one pass.

She'd have to remember to get him a new blade for his razor, though. You couldn't just grow moustaches willy-nilly without looking after them properly!

© Margaret Riddington, 1981

The following five-stage procedure, which I shall work through, provides a guideline of what to look for in a story. As I go through it, check that you can do the analysis yourself; I shall be asking you later to use the method on a story in your copy of *Woman's Own*.

1 *We shall first examine the title, visual and caption introducing the story along the lines we adopted for looking at the covers.*

The style of the visual corresponds to the artistic impression discussed on p. 22. It shows people and a real scene — a breakfast time, primarily signified by the toast rack — that we should all probably recognize, but represents it in a non-naturalistic way. It signifies both fantasy and reality. The cards signify both that it is someone's forty-something birthday and the likelihood, since the cards are flowery ones, that it is a *woman's* birthday. By association, it is likely to be the birthday of the woman who is also represented there. A birthday breakfast it might be, but neither of the couple seems to be celebrating. On the contrary, they seem to be avoiding any specialness of the day. With him dressed in a suit — signifying just-about-to-go-to (white-collar) job — and barricaded behind his newspaper; and she — 'the housewife in a servicing role' (signified by the apron strings down her back, her arm reaching for the jug) — with her *back* to the birthday breakfast, there are all the signs of a coolness, to say the least. They are separated from one another, not communicating; there is the flatness and repetition of the everyday-life ritual of first-thing-in-the-morning.

The caption confirms that all is not as well as it might be in the marital nest. It poses a *problem* and a *question* that the narrative will work through: 'everyone' thinks their marriage is 'perfect' but 'she' (Sue) is dissatisfied: what *does* she expect, what is it exactly that is wrong?

In the light of the visual and this caption, then, the title 'The Good Years' poses another riddle for the narrative to resolve for us: which years are those? Those gone, the current years? The visual and caption suggests otherwise. Or the years ahead?

Thus, attention to the visual, title and caption provides quite a lot of knowledge about the short story's narrative method. The latter sets up certain problems and questions which will interest the reader, and which the reader *will want to know more about*. It can be seen that the method also relies on stereotypes: the husband behind his newspaper, the wife getting breakfast. This use of stereotypes that most readers will recognize facilitates both a quick and ready placing of the scene for the reader, and her *identification* with the problems and questions at issue. By representing the marital breakfast minimally, which is in part what a stereotype does, the reader is allowed to recognize it as breakfast, but is given the opportunity of filling in *her own details* of that experience. Many women will recognize only too well shades of this everyday breakfast scene in their own lives, and acknowledge various degrees of dissatisfaction in their own marriages. The stereotype triggers this recognition.

2 *Now we shall divide the story into its 'phases' or 'scenes': try to characterize its 'structure' or 'shape' and its 'narrative movement' through that structure.*

For this stage of the analysis it is probably best to mark the text with a pencil. Some of the breaks or ends and beginnings of scenes are marked by the author (e.g. the gap near the top of column four, where the restaurant scene begins). Others, some of which are not that clear cut, you can mark by looking at where the 'action' changes. In this story the narrative moves through five phases or scenes, though you might disagree with me slightly about where exactly some of them begin and end: in the bedroom; the children's breakfast; Robert's breakfast; Sue alone doing housework; the restaurant.

● In order to discover the shape or structure of the narrative, I want you to try tracking Sue's mood through these scenes. List her explicit or implicit responses and thoughts to the events that occur or the things she has to do, and try to draw a graph of how her spirits rise and fall. You might begin by noting her recognition of the dreadful day and the fact that 'birthdays are not important now'. Her mood is clearly sinking.

What I wanted you to notice in this exercise is the down and up movement of the narrative. In the first four scenes, the problem for Sue, which is hinted at in the caption, is gradually elaborated by her, and she becomes more and more unhappy as the dissatisfactions pile up. Her spirits sink to an all-time low. Where is that point in the narrative? Mark it on your graph.

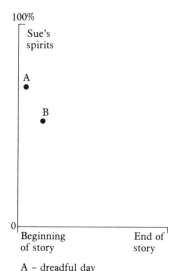

100%

Sue's spirits

A
●

B
●

0

Beginning of story ——————— End of story

A – dreadful day
B – birthdays are not important now

At this low point, towards the bottom of the third column, she asks, 'Is it too much to ask that he cares, just a little?' She has at last made explicit what the nub of the problem is. After that plea, the narrative and Sue's spirits rise again, as the problems are resolved and an equilibrium restored. By the end of the story, her spirits are rather higher than they were at the outset.

Besides this 'down and up' movement of the narrative, we can also see another kind of 'structural balancing', in which the beginning and the end of the story contrast, but also, and importantly, are *comparable*. Thus the 'dark rainy morning', Sue's 'shivering' and Robert's not wanting to get up is distinctly contrasted to the 'bright and clean' restaurant where 'a strong smell of pizzas . . . made you feel hungry, even if you weren't'. But, at the same time, the everydayness of getting up in the morning is balanced by the return to everydayness (from the specialness of the restaurant) in the final paragraph. Sue remembers to buy him a new razor blade: she returns to her 'domestic' role again. If there was a grim note in the opening scene, at the end the tension has dissipated and there is a humour in her thoughts.

3 *We shall now examine how the narrative movement is achieved through a particular method that deploys certain narrative devices. We shall try to decide what these are and how they work.*

● Look again at your pattern of Sue's moods and the events which precipitate that. Can you pick out the events which change the trajectory of the whole story, which I describe as *pivotal moments* in the narrative? Ring them on your graph in another colour.

These pivotal moments are one of the narrative devices of the short story by which the narrative movement and structure is achieved. One example is the telephone call from Robert, which pivots the narrative and Sue from her slough of despond into a steady slope upwards. Short stories frequently deploy such a fortuitous 'outside' event. That is, the change in a woman's fortunes occurs *not* because she has initiated such a change or because this is a 'natural unfolding of events' but because fate or magic intervenes. It is here that the stories move into the realms of 'fantasy' resolutions rather than remaining in the realm of 'real life' battles which often *do not* work out.

The second pivotal moment, which enables an equilibrium to be restored, is *Sue noticing Robert's moustache*. At this moment, the narrative pivots away from Sue's self-pity and attribution of blame to Robert, towards acknowledgement of her *own* blame for what had seemed awry in their relationship.

These two devices, then, allow the couple to be brought back together again: with the first, he begins to demonstrate his care and love; with the second, she acknowledges that it takes two to make a problem. The barriers that were set up between them are now pulled down, sexual attraction flows again, the 'Good Years' are *not* passed.

One other device is the use of *stereotypes*. If you think back for a moment to how, in Unit 5, Richard Allen considered the characters in Doris Lessing's story, you will remember that he looked at the different male characters as certain social types. He suggested that: 'The behaviour and motives of the men and the way their actions are typical of society in general can be read off from the story in a more or less straight-forward way' . . . The woman of the title of the story, however, was much more of a puzzle.

In women's magazine stories, *all* the characters are clearly delineated. They are simply and *typically* characterized with much less detail than Doris Lessing provides. They are not meant to be 'interesting' or 'convincing' characters, but ones that are immediately recognizable social types. Stereotyping is an economical way of referencing characters and other aspects of social life, even if it also has its dangers — the continual flattening of the richness and diversity of social life. It also allows the reader to tune quickly into the story and identify with the scene and characters. For example, despite the probability that most mothers and wives no longer fry bacon for their family's breakfast, such a domestic service still typifies, at the level of representation, being a wife and mother. And most readers will recognise this. To use the term we mentioned in Section 4 on social readings, this is the *preferred meaning* of cooking breakfast. If you look carefully at the story you will also see that the author's cast of Sue, Robert and her two children are all stereotyped constructions.

● Try writing down each of their characteristics. What do they tell you about ideologies of femininity and masculinity? We shall return to these characteristics in a moment.

The final device I want to mention is the story's reliance on Sue's *thoughts and memories*. The story is written in the third person: 'She threw back the covers . . .', yet each description of the action in the story is followed by Sue's personal thoughts and reveries. As you read the story, you are also drawn in to rehearse these thoughts. Though they are said in silence and alone, they are the voice of one woman to another. As Sue says about her fortieth birthday, 'Nobody thinks it deserves special attention, except perhaps a woman, any woman who reaches such a milestone'. The story affirms the relationship of the magazine as a whole to women, that of a woman's *friend*. This rehearsal of the feelings Sue is experiencing is as if she were saying, 'I feel . . .' and it is a further device which allows women readers to identify with the central figure's experiences: the reader too is 'I'.

4 *We shall now examine the problems and contradictions of ideology that are being constructed and dealt with.*

From your stereotyped characterizations above you will have been alerted to the fact that the story takes on the problems of *marriage* for Sue: in the stereotypes, her position as *wife* is contrasted to Robert's as *husband*. Secondarily, it also deals with motherhood: the teenagers in the stereotypes are nonchalant and noisy, using their mother when it suits them, but largely self-sufficient. Being taken for granted as a mother is a problem for Sue. This problem, however, only feeds into the problem of her marriage, of her relationship with Robert. Though this is understated, she feels taken for granted, if not spurned, *sexually*.

The story explores the problem of the long-term nature of the marriage relationship, on the one hand, in which there is a tendency for the relationship between wife and husband to degenerate into one of routine and ritual, without communication or intimacy. On the other hand, and compounding the difficulties of sustaining a 'vital' marriage, there is the problem of ageing and loss of sexual attractiveness for women — a problem that the story makes clear is not experienced by men in the same way. The reduction of their marriage (and family life more generally) to a matter of routine is symbolized by the ritual of breakfast. The lack of love on Robert's part is epitomized, not only by his not giving her a birthday card (since he never did, that was less significant) but also by his not having remembered a present. Sue's life is reduced to performing a long line of domestic chores for which she gets no thanks. She no longer feels sexually attractive to Robert: 'No longer did she feel vital and needed by Robert.': 'Robert didn't seem to notice that he wasn't paying her attention the way he used to. He seemed unaware that something was missing'.

These problems are real enough for many women, but how the story deals with them and resolves them is strictly limited. They are resolved in part *magically;* and they are resolved in part as *individual* problems that *need not* have occurred. In both these ways the problems are not considered to be problems. They are solved magically to the extent that a series of fateful happenings and interventions, outside Sue's control, are the precipitators both of her change of view and the resolution.

Discussing the popular fiction of the 1840s Raymond Williams explains how 'magic ... (is) a simpler way of resolving the conflict between ethic and experience than any radical questioning of the ethic' *(The Long Revolution,* Penguin, 1965, p.83—4). If you think of what he describes as 'ethic' as ideology, then what the magical intervention allows in this story is a resolution of the contradictions between the ideology of marriage and Sue's *experience* and living out of that ideology.

For Sue, at the outset, the ideology of marriage — as being a lifetime partnership of mutual affection and support, and of being a wife and mother as being satisfying — is seriously in question. But, by the end, the ideology has been reaffirmed. The magical intervention first enables Sue to see *her* mistake. But second, the resolution itself — Robert *really* does care, he still finds her sexually attractive after all and suggests going home to make love in the afternoon — is also magical. It *appears* to make everything all right, yet the material conditions of her life have not changed one iota. Magically, the drudgery of her domestic life of routine is elevated and transformed by Robert's renewed responsiveness to her: love makes it all worthwhile again. For better or worse though, she is still dependent on him and her family, and still has to service them.

Further, the chance events that allow Sue to see her mistake — she had misjudged Robert — turn the source of the problem back onto Sue: *she* is responsible for the spark having dimmed in their marriage. The implication is that, if she had been more sensitive and responsive to Robert, the problem would not have arisen in the first place. Not only does this highlight how an ideology of marriage constructs the responsibility for marriage as the woman's, but it also affirms that the ideology is *all right,* so long as individuals adopt the right approach.

What is avoided in the story is an admission that there might be something fundamentally and generally amiss in the state of marriage and the particular sexual division of labour it entails; and it is the raising and solving of these problems as *personal and individual* ones which makes that possible. You might think back here to the Section 3.2.2, on the ideology of paid work, in which these same mechanisms were seen to operate. The story never considers what might be more likely outcomes in 'real life': at worst the marriage would break up, at best she might find a new interest, like a job, and at the least she would get her family to prepare their own breakfast and do some housework. And she could make sure that she invited a woman friend round for a fortieth birthday tea!

Thus, if the first half of the story can be read as an indictment of marriage and family life for women, the second half re-endorses an ideology of the possibility of contented marital life without changing any of its gendered conditions. The problems and solutions are envisaged only as *individual* ones, not problems of marriage itself. Thus the story finally reaffirms a pattern of very traditional femininity, and of a traditional division of labour between wife and husband; with wife as primarily mother, house-wife, and wife, seeking satisfactions within those roles; with husband as primarily breadwinner, sexual and sole emotional provider for his wife.

5   *Now we shall consider how pleasure in constructed in the story.*

Pleasure in the short story is partly derived from its narrative structure and movement: the building up of tension and its gradual resolution, the balance between beginning and end, its completeness. But it is the *personal experience* of Sue which is worked through that structure and movement. There is pleasure not just in recognizing her and in identifying with her problems, but also in those problems being both articulated and satisfactorily worked out for her. When I discussed pleasure earlier, I was critical of this aspect of the production of pleasure, i.e. in order to give pleasure to women it was necessary to represent them as happy. To that extent I am also critical of most women's magazines' stories. Yet I would modify my criticism slightly by saying that I think that for many women the pleasure of the magical endings of these stories is precisely because of that gap — of which *they are only too well aware* — between their own lives and the fantasy world of this fiction and women's magazines as a whole. And women, like anyone else, need their dreams. The sadness is that the dreams of the short stories continue to represent women and men as equal partners in marriage, which is illusory; our analysis has shown that the dreams, in fact, reveal women's *inequality* with men.

● To check that you are clear about these five stages of analysis in the short story, see if you can write them down briefly in your own words, and go through in your mind what is involved at each stage.

5.4 Summary

What we have seen in the fictional form of the short story are many of the elements at work in other parts of the magazine.

1   The story deals in one of the areas of central concern in the weeklies: marriage in its domestic and sexual aspects.

2   The central figure in the story is a woman who is white and middle class.

3 The story works by presenting real problems that women experience. It presents 'solutions' that are wholly unlikely in real life, but have the pleasurable satisfaction of *being* solutions.

4 The problems are presented as ones that *individual* women *experience* and can, therefore, solve as individuals.

5 Women, as readers, are drawn into the story by *identifying* with the personal experiences that are being recounted and by the story's mode of addressing women.

6 The pleasure in reading the story is derived from a combination, which the reader knows well, of the revelation of the problems of everyday life for women and their magical resolution. This allows the reader to recognize the problems women have, but also to escape from them.

I wrote about the story that 'if the first half of the story can be read as an indictment of marriage and family life for women, the second half re-endorses an ideology of the possibility of contented marital life without changing any of its gendered conditions. The problems and solutions are envisaged only as *individual* ones, not as problems of marriage itself. The story finally reaffirms a pattern of very traditional femininity, and of a traditional division of labour between wife and husband: with wife as primarily mother, housewife and wife, seeking her satisfactions within those roles; with husband as primarily breadwinner, sexual and sole emotional provider for his wife'.

That could as well be said about the whole of *Woman* and *Woman's Own*. They currently play around that ambiguity, of pushing towards feminist ideas, and then taken two steps backwards by retreating into individual problems and solutions. In the end, the 'mirror image' they present is of a traditional femininity which is only slightly, but increasingly becoming *more*, cracked around its edges.

● Now turn to the cassette. On it I ask the editors of *Woman's Own* whether they think their fiction is more progressive with respect to its images of women than, say, ten years ago. I also ask you to analyse one short story, focusing on what it has to say about how women experience the difficulties of their position in contemporary society.

⎆ Conclusion

The analysis we have made of women's magazines, and of your copy of *Woman's Own* in particular, has been very extensive. To conclude, I want briefly to draw out three themes which have been running through the material we have been examining in the Unit. First, I want to spell out the most important points about women's magazines that I should like you to take away with you from this Unit. Second, I want to suggest what you might have gained by approaching women's magazines from the particular perspective of cultural studies. Third, I should like to return to the question of women's magazines and pleasure.

First, then, we have considered the women's magazine as a cultural form which is produced by a particular culture and which, in turn, affects that culture. We have examined the relation between the representations of femininity in such magazines and women's experience. Perhaps the most significant point that the Unit has been making is that the representations of femininity found in women's magazines profoundly shape women's experiences of themselves as women, even though women themselves may not realize it. Women's magazines are, therefore not just ephemeral reading matter, which we can choose or choose not to read. If we are concerned about the political and economic position of women, it is as important that this seemingly trivial cultural form of everyday life is understood, questioned and challenged, as it is that women struggle for equal pay and promotion at work. The cultural form of women's magazines is then not just a cultural issue but a *political issue*. Women's experience of themselves as women will only change when the representations of femininity like those found in women's magazines are transformed.

Second, a cultural studies approach has offered a method for beginning to analyse that relation between women's magazines and their readers, and women more generally. At the outset of the Unit, you probably had not cast more than a few moment's thought to the subject of women's magazines. You just took them for granted as the literature that many women in Britain read for light entertainment. Our cultural analysis of decoding and deconstruction has enabled us to see and read into the magazine the ideologies out of which it is produced. In particular, we have focused on how an ideology of femininity is represented in *Woman's Own* and have throughout tried to understand how that ideology is also the product of conditions outside this particular magazine. In a sense, then, a cultural studies approach has undermined the apparent simplicity and straightforwardness of the cultural form with which we began. And it has also enabled us to understand a women's magazine *better*. We now know the factors which have made it as it is; what it means to women readers; and the conditions which might change it. Such knowledge not only tells us about that cultural form but, like any cultural analysis, also contributes to our overall knowledge of women and society. Thus what seems to be an analysis of one very small area has, in fact, delivered knowledge about women of a much more general kind.

Third, though I have urged you to be critical of women's magazines, I have also insisted that they provide a pleasure for women which should not be underestimated. I have suggested not only that women *identify* with the representations of women's magazines, but also *escape* into the fantasy *solutions* the magazine provides. Such solutions, however, do not occur in real life, and the pleasure of reading these women's magazines is often derived precisely because women recognize this disjunction between fantasy and reality.

We hope that this Unit has not destroyed your pleasure in reading; but rather that, for those of you who previously felt guilty or embarrassed about reading women's magazines, working through this Unit has given you ways of thinking about their place in women's lives which allow you the indulgence of buying and reading them without feeling guilty. Moreover, when you read magazines in the future, you may even find that the knowledge you now bring to bear on them makes them an infinitely more fascinating read. I certainly still go to bed armed with my hot water bottle and *Woman's Own* — even after all these months of work on it. So, happy reading!

Objectives

Before moving on to the next Unit you should check that you understand the following concepts by making your own brief notes: cultural representation; deconstruction and decoding of a cultural form; dominant ideology; ideology of femininity; social reading; narrative resolution; narrative devices; stereotypes.

You should now be able to use the methods of cultural studies to approach women's magazines. You should be able to do the following (again make your own notes):

1 Suggest the combination of elements that make up the cover of a women's magazine as opposed to that of a Sunday supplement.

2 Give the categories and suggest the balance that defines the content of women's magazines.

3 Specify several visual forms and styles, and suggest which kind of feature they are used in.

4 Briefly describe the characteristic verbal style and mode of address of women's magazines.

5 Outline how developments in consumption have effected women's lives and women's magazines since the Second World War.

6 Define five characteristics of ideology.

7 Suggest at least three ideologies that comprise an ideology of femininity.

8 Suggest why there might be different social readings of any feature in *Woman's Own*.

9 Outline some of the sources of pleasure for women in reading women's magazines.

10 Suggest the *dominant* mechanism of pleasure for women in reading women's magazines.

11 List the stages involved in analysing a short story.

12 Outline the dominant ideological pattern and solutions of most of the stories in *Woman's Own*, which is also the pattern and solution of *Woman's Own* as a whole.

Answers to questions

TABLE 1 (completed)

	Woman's Weekly	Company	Spare Rib	Ideal Home	Woman	Woman's Own
Home	✓ (circled)	✗	✓	✓	✗	✓?
Beauty	✓	✓		✗	✓	✓
Personal relationships	✗	✓		✗	✓ (circled)	✓ (circled)
Paid Work	✗	✓ (circled)?		✗	✗	✗
Offers/ competitions	✓	✓	✗	✓	✓	✓
Social issues	✗	✓	✓ (circled)	✗	✗	✗

I found it quite difficult to ring the most important category for *Company*, but plumped for personal relationships and paid work, since the photography feature, possibly 'gold diggers' and the emphasis on *not* having the 'urge to breed', pointed to the latter. *Spare Rib* did not really fit the categories and sometimes opposed them. For example, 'Images of Ourselves' could be slotted into an 'anti-beauty' category. Both *Woman* and *Woman's Own* emphasized their personal relations piece by bigger print. I have queried the 'home' slot for *Woman's Own* because you may not think it appropriate to classify 'Embroider a work of art' and 'Clown around with our fun knit' as strictly to do with the home, but they are home-based activities.

TABLE 2 (completed)

	Woman's Weekly	Company	Spare Rib	Ideal Home	Woman	Woman's Own
Age	middle age	young	all ages	not very young	youngish	youngish
Class	middle class	middle class	all classes	middle/ upper	middle/ working	middle

My grounds, perhaps unwarranted, for suggesting *Woman's* address to a working-class readership is its offer of savings on clothes from *Woolworths*.

TABLE 7 Taken from the National Readership Survey 1981

Social grade	social status	Head of household occupation
A	Upper middle class	Higher managerial administrative or professional
B	Middle class	Intermediate managerial administrative or professional
C$_1$	Lower middle class	Supervisory or clerical, and junior managerial administrative or professional
C$_2$	Skilled working class	Skilled manual
D	Working class	Semi and unskilled manual workers
E	Those at lowest level of subsistence	State pensioners or widows (no other earner) casual, lowest grade workers

TABLE 5 (completed)

	Woman's Weekly	Company	Spare Rib	Ideal Home	Woman	Woman's Own
Matter-of-fact	✓	✗	✗	✓	✓	✓
Racy	✗	✓	✗	✗	✓	✓
Investigative *and* serious	✗	✗	✓	✓	✗	✗

TABLE 11

Category	(a)			(b)		
	Ideal Home	Woman	Sunday Times	Ideal Home	Woman	Sunday Times
Home	✓	✓	✓	✓	✓	✗
Cookery/food	✓	✓	✓ (wine)	✓	✓	✗
Beauty/make-up	✗	✗	✗	✗	✗	✗
Fashion	✗	✓	✓	✗	✓	✗
Personal relationships	✗	✓	✗	✗	✗*	✗
People 'ordinary'	✗	✓	✓	✗	✗	✗
People 'celebrities'	✓	✓	✓	✓	✗	✗
Paid work	✗	✗	✗	✗	✗	✗
Offers/competitions	✓	✓	✓	✓	✓	✗
Consumers items	✓	✓	✓	✗	✗	✗
Fiction	✗	✓	✗	✗	✓	✗
Holidays/travel	✓	✓		✗	✓	✗

* In fact *Woman's* 'Feature' category is mainly composed of articles on personal relationships and people.

References

ABRAMS M. (1959) 'The Home Centred Society', *The Listener*, 26/11/59

BERGER J. (1972) *Ways of Seeing*, Penguin

CECIL M. (1974) *Heroines in Love 1750—1974*, Michael Joseph

DIX C. (1978) *Say I'm Sorry to Mother*, Pan

DRAWBELL J. (1968) *Time on My Hands*, Macdonald

GRIEVE M. (1964) *Millions Made My Story*, Gollancz

JOHNSON R. (1979) 'Three Problematics' in *Working Class Culture* (eds) J. CLARKE, C. CHRITCHER, R. JOHNSON, Hutchinson/CCCS

NEWSOM J. (1948) *The Education of Girls*, Faber and Faber

HOPKINS H. (1963) *The New Look*, Secker and Warburg

MITCHELL J. (1971) *Woman's Estate*, Penguin

MONTGOMERY J. (1965) *The Fifties*, Allen and Unwin

PINTO-DUSCHINSKY M. (1970) 'Bread and Circuses? The Conservatives in Office 1951—64', *The Age of Affluence*, (eds) BOGDANOR and SKIDELSKY, Macmillan

RICE M. S. (1981) *Working Class Wives*, (Virago) (First published 1939)

ROWBOTHAM S. (1973) *Woman's Consciousness Man's World*, Penguin

SPENCE J. (1978) 'Facing Up to Myself' in *Spare Rib* No. 68 March 1978

SPENCE J. (1978) 'What do people do all day?' *Screen Education* No. 29 Winter 1978/79

WILLIAM S. (1965) *The Long Revolution*, Penguin

WHITE C. (1970) *Womens Magazines 1693—1968*, Michael Joseph

WHITE C. (1977) *The Women's Periodical Press in Britain*, HMSO

Acknowledgements

Grateful acknowledgement is made to the following sources for permission to reproduce material in this Unit:

Figures

Figure 1 New Statesman; *Figure 2* The *Observer*; *Figure 3 Motor Sport*; *Figure 4 Practical Computing*; *Figure 5 Men Only*/Paul Raymond Publications Limited ; *Figure 6 Woman's Own*/Camera Press; *Figure 7 Woman's Weekly*; *Figure 8* National Magazine Company Limited; *Figure 9* photo Derek Speirs/*Spare Rib*, Issue 111, 27 Clerkenwell Close, . London; *Figures 10 and 13* reproduced by kind permission of *Ideal Home* magazine; *Figure 12 Woman's Own*; *Figures 11 and 14* from *Woman*, October 3, 1981, reproduced by permission; *Figure 15 The Sunday Times Magazine*, June 28, 1981; *Figures 16, 17, 19, 20, 21, 22, 29 and 30 Woman's Own*; *Figure 18* General Foods Ltd.; *Figure 23* Sacha/ *The Sunday Times*; *Figures 24 and 25* Revlon Inc.; *Figure 26* courtesy *Daily Star*; *Figures 27 and 28* photos Jo Spence/*Spare Rib*, Issue 68, 27 Clerkenwell Close, London;

Extracts

Extract 1 courtesy of *My Weekly*; *Extract 2* The National Magazine Company Limited; *Extracts 3, 4, 5, 6, 7, 8, 9 and 10 Woman's Own*.

Cover

'Pencil power', *Woman's Own*.
'The good years', *Woman*.

U221   The Changing Experience of Women